Landlords' Rights & Duties in California

LANDLORDS' RIGHTS & DUTIES IN CALIFORNIA

with forms

John J. Talamo
Mark Warda
Attorneys at Law

SPHINX® PUBLISHING

A Division of Sourcebooks, Inc.®

Naperville, IL • Clearwater, FL

First edition, 1998

Published by: **Sphinx® Publishing: A Division of Sourcebooks, Inc.®**

Naperville Office
P.O. Box 4410
Naperville, Illinois 60567-4410
630-961-3900
Fax: 630-961-2168

Clearwater Office
P.O. Box 25
Clearwater, Florida 33757
727-587-0999
Fax: 727-586-5088

Interior Design and Production: Shannon E. Harrington/Mark Warda, Sourcebooks, Inc.®

This publication is designed to provide accurate and authoritative information in regard to the subject matter covered. It is sold with the understanding that the publisher is not engaged in rendering legal, accounting, or other professional service. If legal advice or other expert assistance is required, the services of a competent professional person should be sought.

From a Declaration of Principles Jointly Adopted by a Committee of the
American Bar Association and a Committee of Publishers and Associations

Library of Congress Cataloging-in-Publication Data
Talamo, John.
    Landlords' rights & duties in California : with forms / John J.
Talamo, Mark Warda.—1st ed.
        p.   cm.
    Includes index.
    ISBN 1-57071-359-6 (pbk.)
    1. Landlord and tenant—California—Popular works.   I. Warda,
Mark.   II. Title.
KFC145.Z9T35   1998
346.7304'34—dc21   98-15277
                                                                                        CIP

Printed and bound in the United States of America.

HS Paperback — 10 9 8 7 6 5 4 3

CONTENTS

Using Self-Help
Law Books

Whenever you shop for a product or service, you are faced with various levels of quality and price. In deciding what product or service to buy, you make a cost/value analysis on the basis of your willingness to pay and the quality you desire.

When buying a car, you decide whether you want transportation, comfort, status, or sex appeal. Accordingly, you decide among such choices as a Neon, a Lincoln, a Rolls Royce, or a Porsche. Before making a decision, you usually weigh the merits of each option against the cost.

When you get a headache, you can take a pain reliever (such as aspirin) or visit a medical specialist for a neurological examination. Given this choice, most people, of course, take a pain reliever, since it costs only pennies; whereas a medical examination costs hundreds of dollars and takes a lot of time. This is usually a logical choice because rarely is anything more than a pain reliever needed for a headache. But in some cases, a headache may indicate a brain tumor and failing to see a specialist right away can result in complications. Should everyone with a headache go to a specialist? Of course not, but people treating their own illnesses must realize that they are betting on the basis of their cost/value analysis of the situation. They are taking the most logical option.

The same cost/value analysis must be made in deciding to do one's own legal work. Many legal situations are very straight forward, requiring a simple form and no complicated analysis. Anyone with a little intelligence and a book of instructions can handle the matter without outside help.

But there is always the chance that complications are involved that only an attorney would notice. To simplify the law into a book like this, several legal cases often must be condensed into a single sentence or paragraph. Otherwise, the book would be several hundred pages longer and too complicated for most people. However, this simplification necessarily leaves out many details and nuances that would apply to special or unusual situations. Also, there are many ways to interpret most legal questions. Your case may come before a judge who disagrees with the analysis of our authors.

Therefore, in deciding to use a self-help law book and to do your own legal work, you must realize that you are making a cost/value analysis. You have decided that the money you will save by doing it yourself outweighs the chance that your case will not turn out to your satisfaction. Most people handling their own simple legal matters never have a problem, but occasionally people find that it ended up costing them more to have an attorney straighten out the situation than it would have if they had hired an attorney in the beginning. Keep this in mind while handling your case, and be sure to consult an attorney if you feel you might need further guidance.

INTRODUCTION

California's landlord/tenant laws are like a double-edged sword. If a landlord does not know about them, or ignores them, he or she can lose thousands of dollars in unpaid rent, penalties, and attorney's fees. However, a landlord who knows the law can use the procedures to simplify life and to save money. Knowledge is power and knowing the laws governing rentals will give you the power to protect your rights and to deal with problems effectively.

Laws are written to be precise, not to be easily readable. This book explains the law in simple language so that California landlords can know what is required of them and know their rights under the law. If you would like more detail about a law, you can check the statutes in appendix A or conduct more detailed research of the California Code and the court cases as explained in the section on "Doing Further Research" in chapter 1.

Nearly every year the California legislature passes new laws regulating landlord/tenant relations and the courts of the state write more opinions defining the rights of landlords and tenants.

No book of this type can be expected to cover every situation that may arise. Laws change and different judges have different interpretations of what the laws mean. Only your lawyer, reviewing the unique characteristics of your situation can give you an opinion of how the laws apply to your case. But this book can give you the legal framework to avoid costly mistakes.

When following the procedures in this book it should be kept in mind that different counties have different customs and some judges have their own way of doing things, so the requirements in your area may differ somewhat from those outlined in this book. Clerks and judge's assistants cannot give you legal advice, but often they can tell you what they require in order to proceed with your case. Before filing any forms, ask if your court provides its own forms or has any special requirements.

We at Sphinx Publishing hope that you find this book useful and we welcome your comments on this or any of our books.

Laws That Govern Rental Property

1

California Landlord/Tenant Law

California landlord/tenant law consists of statutes passed by the legislature and legal opinions written by judges. The statutes usually address specific issues that have come up repeatedly in landlord/tenant relations. The judicial opinions interpret the statutes and decide what the law is in areas not specifically covered by statutes.

When reading the law contained in judges' opinions, be sure to note from which court the opinion originated. If it is not from your district, it might not be binding on your case. Supreme Court of California opinions apply to all courts in California, but court of appeal opinions only apply to the district in which they sit. circuit court appeals of municipal court cases only are binding in the circuit in which that court sits, and municipal court opinions are not binding in other courts, but they may be used as rationale by other municipal courts.

Which California Laws Apply?

California laws, also called *statutes* are passed by the state's legislature. In California, the laws, for research purposes, are grouped in categories called *codes*. Most laws relating to landlords rights and duties are found in the California Civil Code. However, the Health and Safety Code, Business and Professions Code, and other codes also contain laws affecting the landlord/tenant relationship.

LOCAL LAWS AND REGULATIONS

Local (city or county) laws are called *ordinances*. An example of this would be a rent control ordinance. Cities and counties also have agencies, sometimes called departments or boards, that issue rules regarding rental property. Be sure to check with both your city and county governments for any local laws and regulations that may apply to your property.

FEDERAL LAWS AND REGULATIONS

Federal laws that apply to rental of real estate include discrimination laws such as the Civil Rights Act, the Americans With Disabilities Act, and lead-based paint rules of the Environmental Protection Agency. These are explained in chapter 2 of this book.

The United States Department of Housing and Urban Development (HUD) has a handbook that explains the rules applicable to public housing and other HUD programs.

DOING FURTHER RESEARCH

This book contains a summary of most of the statutes and many court cases affecting landlord/tenant law in California. However, the law is an ever changing body of knowledge and information that is influenced by several sources. You may want to research your predicament further by reading the entire statute section or court case. To do this you should use the code title and section number or case citation. California code citations appear as "California" followed by the code title and section number (such as "California Civil Code, section 1951," or "California Business and Professional Code, section 17217"). Many of California's landlord-tenant laws are included in appendix A in this book.

As you will realize after reading this book, all of these laws and regulations can create some confusion. As well as the different laws and rules sometimes overlapping and contradicting each other, many are not well written and their exact meaning is not clear. Cases are actions brought in court to determine what these laws and rules mean, and which control in the event of overlap and conflict.

Court cases are noted by the little book symbol 📖. Case citations include the name of the case, the volume and page of the reporter, and the court and year. For example, *Clark & Lewis v. Gardner*, 109 Cal Rptr. 2d 192 (Cal. 1926) means that the case is found in volume 109 of the California Reporter, 2nd Series, at page 192 and that it is a 1926 case from the California Supreme Court.

To learn more about doing legal research, you can refer to *Legal Research Made Easy*, by Suzan Herskowitz, available at your local bookstore or library or directly from the publisher. Call 1-800-226-5291.

A good rule to follow when attempting legal research is to ask yourself what the consequences will be if you are wrong about the law. If they are minor, attempt the research. If they are serious, consult an attorney who specializes in the problem you are facing.

This book will cover the current law regarding the most common areas concerning a landlord's rights and duties. No book can cover every possible situation. When in doubt, refer to the above rule.

CONFLICTING LAWS

Occasionally you will find that the laws conflict with one another in how they apply to your situation. The general rules to follow are:

- ☞ Federal law controls if it conflicts with state or local law. State law controls when it conflicts with local law. The federal constitution controls when it conflicts with any other law or regulation.

- ☞ When the laws do not directly conflict, the stricter law controls. For example, when the federal maximum speed limit was in effect, states could not permit drivers to exceed 55 mph. However, the states could require motorists to drive at a slower speed, such as 25 mph in a school zone.

We will see another example of this when we look at the state laws and city ordinances regarding rent control.

FICTITIOUS NAMES

Some landlords conduct their rentals under a business, or *fictitious*, name. If you use a fictitious name that appears on your lease or rental agreement, you must register the name with the county. There is a requirement of a small fee paid to the county and publishing in a local newspaper. Check with your county.

The proper county to file in is wherever your primary place of business is located. You may want to file in more than one county if your primary place of business is not in the county where the property is located.

Note. Failure to file or filing in the wrong county could delay eviction.

RENT CONTROL

As of this writing, the following sixteen California cities have some form of rent control.

Berkeley
Beverly Hills
Campbell
Cotati
East Palo Alto
Haywand
Los Angeles
Los Gatos

Oakland
Palm Springs
San Francisco
San Jose
Santa Monica
Thousand Oaks
West Hollywood
Westlake Village

The right of California cities to enact rent control ordinances has not only been decided in the California courts but affirmed by the U. S. Supreme Court (*Fisher v. City of Berkeley*, 475 U.S. 260, 1986).

The problem with discussing rent control is that the laws vary from city to city and they are amended from time to time. To be sure of the current law as it applies to your property you must contact the city or county where your property is located and obtain a copy of the current ordinance and regulations.

EXEMPT PROPERTY

Not all property is subject to rent control. State law (California Civil Code, section 1954.52) exempts any property that had a certificate of occupancy issued after February, 1995. The rent control ordinance may also exempt property constructed after the date of the ordinance (be sure you know the city's interpretation of the date of construction). Some ordinances also exempt property having only one, two, three, or four units and some exempt higher-priced rental units.

WHAT TO LOOK FOR

These are some major areas that should concern you if your property is subject to rent control. Remember that these rules vary from city to city, and some cities frequently change their own rules.

Registration. Some cities require that the property be registered with their rent control department. This will involve paying a fee. Either the landlord or tenant may request the rent control board to notify them in writing as to the proper rent for the property. The board must send the notice to both parties. Either may challenge the amount within fifteen days. The board then has sixty days to review its original decision and notify the parties. Failure of the parties to properly object within fifteen days waives the right to object later unless fraud was involved (California Civil Code, section 1947.8).

Failure to register could result in fines as well as payment of back registration fees, and the return to tenants of any rent increases during the time the property was not registered. State law (California Civil Code, section 1947.7) allows the "illegal" increases to be phased in if the landlord did not deliberately avoid registration (check this statute and any updates to it for the procedure you must follow).

Withholding rent. A tenant may not withhold rent solely because the property is not registered [*Floystrup v. Berkley Rent Stabilization Board,* 219 Cal. App. 3d 1309 (1990)].

Rent increases. The amount and frequency of rent increases will be set out in each ordinance. This may be a percentage of the current rent or some more complicated formula.

Some ordinances do not require adherence to a maximum increase but ask the landlord to voluntarily follow their formula or to use a mediation service to establish a proper rent (mediation, unlike arbitration, is not binding). Don't confuse the word "voluntary" with the word "ignore." Remember that a tenant who can't get help from the city may turn to the courts. The landlord's completely ignoring the guidelines may be considered *bad faith* or *unconscionable.*

Extraordinary rent increases. Under certain circumstances, such as greater expenses related to the property, the rent may be increased over the ordinarily allowable amount. There are two very different rules. Some ordinances allow the rent increase unless the tenant objects within a given time. Only if the tenant objects does the rent control board hold a hearing to decide on the merits of the increase. Other ordinances require the landlord to justify the increase to the rent control board before raising the rent.

If you must attend a hearing, try to observe other hearings before your hearing. You can then decide whether you want to hire an attorney or attempt it on your own.

Tenant's waiver. In most cities a tenant may not agree to a higher than allowable rent in place of a hearing when the ordinance requires a hearing prior to the increase. Any such agreement cannot be enforced. [*Nettles v. Van de land*, 207 cal. App. 3d Supp. 6 (1988)].

Rent decreases. Some ordinances allow a tenant to request rent decreases if the landlord is especially lax in maintenance and repairs.

Vacancy. The effect on rent control of a tenant vacating the property varies greatly depending on the ordinance. There are several factors to consider.

- ☛ If a tenant voluntarily vacates, some ordinances provide for no further rent control. Remember that a landlord's making the tenants occupancy so difficult that the tenant moves out does not qualify as "voluntary."

- ☛ Some ordinances provide that if a tenant voluntarily vacates or is evicted for nonpayment of rent, the landlord may set a new rent without restriction. However, when the next tenant moves in, the rent control laws again apply.

- ☛ Some ordinances control the rental amount even after a voluntary vacancy or eviction for failure to pay rent.

COSTA-
HAWKINGS
RENTAL
HOUSING ACT

California Civil Code, sections 1954.52-53, popularly called the *Costa-Hawkins Rental Housing Act*, provides some very limited standards. The law states that after January 1, 1999, a landlord may set a new rental amount without restriction when a tenant vacates voluntarily or is evicted for nonpayment of rent. Once the new tenant moves in, the property is again subject to rent control when the local ordinance so provides.

The current law, until 1999, is more confusing. The formula for a rent increase after a tenant voluntarily vacates or is evicted for nonpayment of rent is the highest of the following:

☛ fifteen percent more than the rent charged to the last tenant.

☛ seventy percent of the "prevailing market rent for comparable units." California Civil Code, section 1954.53 (3-c).

☛ the amount allowed by the city ordinance.

Trying to find the "prevailing market rent" in a city with rent controls may be a difficult task.

Notice that both the state statutes and city ordinances call for a tenant to voluntarily vacate or be evicted for nonpayment of rent. State law is silent, even after 1999, as to the effect of a tenant being evicted for a reason other than nonpayment of rent. If you are evicting a tenant for a reason other than nonpayment of rent, check with your local rent control board to determine their position. If you don't agree with it, find an attorney familiar with the city and their procedures. You may be able to get them to change their minds without resorting to a lawsuit that you could lose.

Note. A landlord who violates health and safety codes may not be allowed to raise rent, even if a tenant voluntarily vacates or is evicted for nonpayment of rent (California Civil Code, section 1954.53 f).

Note. California Civil Code, section 798.21 exempts mobile homes from rent control under certain conditions.

EVICTIONS AND RENT CONTROL

We cover eviction separately in chapter 10, but the rent control ordinances also include rules that cover evictions. Again there are different rules for different cities. The biggest difference in rent controlled cities is that most of them require "just cause" such as violation of the lease, before a tenant can be evicted. You cannot just decide to terminate the tenancy because you want to rent to someone else.

To evict for just cause you must first give notice to the tenant as required by law, after which the tenant usually has a right to cure the breach. If the tenant fails to cure the breach or vacate, you must then file for eviction in court.

Notice requirements may also be different from state requirements. A tenant may, for example, have to be given notice and a time period to correct the problem or stop the offensive behavior before the actual notice to quit (vacate) is given.

Even though also prohibited by state law, some ordinances specifically address retaliatory evictions and the penalties for such evictions. Retaliatory evictions are discussed separately.

Other allowable reasons to evict include:

- ☛ The landlord wishes to occupy the property or rent it to an immediate family member. Who is a member of the landlord's "immediate" family is not the same in all ordinances. Also, some cities require that no similar unit owned by the landlord is available for this purpose. **Note:** Heavy fines and large judgments have resulted from landlords using this reason as a ploy to evict tenants. See: *Beeman v. Burling* 265 Cal. Rptr. 719 (1990).

- ☛ The landlord is going to do extensive remodeling of the property. The tenant will usually be given the right to again rent the property after the remodeling, although the ordinance may allow for a rent increase.

- ☛ The landlord has received all necessary permits and is converting the rental unit to a condominium unit.

- ☛ The property is being removed from the rental market under the provisions of the Ellis Act (California Government Code, sections 7060 to 7060.7).

Even when eviction is allowed, relocation costs for the tenant may have to be paid by the landlord. The costs may be higher for older tenants.

SECURITY
DEPOSITS AND
RENT CONTROL

Some rent control ordinances have stricter controls on security deposits than state law requires (security deposits are covered in more detail in chapter 3). There may be a requirement that the money be deposited in an interest bearing account and the interest be paid or credited to the tenant. Remember that all monies collected from the tenant, whether called deposits, fees, or last month's rent are considered security deposits.

Failure to comply with security deposit requirements may result in the landlord paying interest to the tenant out-of-pocket.

Note. Some cities without rent control may have requirements for security deposits that differ from state requirements. When checking for rent control, ask specifically about security deposits.

MANAGERS

In California, a landlord is required to provide an on site manager (one who lives on the property) for a residential complex over fifteen units (California Code of Regulations, Title 25). Some landlords desire to have a manager for fifteen or fewer units. This manager may, of course, be the landlord. If you decide to hire a manager, how must you do it and how should you do it? The following guidelines are important:

☛ You must treat the manager as an employee even if the manager's only payment is reduced rent. This means following all rules regarding withholding taxes and social security, any insurance requirements, safety requirements, and applicable immigration laws.

☛ You must notify the tenants who the manager is and how and when they may serve notices to the manager.

You should understand the role a manager will play in your building. The manager, in addition to making some repairs and generally keeping an eye on things, will be your agent. This means that your manager's actions may be legally attributable to you. This will be true for those actions by the manager specifically authorized by you. More importantly, you will be liable for the manager's actions not authorized by you if a court decides you impliedly authorized them or it appeared that you authorized them.

You may also be liable if you fail to use reasonable care in hiring. For example, you hire a manager with a conviction for assault. The manager then assaults a tenant. You could be liable even if you didn't know of the conviction if a court thinks you didn't do a sufficient background check.

What does this mean? It means be careful when you hire a manager.

☞ Run all the checks you would normally run for a new tenant. In addition, look for the qualities you would want in an employee who will receive very little day to day supervision.

☞ Make a contract with the manager. This should set out both the manager's duties and compensation.

☞ Use a separate rental agreement if the building's office is in a separate unit and not part of the manager's residence. This will avoid confusion if the employment terminates. Don't give the manager reduced or free rent as compensation.

☞ If the building's office and manager's residence are in the same unit, a combination employment contract-lease may be used.

☞ Attempt to limit liability by letting the tenants know anything you have not authorized. For example, if the manager is authorized to collect rent, let the tenants know that the manager is not authorized to accept cash or checks made out to anyone except you. This can be done in your required notice.

☞ Give the tenants a way to reach you by mail. You don't want your first knowledge of a complaint to come from a tenant's lawyer because the tenant had trouble with your manager and couldn't reach you.

☞ Insure against those liabilities you can't eliminate. Consult your insurance agent.

Unless you enjoy taking a very active role in your property or the cost is prohibitive, hire a management company. Any reliable management company will have several advantages.

☞ The on site manager is the employee of the management company, not your employee.

☞ They will have experience in hiring, training, and firing managers.

☞ The company will have a contract spelling out exactly what they are required and authorized to do.

☞ They will have liability insurance.

You are still going to have to make sure you hire a good company. Checking other landlords who use them and a financial rating service are suggested ways.

OTHER LAWS

TELEPHONE JACKS

The landlord is required under California Civil Code, section 1941, to maintain all interior telephone wiring and to supply at least one workable telephone jack.

SMOKE DETECTORS

The landlord is required to have installed a workable smoke detector as defined by the California Health and Safety Code, section 13113. The Code states that stricter local laws are valid, so check your county or city for the local standard.

CREATING THE LANDLORD/TENANT RELATIONSHIP 2

SCREENING PROSPECTIVE TENANTS

The first step in avoiding legal problems with tenants is to carefully choose who will be your tenant. Taking the time to do this right is the key to being a successful landlord. As long as you do not discriminate based on such categories as race, sex, and age (see pages 19-25) you can be selective in renting your property. A tenant who has had the same apartment and job for the last five years will probably be a better risk than one who has been evicted several times.

You should get a written application from all prospective tenants. Be sure it allows you to contact employers, banks, and former landlords, and to run a credit check. Besides allowing you to check their past record as tenants, the information can be helpful in tracking them down if they disappear owing you rent or damages. (See Form 1.) Be sure that the form you use does not ask illegal questions, such as nationality.

Make it clear to the prospective tenant that you intend to do a thorough background check. This is when you can expect to hear the problems and excuses. Although it is preferable to have the application filled out on the spot, you may give the prospective tenant the application to complete and return to you the following day. You may never hear from him or her again. The prospective tenant's reaction to the threat of a background check may even save you the trouble of actually doing the background investigation.

INVESTIGATION CHARGES
You may charge a fee for the expense of a credit report and for your investigation work. The current maximum allowed is $30.00 for each applicant (California Civil Code, section 1950.6). The law says you can't charge for a credit report unless you actually get one, you can't charge for work you do unless you *do* the work, and you can't charge if you do not have any vacancies (i.e., the tenants will go on a waiting list). Good sense says that you don't want to seem unfair to a prospective tenant, so only charge your actual costs.

CREDIT REPORTS
One of the most important pieces of information available is the credit report. There are primarily two things to look for that are warning flags. The first is obvious: they don't pay their bills. The second is more subtle: they pay their bills, but are financially overextended. If you are dealing with young people who have only received credit recently, how much do they owe? Do you get the feeling that they're going to have future credit problems? If you have a large number of vacant units, you may not have the luxury of being so careful. However, if you are renting a second house and depend on the income, you may be asking for trouble by renting to them if your common sense tells you that these people don't know how to manage credit.

COURT RECORDS
You should check the defendant index of the court records (not just the "official records") of your county or the last county they lived in to see if they have ever been evicted or sued. It would also be wise to check the plaintiff index to see if they have sued a landlord. In some counties these indexes are combined.

PRIOR LANDLORDS
You should check with a prior landlord to see if she would rent to them again. Don't bother checking with their present landlord. He may lie just to get rid of them! And be sure the people you talk to are really landlords. Some tenants use friends who lie for them. One thing to consider is how long the tenants have stayed at their previous addresses. If they have a history of moving every few months, they may not be

desirable even if they do pay their rent for the short period of time they stay in your property.

TENANT
INVESTIGATION
COMPANIES

There are some companies that, for a fee, will investigate tenants including employment, previous landlords, court cases, and their own files of "bad tenants." Some landlords require a non-refundable application fee to cover such an investigation. Check your phone book under Credit Reporting Agencies.

EMERGENCIES

Occasionally tenants may apply to rent the apartment and say that they need a place to stay immediately for some reason. They may ask to move in on a temporary basis until you have a chance to check references. This is a very bad idea. Once they are in your property, it may take months to get them out. Be sure you check them out before you allow them to move anything into the unit.

DISCRIMINATION

Since Congress passed the Fair Housing Act, it has been a federal crime for a landlord to discriminate in the rental or sale of property on the basis of race, religion, sex, or national origin. In addition, California has passed its own anti-discrimination statute. In 1988, the United States Congress passed an amendment to the act that bans discrimination against both the handicapped and families with children. Except for apartment complexes which fall into the special exceptions, all rentals must now allow children in all units.

CIVIL RIGHTS
ACT §1982

The Civil Rights Act §1982 (42 USC 1982) passed in 1866 applies only where it can be proved that the person had an intent to discriminate.

PENALTY. Actual damages plus unlimited punitive damages. ***Example:*** In 1992, a jury in Washington, D.C., awarded civil rights groups $850,000 damages against a developer who only used white models in rental advertising. *The Washington Post* now requires that the models in ads it accepts must be twenty-five percent black to reflect the percentage of blacks in the Washington area.

LIMITATION. None.

EXEMPTIONS. None.

FAIR HOUSING ACT

Under the Fair Housing Act (42 USC 3601-19) any policy that has a discriminatory effect is illegal. Failure to attend a hearing or to produce records can subject you to up to a year in prison or $1,000 fine.

PENALTY. A victim of discrimination under this section can file a civil suit, a HUD complaint, or request the U.S. Attorney General to prosecute. Damages can include actual losses and punitive damages of up to $1,000.

LIMITATION. The complaint must be brought within 180 days.

EXEMPTIONS. This law does not apply to single family homes if the owner owns three or less, if there is no more than one sale within twenty-four months, if the person does not own any interest in more than three at one time, and if no real estate agent or discriminatory advertisement is used. It also does not apply to a property that the owner lives in if it has four or fewer units.

COERCION OR INTIMIDATION. Where coercion or intimidation is used to effectuate discrimination, there is no limit to when the action can be brought or the amount of damages. *Example:* Real estate agent fired for renting to African-Americans. *Wilkey v. Pyramid Construction Co.*, 619 F.Supp. 1453 (D. Conn. 1983).

FAIR HOUSING ACT 1988 AMENDMENT

The 1988 Amendment to the Civil Rights Act (42 USC 3601) bans discrimination against the handicapped and families with children.

Residential premises. Unless a property falls into one of the exemptions, it is illegal under this law to refuse to rent to persons because of age or to refuse to rent to children. While landlords may be justified in feeling that children cause damage to their property which they wish to avoid, Congress has ruled that the right of families to find housing is more important than the rights of landlords in the condition of their property. The exemptions are for two types of housing: 1) Where units are rented solely by persons sixty-two or older; 2) Where eighty percent of the units are rented to persons fifty-five or older. In late 1995, the law was amended so that the property does not need special facilities for such persons' needs.

Regarding the disabled, the law allows them to remodel the unit to suit their needs as long as they return it to the original condition upon leaving. It also requires new buildings of four units or more to have electrical facilities and common areas accessible to the disabled.

PENALTY. $10,000 for first offense, $25,000 for second violation within five years, and up to $50,000 for three or more violations within seven years. Unlimited punitive damages in private actions.

LIMITATION. Complaint can be brought within two years for private actions.

EXEMPTIONS. This law does not apply to single family homes if the owner owns three or less, if there is no more than one sale within twenty-four months, if the person does not own any interest in more than three at one time, and if no real estate agent or discriminatory advertisement is used. (A condominium unit is not a single-family home so is not exempt.) It also does not apply to property that the owner lives in if it has four or fewer units. Additionally, there are exemptions for 1) dwellings in state and federal programs for the elderly, 2) complexes that are solely used by persons sixty-two or older, and 3) complexes used solely by persons fifty-five or over, if there are substantial facilities designed for the elderly, for religious housing, and for private clubs.

Commercial premises. If any commercial premises are remodeled, then the remodeling must include modifications that make the premises accessible. All new construction must also be made accessible.

The law does not clearly define what these terms mean and does not even explain exactly who will qualify as handicapped. Some claim that up to forty percent of America's labor force may qualify as handicapped. The law includes people with emotional illnesses, AIDS, dyslexia, past alcohol or drug addictions, as well as hearing, sight, and mobility impairments. Of course, this law will provide lots of work for lawyers who will sue landlords and businesses.

What is reasonable will usually depend upon the size of the business. Small businesses will not have to make major alterations to their premises if the expense would be an undue hardship. Even large businesses would not have to have shelving low enough for people in wheelchairs to reach as long as there was an employee to assist the person. In addition, there are tax credits for businesses of less than thirty employees and less than one million dollars in sales. For more information on these credits obtain IRS forms 8826 and 3800 and their instructions.

Some of the changes that must be made to property to make it more accessible to the disabled are:

- ☛ installing ramps,

- ☛ widening doorways,

- ☛ making curb cuts in sidewalks,

- ☛ repositioning shelves,

- ☛ repositioning telephones,

- ☛ removing high pile, low density carpeting, and

- ☛ installing a full-length bathroom mirror.

Both the landlord and the tenant can be liable if the changes are not made to the premises. Most likely the landlord would be liable for common areas and the tenant for the area under her control. However, since previous leases did not address this new statute either party could conceivably be held liable.

PENALTY. Injunctions and fines of $50,000 for the first offense or $100,000 for subsequent offenses.

EXEMPTIONS. Private clubs and religious organizations are exempt from this law.

HUD CONTACT

If you wish to contact HUD for more information about the laws their web site, address, and phone numbers are:

> http://www.hud.gov/fhe/fheact.html

> HUD
> 450 Golden Gate Ave.
> San Francisco, CA 94102
> 415-436-6550
> 800-343-3442

CALIFORNIA LAWS

In addition to federal laws, California has enacted the Fair Employment and Housing Act, enforced by the California Department of Fair Employment and Housing.

Even more far reaching is California Civil Code Section 51, known as the Unruh Act, which prohibits discrimination on the basis of race, religion, national origin, ethnic background, gender, marital status, age, disability, sexual orientation, income from government assistance, personal traits, and families with children.

Discrimination can take place at any time during the rental process. This includes advertising, negotiating the agreement, after the tenant moves in (raising the rent, for example), and eviction.

A few common sense rules to follow are:

- ☛ Treat all applicants and tenants alike.

- ☛ Keep good records.

- ☛ Run credit checks on all prospective tenants.

- ☛ Require approximately the same rent and security deposit from all tenants.

☛ Raise rents and security deposits equally.

☛ Do not evict one tenant for something you ignored when done by another tenant.

☛ Document all instances that may negatively affect a tenant. This means keeping accurate records of exactly why you refused to rent to a prospective tenant, or exactly what a tenant did to deserve eviction.

California allows discrimination based on age by allowing senior citizen only housing. California Civil Code, sections 51.3 and 51.4 set out the rules. If you plan to acquire, build, or convert to senior citizen housing, consult an attorney.

You cannot prohibit a dog used to alleviate the handicap of a blind, deaf, or otherwise handicapped person, even in a "no pet" building.

You cannot refuse to rent to a person convicted of drug use or possession. Drug addiction is considered a disability. Don't confuse this with a drug dealing tenant. A conviction for the manufacture or sale of drugs would be a legitimate reason to refuse to rent. The landlord must act to stop the drug dealing, typically by eviction, or be subject to liability.

LOCAL LAWS
Landlords should check their city and county ordinances before adopting a discriminatory policy such as an "adult only" complex.

EXAMPLE COURT CASES
The following cases can give some guidance as to what types of actions may be outlawed.

📖 Not including child support and alimony in an applicant's income is sex discrimination. *U.S. v. Reese*, 457 F.Supp. 43 (D. Mont. 1978).

📖 It is not illegal to require a single parent and a child of the opposite sex to rent a two-bedroom rather than a one-bedroom apartment. *Braunstein v. Dwelling Managers, Inc.*, 476 F.Supp. 1323 (S.D.N.Y. 1979).

📖 It was found not to be illegal to limit the number of children allowed. *Fred v. Koknokos*, 347 F.Supp. 942 (E.D.N.Y. 1972). (But there may be a different interpretation under the 1988 amendment. Also, be sure to check local ordinances.)

📖 It is illegal to segregate the people in an apartment complex. *Blackshear Residents Organization v. Housing Authority of the City of Austin*, 347 F.Supp. 1138 (W.D.Tex. 1972).

📖 A company that used only caucasian models in its housing ads was ordered to pay $30,000 in damages. (The judge overruled the jury's recommended $262,000!) *Ragin v. Macklowe*, No. 88 Civ. 5665(RWS), U.S. D.C. S.D.N.Y., Aug. 25, 1992.

AGREEMENTS TO LEASE

What are your rights if a tenant agrees to rent your unit but then backs out? An agreement to enter into a lease may be a valid and binding contract even if a lease has not yet been signed. As a practical matter, it will probably not be worth the time and expense to sue someone for breaching an oral agreement to lease.

What if a prospective tenant puts a deposit on a unit, changes his mind and then wants the deposit back? If you quickly find another tenant and have no financial loss, the tenant might be able to get the deposit back if the matter went to court. The law is not clear and the result would depend on all the facts of the case.

To avoid a misunderstanding you should put on the receipt whether the deposit is refundable. Also, if you give a refund, make sure the tenant's check has cleared first.

LEASES AND RENTAL AGREEMENTS

A lease or rental agreement is a contract. A contract, simply put, is an agreement between two or more parties that is enforceable in court. A contract (your lease or rental agreement) may contain anything you want, as long as your tenant agrees to it, except a contract may not have a provision that:

- ☞ violates the law. For example, you could not rent your property in violation of a rent control ordinance.

- ☞ is against public policy. This is less clear, because the purpose may be legal, but not something a court would want to encourage. For example, your city has rent control "voluntary guidelines." You rent your property at a substantially higher rent than the guidelines "suggest." Does the court wish to encourage this behavior by enforcing the contract? Probably not.

- ☞ is unconscionable. This means the court finds the provision to be so unfair that it cannot, in good conscience, enforce it. Remember this one when you get a tenant who will agree to anything.

There are different opinions as to whether or not a landlord should use a *lease* with a set term, such as one year, or an open ended *rental agreement*. Some argue that they would rather not have a lease so they can get rid of a tenant at any time. The disadvantage is that the tenant can also leave at any time which means the unit may be vacant during the slow season.

The difference between a lease and a rental agreement is how long the tenant is *required* to stay; not how long the tenant *actually* stays. For example, you could have a lease for three weeks, or a month-to-month rental agreement that lasts for many years. The lease would be for the fixed term of three weeks, and would end at the end of the third week.

Under the rental agreement, the tenant could move out at any time after giving proper notice.

RENTAL
AGREEMENTS

In all cases, even month to month tenancies, there should be some type of written agreement between the parties. If the landlord does not want to tie up the property for a long period of time, he can use a rental agreement stating that the tenancy is month to month, but which also includes rules and regulations that protect the landlord. (See Form 8.) A rental agreement may include the same rights and duties for the landlord and tenant as a lease. The difference is that a rental agreement is based on the rental period (e.g., weekly or monthly). This creates two important differences from a lease:

1.   Either the landlord or tenant may terminate the agreement by simply giving notice to the other. The usual required notice is thirty days for a month-to-month tenancy.

2.   The agreement may be changed by giving the same notice. Most often, this means raising the rent, although any other part of the agreement could also be changed.

Remember that different rules may apply if your property is under rent control or other government regulations such as subsidized housing. Federal laws will supersede state laws, and state laws will supersede city or county laws or ordinances. California Civil Code, section 827 provides for a thirty-day notice. In *Tri County Apartment Association v. City of Mountain View*, 196 Cal. App. 3d 1283 (1987), the court held that the city could not require a longer notice period for a rent increase.

Note: There is pending state legislation (SB 82) that would require a sixty-day notice to be given to residential month-to-month tenants to change the terms of a rental agreement.

LEASES

As stated earlier, a lease is a rental agreement for a set term. It can be as short as a few weeks or for several years, but it requires the tenant to stay for the entire period. A rental agreement does not require the tenant to stay beyond each rental period.

Most California landlords opt for the rental agreement.

The disadvantages of a lease are:

☞ The landlord cannot take back the property until the lease expires or the tenant breaches the lease. For example, the landlord could not evict the tenant in order to move into the property himself.

☞ If a tenant moves out before the lease expires, the landlord is required to mitigate (minimize) damages by making a reasonable effort to rent the property. Failure to do so will relieve the tenant of the obligation to pay rent. A judge may even say you didn't try hard enough if you are unable to rent the property.

☞ Collection of back rent is difficult at best, especially since most tenants move because they can't afford the rent.

On the other hand, a lease may be desirable:

☞ if you spend money on improvement specifically for this tenant. This would be common in commercial leasing, but unusual in leasing residential property.

☞ if your property is difficult to rent. Even the psychological obligation may result in the tenant staying longer than with a rental agreement. Also, you may be able to get back rent if the tenant moves out before the lease expires. If the property is tough to rent, you don't lose much.

If you use a lease, how long of a term should you require? The most common lengths of a lease are six months and one year. If you lease for a longer term, or if the tenant has the right to renew the lease, you may want to include a rental increase. There are two common ways to do this:

1. Simply state the increase in the lease. For example, state that the rent beginning on the first day of the thirteenth month of the lease shall automatically increase from $1,000 per month to

$1,100 per month. You may want to express this by giving the exact date of the increase.

2. Tie the rent to a government inflation index. Pick one of the indices that measures inflation, and state that the rent shall increase by the same percentage that the index increased for the prior twelve months.

There are many other ways to increase rent by passing on to the tenant the landlord's increased costs of the property. This could include increases in taxes, insurance, maintenance, etc. These formulas may also be combined. However, these are commonly used in commercial leasing and are beyond the scope of this book.

REQUIRED
CLAUSES

There is no special form to create a lease or rental agreement. However, a lease must contain the following minimum information to be valid:

☛ name of lessor (landlord) or agent,

☛ name of lessee (tenant),

☛ description of the premises,

☛ rental rate,

☛ starting date,

☛ termination date (lease only), and

☛ granting clause ("Lessor hereby leases to Lessee...").

(Actually, there have been cases where a lease has been held to be valid where one or more of these terms has been omitted if there was an objective means to determine the missing term, but such exceptions are beyond the scope of this book.)

DISCLOSURE
REQUIREMENTS

Landlords in California must make certain disclosures to prospective tenants. All disclosures should be made in writing, and a disclosure form is included as Form 13 in appendix D of this book. Disclosures may also be made in the lease or rental agreement itself. These disclosures include:

☞ If your property is within one mile of a former military base where ammunition or explosives were kept, you must disclose this to a prospective tenant. You can find out if the government ever owned property within a one mile radius of your property from the county recorder's office or from a title company.

☞ If a tenant is going to pay for utilities outside of the tenant's unit, you must disclose this. Most modern units are separately metered. However, if the tenant's meter includes utilities for which the tenant is not normally responsible, disclose it in writing and make some arrangement in writing for proration or reimbursement.

☞ The presence of environmental hazards, such as asbestos and lead-based paint, must be disclosed. If your building was constructed prior to 1981, assume there is asbestos present. If your building was constructed before 1979, there is a good chance it has both asbestos and lead-based paint.

The U.S. Occupational Safety and Health Administration (OSHA) has both written information and software that will help you identify the presence of asbestos, and give you legal ways to eliminate the potential danger. Remember that you may be liable to workmen, as well as to tenants.

Both the U.S. Environmental Protection Agency (EPA) and the California Department of Health Services can help you determine if your property has lead-based paint, and what to do about it. Both agencies have booklets that must be given to tenants.

In 1996, the EPA and the U.S. Department of Housing and Urban Development issued regulations requiring notices to be given to tenants of rental housing built before 1978 that there may be lead-based paint present and that it could pose a health hazard to children. This applies to all housing except housing for the elderly or 0-bedroom units (efficiencies, studio apartments, etc.) It also requires that a pamphlet about lead-based paint, titled *Protect Your Family from Lead in Your Home* be given to prospective tenants. The recommended disclosure form is included in appendix C as Form 12.

The rule is contained in the *Federal Register*, Vol. 61, No. 45, March 6, 1996, pages 9064-9088. More information, and copies of the pamphlet, can be obtained from the National Lead Information Clearinghouse at (800)424-5323. The information can also be obtained on the world wide web at http://www.nsc.org/ehc.html.

☞ You must disclose the name and address of the owner or manager of the property who can receive legal service, notices, and demands. Section 1962 of the California Civil Code states that such disclosure can be made in the lease or rental agreement, or by conspicuous posting at the rental property as set forth in section 1962.5 of the California Civil Code. It is easier and safer to disclose it in the lease or rental agreement.

☞ If the building is over one story high, emergency safety procedures must be posted, and tenants must be given a booklet or pamphlet describing the procedures. These must not only conform to the Health and Safety Code, but also be approved by the fire marshall. It may also be required that these disclosures be in a language other than English if the lease or rental agreement was negotiated in another language.

SUGGESTED CLAUSES

The following clauses are not required by any law, but are suggested by the authors to help you avoid potential problems during the tenancy:

☞ security or damage deposit.

☞ use clause. This is a provision limiting use of the property.

Note: Under the California Health and Safety Code, section 1598.40, a tenant may use the property as a day care business even if prohibited by the lease or local zoning ordinances. The tenant must first obtain a state license to operate a day care facility on the property, and, after obtaining the license, give the landlord at least a thirty day notice before starting the business. The maximum security deposit laws still apply, but the landlord may raise the deposit above that of other tenants.

☛ maintenance clause. (Spelling out who is responsible for which maintenance.)

☛ limitation on landlord's liability for acts beyond his or her control. It is not legal for a landlord to attempt to limit liability for his or her own acts, but a landlord may limit liability for acts of others beyond his or her control.

☛ limitation on assignment of the lease, or subletting by tenant.

☛ clause granting attorney's fees for enforcement of the lease.

☛ clause putting duty on tenant for own insurance.

☛ late fee and fee for bounced checks.

☛ limitation on number of persons living in the unit. This can be a reasonable number based upon the size of the unit, but if it causes discrimination against families with children, it could be illegal and subject the landlord to fines.

The safe-harbor rule is a limit of two persons per bedroom plus one additional. A landlord could go below that if the landlord had a record of renting to families with children and didn't use the limit to avoid children.

☛ in a condominium, a clause stating that tenant must comply with all rules and regulations of the condominium.

☛ requirement that if locks are changed, the landlord is given a key. (Forbidding tenants to change locks may subject the landlord to liability for a break-in.)

☞ limitation on pets. Landlords may and usually do prohibit pets except with the landlord's written permission. If you allow pets, be aware of some possible problems.

A landlord may be liable for an injury caused by a tenant's dog if the landlord knew or should have known of the animal's dangerous tendencies and did nothing about it. [*Uccello v. Laudenslayer*, 44 Cal.App.3rd 504, (1975)]. If the pet is a "wild animal," you only have to know that the tenant is keeping it—it is presumed dangerous (i.e., you are *strictly liable*). If the tenant posts signs warning of a dangerous dog, your insurance may refuse to cover the damage, arguing that the danger was known.

You may not forbid dogs necessary for a blind, deaf, or otherwise disabled tenant, nor increase the security deposit.

You may increase the security deposit for pets, but it is not advised that you specify it is to be used for damage caused by the pet as this may prevent you from using the extra deposit to cover damages caused by the tenant.

You may not raise the security deposit beyond the legal limit, regardless of the tenant's pets. This will be further discussed in chapter 3 on security deposits.

A pet agreement form is contained in appendix D as Form 4.

☞ limitation on where cars may be parked (not on the lawn, etc.).

☞ limitation on storage of boats, RVs, etc., on the property.

☞ in commercial leases there should be clauses regarding the fixtures, insurance, signs, renewal, eminent domain, and other factors related to the business use of the premises.

☞ to protect the landlord if it is necessary to dispose of property left behind by a tenant. (See ABANDONED PROPERTY BY TENANT in chapter 8.)

☞ attorney's fees. The lease will control attorney's fees. If the landlord requires the tenant to pay reasonable attorney's fees if the landlord sues and wins, the landlord is automatically required to pay tenants reasonable attorney's fees if the tenant wins.

Landlords put payment of attorney's fees into the lease because most suits are brought by the landlord and won by default. The problem is that most of the judgments won are not collectable.

Note. A court may award attorney's fees even if not required by the lease. This usually happens when the court feels that one of the parties should be punished for especially bad behavior.

For an explanation and analysis of each of the different clauses used in residential and commercial leases, and suggestions on how to negotiate, see *How to Negotiate Real Estate Leases*, by Mark Warda, available at most bookstores or directly from Sourcebooks, Inc.

ORAL
LEASES

A rental agreement or lease of property for one year or less does not have to be in writing to be valid. The problem, of course, is proving the terms of the oral agreement. Even the most honest people often remember things differently, especially as time passes. Oral leases have been held up in court. It just depends upon who sounds more believable to the judge.

Good advice is: don't use oral leases or rental agreements, even with friends or relatives. Better advice might be: don't use oral leases or rental agreements, *especially* with friends or relatives.

PROBLEM CLAUSES

UNCONSCIONABLE
CLAUSES

If a judge feels that a clause in a rental agreement is grossly unfair, she may rule that it is *unconscionable*. Certain provisions in leases are simply prohibited. These fall into two broad categories:

☞ A tenant cannot waive the right to a habitable dwelling. These rights are set forth in the California Civil Code, sections 1941 and 1942. However, the landlord and tenant may agree to the tenant maintaining, repairing, or improving the property. Also, the California Civil Code, section 1942.1, allows the parties to agree in writing to submit to arbitration any controversy over the condition of the property.

☞ The tenant cannot waive the legal remedies provided for in the California Civil Code, sections 1942.4 and 1953, such as the right to withhold rent or to sue the landlord.

Another problem is a clause in a lease that gives the landlord an illegal advantage over the tenant. A court could decide that the offending clause is unenforceable, or declare the entire lease invalid.

Clauses by which the tenant agrees to give up a legal right are the most common. Examples are clauses that have the tenant agreeing to pay more rent than the local rent control ordinance allows, agreeing to a *non-refundable* security deposit, agreeing not to sue the landlord for improper maintenance that causes injury, giving up the right to withhold rent as allowed by law, allowing the landlord to enter the property without giving adequate notice, and giving the landlord the right to evict by "self help" or without following the legal notice requirements. Any such clauses, as well as others that a court determines are illegal, against public policy, or unconscionable will not be enforced.

California Civil Code, section 1632, requires that if a lease or rental agreement is negotiated in Spanish, the tenant must receive a Spanish translation of the lease or agreement before signing. The English language lease or agreement is then binding. The translation may be submitted to the Department of Consumer Affairs for an opinion as to whether it is an accurate translation. The California Apartment Association has lease forms with approved Spanish translations.

BURIED CLAUSES   If a lease contains a clause which adversely affects a tenant, or might be considered controversial, it should not be buried in the lease. It should be pointed out to, and initialed by, the tenant. If not, a court would be more likely to refuse to enforce the provision.

SECURITY
DEPOSITS

Under California law, any money given to the landlord by the tenant that is above the normal rent is considered a refundable security deposit. It doesn't matter whether you call it non-refundable, a fee, last month's rent, or a larger first month's rent.

The maximum amount allowed is two month's rent for an unfurnished unit, and three month's rent for a furnished unit. A tenant with a pet may be charged a deposit greater than that of tenants without pets and not be discriminatory, but it may not exceed the allowable amount. A tenant with a waterbed may be charged a maximum of one-half month's rent over the amounts stated above.

WATER BEDS

Under the California Civil Code, section 1940.5, if your certificate of occupancy was issued after January 1, 1973, you may not prohibit a tenant from having a water bed. However, the bed must conform to industry standards, and the tenant must protect the landlord with insurance. Also, you can require up to the amount of one-half month's rent as an additional security deposit.

GUARANTEES

One way to protect yourself, especially when renting to young tenants, is to require a guaranty of the lease or rental agreement. With a parent or other relative on the hook, a tenant would be much less likely to damage the premises or to abscond without paying the rent. A guaranty form is included in this book as Form 11 in appendix D.

OPTIONS

Both residential and nonresidential leases may contain clauses which grant the tenant an option to extend the lease for another term or several terms. Often these options provide for an increase in rent during the renewal periods.

☛ A clause that automatically renews a lease is required to be in at least eight-point, bold-face type (California Civil Code, section 1945.5).

OPTION TO
PURCHASE

An option to purchase gives the tenant the right, but not the obligation, to purchase the property at some future date, at a preset price. The tenant may elect to *exercise the option* (i.e., buy the property) at any time during the lease, or be limited to some more specific time. If a lease contains an option to purchase, it will usually be enforceable exactly according to its terms.

📖 Where a tenant continued renting the property as a tenant-at-will after his lease expired, the court ruled his option to purchase the property expired at the end of the lease.

An option to purchase is usually not a good deal for the landlord. The disadvantage of an option to purchase is that if the option price is less than the market value, the tenant exercises the option (buys). If the option price is greater than the market value, the tenant doesn't buy.

The advantages of an option to purchase are that a tenant may be willing to sign a longer lease, pay higher rent, and take better care of the property.

RIGHT OF FIRST
REFUSAL

The *right of first refusal* may be used as an alternative. Tenants will often express an interest in purchasing the property if the landlord ever decides to sell. With a right of first refusal you give the tenant the right to match any offer you receive and are willing to accept from another buyer.

If you wish to give the tenants any rights to purchase as part of the lease, it is suggested that you either have an attorney prepare the agreement or consult a book such as *How to Negotiate Real Estate Contracts*, by Mark Warda, available at your local bookstore or directly from the publisher. Call 1-800-226-5291.

FORMS

There is no special form to create a lease or rental agreement. However, there are minimum requirements, as explained earlier. An exchange of letters, for example, which contained these requirements, would be sufficient to create a contract. This book contains suggested lease forms. Forms may also be obtained from the California Apartment Association in Sacramento. Forms regarding court procedures can usually be obtained from the court clerk. Several other books on the subject contain forms and lease clauses. If your situation requires special clauses, you should either consult such a book or a real estate attorney.

Be careful to choose a good lease form. Some forms on the market do not comply with California law and can be dangerous to use.

Forms 6-9 in this book are leases and rental agreements developed and used by the author. They are free of legalese and intended to be easily understandable by both parties. You may also need to use Forms 12 and 13.

PAYMENT

When accepting the deposit from a first time tenant you should be sure to get only cash, a cashier's check, or money order. If you accept a personal check and it bounces, it may take months to get the tenants out.

PHOTOS

If you want to be able to make a claim against the tenants in the event of any damage to the unit, you should take photos of the unit before the tenants move in. Without such photos it would be more difficult to prove in court that the tenants actually caused the damage.

SIGNATURES

If you do not have the proper signatures on the lease, you could have problems enforcing it, or evicting the tenants.

LANDLORD   If the property is owned by more than one person, then it is best to have all owners sign the lease.

TENANTS   In most cases it is best to have all adult occupants sign the lease so that more people will be liable for the rent.

INITIALS   Some landlords have places on the lease for the tenants to place their initials. This is usually done next to clauses that are unusual or very strongly pro-landlord, such as where the tenant is paying utilities for more than just the tenant's unit.

Initials of both landlord and tenant should also be placed wherever any part of the printed form is changed.

NOTARY   A lease does not need to be notarized to be valid. A landlord should not allow his signature on a lease to be notarized because the lease could then be recorded in the public records, which would be a cloud on his title and could cause a problem when the property is sold.

CO-SIGNERS AND GUARANTORS   If you have someone sign the lease or rental agreement to ensure payment by the tenant, they must also sign any subsequent changes to the agreement, especially rent increases.

BACKING OUT OF A LEASE

RESCISSION   Contrary to the beliefs of some tenants, there is no law allowing a rescission period for a lease. Once a lease has been signed by both parties it is legally binding on them.

ILLEGALITY   If a lease is entered into for an illegal purpose then it is void and unenforceable by either party. For example, you could not legally lease your property for the storage of stolen goods or for a house of prostitution.

HANDLING SECURITY DEPOSITS 3

The law regarding security deposits is controlled by the California Civil Code, section 1950. It applies to rentals that are longer than thirty days, but not to short term rentals such as hotels, motels, and vacation homes.

AMOUNT

Under California law, any money given to the landlord by the tenant above the normal rent is considered a refundable security deposit. It doesn't matter if you call it non-refundable, a cleaning fee, moving in fee, last month's rent or a larger first month's rent payment. Any amount paid at the beginning of the tenancy which is above one month's rent is considered a security deposit and must comply with the law.

The maximum amount allowed is two months' rent for an unfurnished unit, and three months' rent for a furnished unit. A tenant with a pet may be charged a larger one than a tenant without a pet, without liability for discrimination, but in either case the amount may not exceed the two or three months limit. A tenant with a waterbed may be charged a maximum of one-half month's rent over the amounts stated above.

INTEREST AND BANK ACCOUNT

California law does not require security deposits to be kept in a trust account or to keep them separate from other money of the landlord. Also, there is no state law that the landlord pay interest on the deposits. However, some cities have local ordinances with such requirements. At the time of publication the following cities had ordinances covering deposits. If you rent property in any of these cities you should obtain a copy of the ordinance.

Berkeley	San Francisco
Cotati	Santa Cruz
East Palo Alto	Santa Monica
Hayward	Watsonville
Los Angeles	West Hollywood

KEEPING THE DEPOSIT

California Civil Code, section 1950.5, allows a landlord to deduct only the following items from the security deposit:

- unpaid rent

- repair for damages caused by the tenant, tenant's guest or licensee, exclusive of normal wear and tear.

- cleaning after the tenant leaves.

- return of personal property or appurtenances if the security deposit agreement calls for it.

The landlord may deduct *damages* from a security deposit, but may not deduct normal wear and tear. What is normal is a question of fact which only a judge or jury can decide using a standard of reasonableness. A hole in a wall is clearly not normal. An apartment needing painting after a tenant lived there ten years is normal. Between those you have to use your best judgment. If you have any doubts, you should get a second opinion from a disinterested person or an attorney. A landlord making a claim on a deposit should *always* take pictures of the damage.

    📖   An Illinois court allowed a landlord to deduct $40 for cleaning a stove and refrigerator himself. *Evans v. International Village Apts.*, 520 N.E.2d 919 (Ill.App. 1988). Of course, it would be helpful to get a written estimate before doing the work yourself.

    📖   A Florida court allowed a landlord to charge a tenant for the cost of a real estate agent's fee for finding a new tenant for a rental unit. *McLennan v. Rozniak*, 15 Fla.Supp.2d 42 (Palm Beach 1985).

Some leases have clauses allowing a landlord to keep the entire deposit or a certain portion of it if the tenant leaves before the lease is up. Where the clause has been considered a liquidated damages clause, it has usually been upheld, but where it has been considered a penalty, it has been thrown out. It is not possible to say for certain whether a clause will be considered one or the other because judges have a wide leeway in their rulings. Usually the decision depends upon who the judge considers the good guy and the bad guy in the case.

    📖   In one case an automatic $200 re-rental fee was considered acceptable. *Lesatz v. Standard Green Meadows*, 416 N.W.2d 334 (Mich.App. 1987).

    📖   In another case an automatic $60 cleaning fee was considered a penalty and therefore illegal. *Albregt v. Chen*, 477 N.E.2d 1150 (Ohio App. 1985).

    📖   In a California case an additional $65 fee in a lease resulted in a civil penalty against the landlord of $271,000 plus $40,000 in attorney fees. *People v. Parkmerced Co.*, 244 Cal.Rptr. 22 (Cal.App.Div. 1988).

If a security deposit claim goes to court, it is also good to have receipts for the repairs that were done.

NOTICE

In order to make the deductions, the landlord must send the tenant an itemized statement of the deductions. This must be mailed to the tenant's last known address not later than three weeks after the tenant vacates the property. This applies to a tenant who leaves voluntarily or by eviction, even if the tenant owes rent which exceeds the deposit.

In order to legally keep all or a portion of a tenant's deposit you must send notice of the amounts you are keeping and the reasons. You should be as detailed as possible in case you are later taken to court by the tenant. You should only take legitimate deductions from the deposit. If you claim things that are not legitimate, the court can assess a penalty of $600 in addition to forcing you to return the deposit. A notice form is included in this book as Form 22. When noting the damages to the premises, you should take photographs or have someone who is disinterested observe the damage.

ADDRESS

If the tenant provided you with a new address, you should send the notice there. If not, you should send it to the address of the property. If the tenant has not filed a change of address notice with the post office, your notice will be returned to you and will serve as your proof that you complied with the law.

If you wish to learn the tenant's new address, you should write "Address Correction Requested" on the envelope and you will receive the new address from the post office for a very small fee.

If you try to send the tenant the balance of a deposit but cannot find the tenant, then the money is considered abandoned and is supposed to be turned over to the state of California.

CERTIFIED MAIL

If you send the notice by certified mail, you will have proof that you made a good faith effort to comply with the law and sent the notice in a timely manner.

DAMAGE EXCEEDS DEPOSIT

If, as happens in many cases, the damages exceed the deposit, then you should show this in the notice. You can sue the tenant in small claims court for the balance, but this is rarely worth the effort and expense.

EVICTION   You must send this notice to the tenant within three weeks of departure even if you have evicted the tenant.

FULL SETTLEMENT   The landlord might want to write on the back of the check, "Accepted in full payment of claims against security deposit." However, this might make a tenant want to immediately sue. A check without this language might be cashed by the tenant who plans to sue later but never gets around to it.

SELLING OR BUYING A PROPERTY

If you sell a property while holding a security deposit, you should transfer the security deposits to the new owner. You are allowed to deduct for rent owed and for damages caused by the tenant.

If you buy property where tenants have put up security deposits, you should be sure to get a correct accounting from the seller and have the deposits transferred to you at closing or have them deducted from your amount owed. If you do not, you may be liable for them when the tenants move out. To protect themselves, buyers sometimes request statements from each tenant confirming the amount of the deposits.

RESPONSIBILITY FOR MAINTENANCE 4

LANDLORD'S DUTIES

CONTRACT   The contract between the parties, whether a written lease or a verbal agreement, can impose an obligation on the landlord to provide certain types of maintenance. For example, if the lease allows use of a swimming pool or states that the landlord will paint the unit, then the landlord would be obligated under the lease to maintain the pool and to paint as agreed. However, since landlords typically provide the lease agreements, excessive promises are not usual and this issue rarely comes up.

STATUTES   State law requires the landlord to keep the premises *habitable*. California Civil Code, section 1941.1, defines *habitability* as having:

(a) effective waterproofing and weather protection of roof and exterior walls, including unbroken windows and doors.

(b) plumbing or gas facilities which conform to applicable law in effect at the time of installation, maintained in good working order.

(c) a water supply approved under applicable law, which is under control of the resident, capable of producing hot and cold running water, furnished to appropriate fixtures, and connected to a sewage disposal system approved under applicable law.

(d) heating facilities which conformed with applicable law at the time of installation, maintained in good worker order.

(e) electrical lighting, with wiring and electrical equipment which conformed with applicable law at the time of installation, maintained in good working order.

(f) building, grounds, and appurtenances at the time of the commencement of the lease or rental agreement in every part clean, sanitary, and free from all accumulations of debris, filth, rubbish, garbage, rodents, and vermin, and all areas under control of the owner kept in every part clean, sanitary, and free from all accumulations of debris, filth, rubbish, garbage, rodents, and vermin.

(g) an adequate number of appropriate receptacles for garbage and rubbish, in clean condition and good repair at the time of the commencement of the lease or rental agreement, with the owner providing appropriate serviceable receptacles thereafter, and being responsible for the clean condition and good repair of such receptacles under his control.

(h) floors, stairways, and railings maintained in good repair.

(i) as of July 1, 1998, dead bolt locks on unit entrances are required by Civil Code Section 141.3 (see pages 124-125)

The common sense definition of lacking habitability is having serious defects which make it very difficult or impossible for the tenant to reside on the property. Cosmetic defects are not included. As explained above, the landlord may create a duty for cosmetic defects by agreement.

CODE
VIOLATIONS

Besides the habitability requirement of the statutes, there are various health codes both at the state and local level. Some of these are contained in the California Health and Safety Code, section 17920.3, and title 25 and the California Code of Regulations. Most local governments also have building codes, such as the Uniform Housing Code.

Landlords should be aware that governmental bodies can levy fines of hundreds of dollars a day for minor violations. Ignoring notices of violation can be expensive.

Whenever you receive a governmental notice, you should read it very carefully and follow it to the letter. One landlord who sold his property and thought the problem was solved, was fined $11,000 ($500 a day for the last twenty-two days he owned the property) for a violation. After you correct a violation, be sure that the governmental body which sent the notice gives you written confirmation that you are in compliance.

WAIVER OF LANDLORD'S DUTIES

As a basic rule, landlords cannot get out of their duty to do maintenance by putting it on the tenant. This is set out in California Civil Code, section 1942.1. However, the statute contains an exception where the parties agree that the tenant shall do the maintenance in exchange for lower rent.

As a practical matter, only a small number of units would be suitable for tenant maintenance. The usual situation is the single family house.

Note. There must be a true agreement for reduced rent. If the court decides that the tenant has simply waived the right to the landlord's duty to repair and maintain the property, the agreement will not be enforced.

TENANT'S DUTIES

The duties of a tenant are set forth by California Civil Code, section 1941.2, which provides:

(a) No duty on the part of the owner to repair a dilapidation shall raise under Section 1941 or 1942 if the resident is in substantial violation of any of the following affirmative obligations, provided the resident's violation contributes substantially to the existence of the dilapidation or interferes substantially with the owner's obligation under Section 1941 to effect the necessary repairs:

(1) to keep that part of the premises which he occupies and uses clean and sanitary as the condition of the premises permits.

(2) to dispose from his dwelling unit of all rubbish, garbage and other waste, in a clean and sanitary manner.

(3) to properly use and operate all electrical, gas, and plumbing fixtures and keep them as clean and sanitary as their condition permits.

(4) not to permit any person on the premises, with his permission to willfully or wantonly destroy, deface, damage, impair, or remove any part of the structure or dwelling unit or the facilities, equipment, or appurtenances thereto, nor himself do any such thing.

(5) to occupy the premises as his abode, utilizing portions thereof for living, sleeping, cooking, or dining purposes only which were respectively designed or intended to be used for such occupancies.

(b) Paragraphs (1) and (2) of subdivision (a) shall not apply if the owner has expressly agreed in writing to perform the act or acts mentioned therein.

The landlord may agree to perform the requirements of paragraphs (1) and (2). The agreement must be in writing.

TENANTS' REMEDIES

If the landlord has failed to comply with his or her duty to do proper maintenance, the law offers the tenant several possible remedies, depending upon the severity of the situation.

WITHHOLDING RENT

If a landlord violates the maintenance requirements of the statutes or the health and safety codes and such violation renders the premises "uninhabitable," then the tenant can withhold all or part of the rent until proper repairs are made.

Whether the tenant is legally entitled to withhold rent can only be determined in court, meaning the landlord would need to bring an action to either collect the rent or evict the tenant. Since this is time-consuming, expensive, and risky, the landlord would be well advised to work with the tenant to correct the alleged problems and have the rent paid voluntarily.

However, the claim that rent is being withheld for a maintenance violation is most often made after the tenant has been taken to court for failure to pay rent. Unfortunately, the law does not require the tenant to give the notice in writing or to produce proof of delivery, so a tenant can claim to have given notice after an eviction has been started.

REPAIR AND DEDUCT

If the problem with the premises renders the premises "untenantable" and the landlord fails to remedy it within a reasonable time, then the tenant is allowed to make the repair and deduct the cost from the next month's rent under California Civil Code, section 1942. This remedy cannot be used more than twice in a twelve month period.

Whether the premises are untenantable is a legal question which would depend upon the facts of the situation. A clogged toilet or a broken window in the winter would most likely make the premises untenantable, while a slight drip in a faucet or a burned out bulb where other light is available probably would not.

What is a reasonable time is also a legal question that depends upon the facts. The law says that thirty days is clearly reasonable. But a much shorter time would also be reasonable for many problems.

The tenant must give the landlord reasonable notice of the problem before using this remedy. The notice can be verbal and not in writing. The problem cannot be caused by the tenant or a violation of the tenant's duties.

MOVING OUT   If the premises are actually untenantable and the landlord refuses after a reasonable amount of time to remedy the situation, the tenant also has the option of moving out. A tenant using this remedy where there is substantial time remaining on the lease is taking a risk that he or she will be sued for breach of the lease.

If the premises are actually untenantable, then the landlord would be wasting time tracking the tenant down and filing a suit. If the situation is minor and used as an excuse to break the lease, the landlord might want to take the matter to court. If so, the landlord should be prepared with photographs and witnesses to prove that the condition of the premises was not as bad as claimed.

LANDLORDS' LIABILITIES 5

The law of liability for injuries and crime on rental property has changed considerably over the last couple decades. The law for hundreds of years, that landlords are not liable, was overturned and landlords are now often liable, even for conditions that are not their fault. This change was not made by elected legislators representing their constituents, but by appointed judges who felt tenants needed protection and landlords should give it to them.

GENERAL RULES OF LANDLORD LIABILITY

The landlord has a duty to make safe conditions or adequately warn of dangerous conditions. However, warning is only a temporary safeguard until the premises can be made safe. This duty applies not only to what we usually think of as dangerous conditions, such as a broken step or cracked walkway, but to the actions of others. This means criminal acts by tenants and non-tenants may create liability for the landlord.

There are three ways to create liability.

☛ ***Intentional acts.*** For example, a landlord assaults a tenant.

☞ *Negligence.* The basis of the vast majority of liability is negligence. In order to have liability for negligence, four elements must be present:

1. Duty: The defendant (landlord) must owe a duty to the plaintiff (the one who is suing). Today that duty will extend to almost anyone who is injured on the property, not just a tenant.

   A duty may sometimes be created by the landlord where none previously existed. For example, there may be no duty to have an alarm system in the building. However, if you install one, you may be liable if you fail to keep it in good working order and someone is injured because it failed.

2. Breach of duty: A breach of duty is the failure to use *reasonable care.* This is usually what is contested. If the landlord did everything he reasonably could to prevent the damage or injury to the plaintiff, he is not liable.

   The problem is that "reasonableness" is subjective. A judge or jury may have a much different idea than the landlord's idea of what is reasonable.

   The standard of care may be greater if the landlord makes promises beyond the normal standards. These promises commonly concern safety from crime and are contained in advertisements as well as direct communication with the tenant.

3. Causation: The breach of duty by the landlord must have caused the plaintiff's injury or damages. If you had an inadequate lock on a door (failure to use reasonable care) but the burglar came in through the window, there was no causation.

4. Damages: The plaintiff must be injured or suffer some loss as a result of the negligent conduct of the landlord.

Another common basis for a landlord's liability is what is called *negligence per se*. This is a presumed or automatic failure to use reasonable care. It arises when a landlord violates a law. A common example would be failing to fence off a swimming pool.

☞ **Strict liability.** This is like negligence except there is no need to prove breach of duty. The basis of strict liability is an unusually dangerous activity. If a landlord were having a fireworks display and something went wrong which caused injury, the fact that the landlord used reasonable care would not be a defense. The same would be true of injury caused by an animal normally considered a wild animal.

ACCIDENTS

AREAS UNDER LANDLORD'S CONTROL

A landlord is liable for failure to use reasonable care in keeping areas under the landlord's control safe for the tenants and others who may use them. This means that the landlord is liable if:

☞ the landlord created the dangerous condition.

☞ the dangerous condition would have been discovered by a reasonable inspection.

☞ the landlord knew of the dangerous condition.

In the 1995 case of *Peterson v. Superior Court of Riverside County* (10 Cal. 4th 1185), the California Supreme Court reversed their previous ruling that a landlord could be strictly liable for a dangerous condition which did not meet the above test of liability.

AREAS NOT UNDER THE LANDLORD'S CONTROL

The general rule is that a landlord is not liable for injuries on parts of the premises not under his control, except:

☞ where there is a danger known to the landlord.

☞ where there is a violation of law in the condition of the premises.

☞ where there is a preexisting defect in construction.

☞ where the landlord undertakes to repair the premises or is required by the lease to make the repairs.

PETS

The same rules that apply to accidents caused by dangerous conditions apply to injuries caused by pets. If the landlord knows that a pet owned by a tenant is dangerous, then the landlord can be liable if the pet injures someone. Some courts have even held landlords liable when a tenant's dog bit a friend of the tenant who was visiting.

How can a landlord know if a tenant's pet is dangerous? With most common types of cats and dogs the landlord won't know unless someone reports to the landlord that the pet is vicious.

However, if the pet is obviously dangerous, such as possibly a pit bull or definitely a poisonous snake, then the landlord is assumed to know the condition is dangerous and would be liable for any injuries.

CRIMES AGAINST TENANTS

Another area where liability of landlords has been greatly expanded is in the area of crimes against tenants. The former theory of law was that a person cannot be held liable for deliberate acts of third parties. This had been the theory for hundreds of years, but has recently been abandoned in favor of a theory that a landlord must protect tenants from crimes.

The theory has been stated to be that where the landlord can foresee the possibility of criminal attack, the landlord must take precautions to prevent it. But the law is still evolving in this area and some courts have said that this means any time an attack is possible the landlord must protect the tenant. This would include nearly every tenancy, especially in urban areas. New Jersey has gone so far as to hold landlords strictly liable for every crime committed on their property, whether or not they knew there was a risk or took any precautions. (This liability for crime, unlike the warranty of habitability, applies to both residential and commercial tenancies in New Jersey, but has not been extended to single family homes yet.)

There are several ways a landlord may be liable for crimes committed on the premises:

- ☛ renting to a tenant who is dangerous where the landlord knows or should have known of the danger. Of course it is difficult to know whether an applicant is dangerous and using a persons looks to make such determination could make the landlord liable for discrimination. If a tenant turns out to be dangerous after beginning a rental and the landlord fails to terminate the tenancy, the landlord could be liable for crimes committed by the tenant.

- ☛ dangerous conditions. If windows don't lock properly, halls are not well lit, or bushes create good hiding places for muggers, this can create liability for the landlord.

- ☛ inadequate security. In high crime urban areas some courts have ruled that landlords can be liable for crimes if they fail to provide protection for their tenants and their guests in the form of security guards.

- ☛ broken promises. If a lease or advertisement for the property promises certain types of security, such as locked garages or security guards, then the landlord can be liable for failing to provide these, or for letting them fall out of repair.

CRIMES BY TENANTS AGAINST NON-TENANTS

This is another evolving area of law where landlords were previously safe but now subject to liability. In one case where a commercial tenant was selling counterfeit goods with such trademarks as Rolex and Polo, a federal court held that the landlords could be held liable if they knew of the activities of the tenants and did nothing to stop them. *Polo Ralph Lauren Corp. v. Chinatown Gift Shop*, 93 CIV 6783 TPG (United States District Court for the Southern District of New York, June 21, 1994).

PROTECTION FROM LIABILITY

With juries awarding multi-million dollar verdicts, the owner of rental property is at great risk in the event of an injury to a tenant. The following sections cover some of the ways a landlord can protect himself.

INSURANCE
Insurance is the most important thing a landlord can have for protection from liability. Even the most careful landlord can have problems on his property. Fortunately an umbrella liability policy, offering coverage of a million dollars or more, can be available at a reasonable fee. However, insurance alone is not enough. There are many verdicts awarded each year that exceed insurance limits.

TENANT RELATIONS
By maintaining good relations with tenants a landlord can avoid bad feelings which inspire lawsuits. Even serious matters are often overlooked or settled easily when people have a good relationship. If at all possible, you should seek to stay on good terms with your tenants.

ASSET PROTECTION
Every person with substantial assets, especially risky assets like rental property, should use asset protection techniques. Such techniques make personal assets untouchable from all types of claims. Some of the techniques that can be used are keeping equity in a homestead, pension plan, family limited partnership, or certain types of trusts. See *Simple Ways to Protect Yourself from Lawsuits* available from Sphinx Publishing.

CONTRACTUAL
PROTECTIONS

It is not legal for a landlord to provide in his leases that he is not liable for his own acts of negligence or for other liabilities that the law specifically places on him. However, the landlord can sometimes avoid liability by putting duties, which can result in liability, on the tenant. For example, if a lease put the responsibility for certain maintenance or for repair of the lock on the tenant, then the landlord *might* be free from liability if a defect in either of these causes an injury.

This might not be upheld by a court in every case, but it offers one more line of defense, which might dissuade a trial lawyer from taking the case. It would be most useful in a single family home or duplex, but might not work well in a building with more apartment units.

SECURITY
GUARDS

In some inner-city apartment complexes where crime is common, landlords may be required to provide armed guards or face liability. Again, insurance is a must and this additional cost will have to be covered by rent increases.

Changing the Terms of the Tenancy 6

Assignment or Sublease by Tenant

Sometimes a tenant will seek to turnover all or part of the premises to a third party. This can be done in one of two ways: an assignment or a sublease.

ASSIGNMENT

An *assignment* is where a tenant assigns all of her interest in a lease to another party, who takes over the tenant's position. The new tenant takes the place of the original tenant and deals directly with the landlord. The new tenant pays rent directly to the landlord.

SUBLEASE

A *sublease* is where the original tenant leases all or part of the property to a third party. This new party (called a *subtenant* or *sublessee*) is responsible to the original tenant (called the *sublessor*). The original tenant is still responsible to the landlord. The sublessee pays his or her rent to the sublessor, who then pays his or her rent to the landlord.

VALIDITY

Subleases and assignments are allowed unless prohibited by the terms of the lease. However, even if prohibited by the lease, a problem arises as California law places a *duty to mitigate* on the landlord. A landlord has a duty to make reasonable efforts to rent the property in the event the tenant leaves before the end of the lease term. If your tenant offers you a new tenant who is reasonably acceptable, you can't say "no," and still hold the original tenant liable for rent for the balance of the lease term.

APPROVAL The safest way to handle a sublease or assignment is to require the landlord's written consent. This way you can screen the proposed new tenant and make a more informed decision as to whether to allow the sublease or assignment. This will also help in the event of eviction. You must specifically evict an assignee or sub-tenant.

WAIVER Express consent (with words) may be waived by implied consent (by conduct). Accepting rent from the new tenant, or knowingly allowing a "guest" to stay beyond the time specified in the lease or rental agreement, may waive your right to later object.

MODIFYING THE LEASE You may also raise the rent or security deposit if more people are going to occupy the unit. You may draw a new lease which all adult occupants will sign, or you may use a thirty-day notice for a rental agreement. Be careful to check rent control laws, if applicable to your property, and do not exceed the maximum allowed security deposit.

SALE OF PROPERTY BY LANDLORD

A landlord has the right to sell property covered by a lease, but the new owner takes the property subject to the terms of any existing lease.

The new owner cannot cancel the old lease or raise the rent while the lease is still in effect (unless the lease has provisions allowing the landlord to do so).

When selling property, the contract should make it clear to the buyer that the sale is subject to existing leases. Otherwise the buyer may sue for failure to deliver the premises free and clear of other claims. At closing, the leases should be assigned to the buyer. Also, any security deposits need to be transferred to the buyer or returned to the tenants. When the buyer inspects the property, any damage found should be deducted from the deposit if it is to be returned to the tenant.

If you transfer the security deposit to the buyer, send the tenant a letter containing the buyer's name and address, notification of the transfer of the security deposit, and an itemized statement of any deductions for unpaid rent or damage to the property. The buyer may then demand that the tenant bring the security deposit back up to the agreed upon amount.

FORECLOSURES

When property is purchased at a foreclosure sale, the leases of the tenants are terminated if they were signed after the date of the mortgage.

RAISING THE RENT

WHEN YOU
MAY RAISE THE
RENT

If a tenancy is for a set term (such as a one year lease) at a specified rent, then the landlord cannot raise the rent until the term ends, unless such right is spelled out in the lease. If the tenancy is month to month, then the landlord would be able to raise the rent by giving notice at least thirty days in advance. This is based upon the requirement of thirty days notice to terminate the tenancy.

To raise the rent in a month-to-month tenancy you can use Form 14. In such case, the tenant would probably not have to give thirty days notice if she decided not to stay until the end of the month. This is because by raising the rent the landlord would be terminating the previous tenancy and making the tenant an offer to enter into a new tenancy at a different rental rate.

California Civil Code, section 1946, allows the parties to shorten the notice period when the lease is created to as little as seven days. There is confusion about raising rent by a seven day notice, therefore, a thirty day agreement in the lease is advised. You may also raise the security deposit to reflect the increase in rent. The same notice requirements apply.

Most commonly, rent is increased on the date it is due (usually the first of the month). This is not a legal requirement, and rent may be raised on any date if the proper notice is given. If you raise the rent in the middle of a rental period, you must prorate the rent. This means you must figure how much rent is due before and after the increase to the next usual rent payment date.

HOW TO RAISE
THE RENT

Most rent increases are accomplished by sending a letter to the tenant stating that the rent will be increased to a certain amount as of a certain date. This does not, however, comply with California law and only works because the tenant doesn't object.

The California Code of Civil Procedure, section 1162 is very specific about serving the notice. There are three types of acceptable service:

☞ personal service. This is where you hand the notice to the tenant. Even if the tenant refuses to accept it, it's okay. Leave it near the tenant. You may have someone else do this. It is advisable that you do it yourself unless you have a manager.

☞ substituted service. This is where you leave the notice with someone else at the tenant's home or workplace. The statute requires it be left with someone of "suitable age and discretion." Use common sense.

Before you can use substituted service, you must have attempted to serve the tenant personally both at home and at work. You must also mail a copy of the notice to the tenant's residence (the rental property).

☞ posting and mailing, also known as "nail and mail." This is where you post the notice on the front door of the rental unit *and* mail a copy to that address. Just as with substituted service, you must first attempt personal service.

As soon as the tenant pays the rent increase, the tenant's right to assert improper notice is lost.

Again the usual caution: Rent control or any other government program such as subsidized housing may effect your ability to raise rents and security deposits, as well as effect the procedure for doing so.

MODIFYING THE LEASE

If you agree to modify the terms of your lease with a tenant, you should put it in writing. If you do not and you allow a tenant to do things forbidden in the lease, you may be found to have waived your rights. A simple modification form, AMENDMENT TO LEASE/RENTAL AGREEMENT is included in this book as Form 10.

PROBLEMS DURING THE TENANCY

7

LANDLORD'S ACCESS TO THE PREMISES

RIGHT TO ENTER

California Civil Code, section 1954 is specific as to a landlord's right to enter a tenant's unit. The circumstances set out in the statute are:

- ☛ in an emergency. The statute does not define *emergency*.

- ☛ to make necessary or agreed upon repairs, decorations, alterations, improvements, or services.

- ☛ to show the unit to prospective buyers, mortgagees, tenants, or workmen.

- ☛ when the unit has been abandoned or surrendered.

- ☛ pursuant to a court order.

- ☛ by invitation or consent of the tenant.

Except in cases of emergency, abandonment, or surrender, the landlord can enter only during normal business hours. The statute does not define normal business hours. Some lease forms call for entry between 8am and 6pm, Monday through Saturday.

NOTICE

Except in cases of emergency, abandonment or surrender, or when it is impracticable, reasonable notice must be given. The statute defines reasonable notice as twenty-four-hour notice.

Note. California Civil Code, section 1953 prohibits a tenant's waiver of rights under section 1954.

VIOLATIONS BY THE TENANT

RENT DUE
DATE

Under California law (CC §1947), unless otherwise stated in a lease or rental agreement, rent is due on the last day of each rental period, unless otherwise agreed. For this reason landlords should clearly spell out in the lease that the rent is due at the beginning of each rental period.

VACATING
EARLY

If a tenant vacates the property before the end of the lease, she is still liable for the rent until the end of the lease. However, the landlord cannot just sit back and wait for the end of the lease. He has a duty to try to find a new tenant and credit the rent received from the new tenant to the amount owed by the old tenant. The landlord may also hold the old tenant liable for any reasonable costs of finding a new tenant, such as running an ad or doing a credit check on the new tenant.

BAD CHECKS

Your policy concerning payment by check and bounced checks should be set out in your rental agreement. In addition you should post your charges, if any, where the rents are paid.

If you get a bad check, you may consider the rent to be unpaid and may serve the tenant with a three day notice to pay rent or quit.

Under California Civil Code, section 1719, you may also demand payment from the tenant by sending certified mail which states the amount of the check and the amount of any charges. If you make this demand and the check is not made good within thirty days, you are entitled to three times the amount of the check up, to $1,500.

A bad check notice is included in this book as Form 21 in appendix D. Use this form only for bad checks due to insufficient funds or a closed account. If the tenant stopped payment, you must use a different procedure as explained in California Civil Code §1719 in appendix B.

Keep in mind that if a rent check bounces, you are much better off giving the tenant a THREE DAY NOTICE TO PAY RENT OR QUIT (Form 23) than a thirty-day notice to make a check good. But you can do both and possibly collect triple damages after the tenant leaves.

If a tenant gives you a bad check and then moves before making the check good, you may want to hold the check and periodically call the bank to see if any money is in the account. You can usually get a bank to cash a check less than six months old. If you redeposit a bounced check and it bounces again, the bank will mutilate it (punch holes in it) and you won't be able to later cash it.

DAMAGE TO
THE PREMISES

Minor damage by the tenant, even if intentional, must be repaired by the landlord. The tenant may be billed for the cost involved. If the tenant doesn't pay, the landlord may sue for the amount due.

Major damage done by the tenant may relieve the landlord of the duty to keep the unit habitable. This is discussed further in chapter 4. The landlord may bill the tenant for the damage, and sue if it is not paid.

The landlord may also serve the tenant with a THREE DAY NOTICE TO COMPLY OR QUIT (Form 24), or obtain an injunction against the tenant doing further damage. These are difficult options without an attorney.

LEASE
VIOLATIONS

If the tenant violates the lease, for example by making too much noise, having a pet or allowing too many people to live in the premises, the landlord has three options. If the breach is curable, she can send a THREE DAY NOTICE TO COMPLY OR QUIT. If the breach is incurable, she can give either a three or thirty day notice to quit. The procedure is explained in detail in chapter 9, "Terminating a Tenancy."

VIOLATIONS BY THE LANDLORD

RETALIATORY
CONDUCT

The landlord may not retaliate against a tenant who has exercised any rights under California Civil Code, section 1942. These rights would include:

☛ a written or verbal complaint to the landlord.

☛ a complaint to any government agency.

☛ filing a lawsuit or arbitration proceeding.

☛ receiving a judgment or arbitration award.

Retaliation would include raising rent, decreasing services, and eviction. The burden is on the tenant to prove that the landlord is retaliating and not acting for some legitimate reason. The landlord's action must be within 180 days of the tenants action against which the tenant claims that the landlord is retaliating.

The section then goes on to say that if a landlord's action to raise rent, decrease services, or evict is controverted, the landlord must prove the legitimate purpose.

As a practical matter, a landlord must have a provable reason which is not retaliatory in order to raise rent, reduce services, or evict.

Penalties for violation may include punitive damages and attorney's fees.

INTERRUPTING UTILITIES

Under California Civil Code, section 789.3, a landlord who terminates or interrupts utilities such as water, heat, light, electricity, gas, elevator, garbage collection, or refrigeration can be held liable for up to $100 per day in damages, plus attorney's fees and actual damages suffered by the tenant.

FAILURE TO MAKE REPAIRS

If the building becomes uninhabitable, the tenant has two duties and then three options. The two duties are:

1. notify the landlord. This may be done orally or in writing.

2. give the landlord a reasonable time to make the repairs. A reasonable time will vary with the type of repair necessary. More than thirty days is generally considered unreasonable for most repairs. The time may be much shorter for repairs such as no heat in the winter or broken water pipes.

If the landlord fails to repair in a reasonable time, the tenant may:

1. move, even if this would violate the terms of a lease or rental agreement.

2. repair and deduct. The tenant may make the necessary repairs and deduct an amount not to exceed one month's rent. This may be done not more than twice in a twelve month period. California Civil Code, section 1942.

3. withhold rent. This is a more complex remedy. Not only may the tenant refuse to pay rent until the defect is corrected, the tenant may demand reduced rent for the time that the property was not in proper condition.

The tenant must have the rent available, and cannot use this as a way to avoid paying rent. If a court decides, or the landlord and tenant agree, to a reduced rent, the tenant must pay the reduced rent, within three days if notice is given.

Receivership and relocation. In extreme cases, the California Health and Safety Code, section 17980.7, allows for a receiver to be appointed to take over operation of the building, make necessary repairs, and pay for tenants moving and relocation until the repairs are made.

Tax consequences of failure to repair. If the condition of the property violates state or local codes and the landlord does not make the necessary repairs within six months, the landlord may lose the tax advantages of the property, such as deductions for interest and depreciation. California Revenue and Taxation Code, sections 17274 and 24436.6. Note that these are state and not federal rules.

DESTRUCTION OF THE PREMISES

If the premises are damaged by fire, earthquake or other casualty, the rights of both landlord and tenant are usually spelled out in the lease. If the lease does not cover this situation, or if the rental is under an oral agreement, then California law provides that upon total destruction of the premises the lease terminates (CC §1933). If the premises are only partially destroyed then the tenant has the option of terminating the tenancy upon giving notice (CC §1932).

PROBLEMS AT THE END OF THE TENANCY 8

TENANT HOLDING OVER

Sometimes a tenant will refuse to vacate the premises at the end of the lease or rental period. Accepting rent after a lease expires creates a month to month tenancy.

At the end of a lease term, no notice is required by either landlord or tenant. However, it has become so common for the tenant to stay after the end of the lease that is wise to take a practical approach.

- ☛ If you do not want the tenant to leave, accept rent. If you wish to raise the rent, serve a thirty day notice before the lease term expires.

- ☛ If you want the tenant to leave, serve a thirty day notice to quit which will take effect at the end of the lease term.

DAMAGE TO THE PREMISES

If the landlord finds damage at the end of a tenancy, he may deduct the amount of the damage from the security deposit. However, he must follow the notice requirements as spelled out in chapter 3.

If the damages exceed the amount of the security deposit the landlord may sue the tenant, and if they are under $5,000 the landlord can file the case in small claims court.

PROPERTY ABANDONED BY TENANT

Tenants often leave personal property behind when they move. It is usually of little value and in most cases the landlord throws it away. This is not, however, what the law requires. You must mail to the former tenant or other person who may own the property a NOTICE OF RIGHT TO RECLAIM ABANDONED PROPERTY (Forms 44 and 45). The tenant then has eighteen days from the date of the mailing to reply. The notice may be sent to the property if you don't know where the former tenant may be.

If there is no reply to the notice, there are requirements based on the value of the property.

☞ If the property is worth less than $300, you may do as you please with it.

☞ If the property is worth $300 or more, you must sell it at a public auction and the proceeds, less your costs for storage, advertising and selling the property, must be turned over to the local county. The owner of the property then has one year to claim the money.

There are specific requirements including notice of the sale to the former tenant, advertising and hiring a bonded public auctioneer pursuant to Government Code, section 6066, and Civil Code, section 1988. Check these sections for the details. Also consult with the auctioneer, who may be familiar with the procedure.

As a practical matter, these auctions rarely occur. The tenant usually either does not leave personal property valued at $300 or more behind or comes back to claim it.

BACK RENT   If the tenant owes rent, you may recover it from the proceeds of the auction only if you have a judgment against the tenant and properly execute the judgment. If you have a judgement, contact the court clerk or Marshal's office for the procedure to levy against the proceeds of the auction.

If the tenant contacts you for the return of the property, you may not refuse to return it until unpaid rent is paid. You may insist on storage charges. This may not be worth the possibility of a lawsuit, even if you win.

VEHICLES   If the tenant leaves a motor vehicle on the property you can often get the police to tow it away and take responsibility for its disposal. However, some cities have different procedures and they may tell you it is your responsibility. If so, you can usually find out the procedure from a towing company. Most likely they will tow it, sell it and deduct their fees from the proceeds. If there are excess proceeds, you may be able to levy on them for any back rent judgment.

TERMINATING A TENANCY 9

A tenancy may be terminated in several ways. Unless the tenancy is terminated properly, you cannot regain possession of the premises. If you file an eviction without properly terminating the tenancy, the tenant may win the case and you may be ordered to pay damages to the tenant as well as the tenant's attorney fees.

TENANCIES WITH NO SPECIFIC TERM

When there is no specific term, either party may terminate by giving written notice based upon the rental period. A month-to-month tenancy requires at least a thirty day notice. A week-to-week tenancy requires at least a seven day notice. California Civil Code, section 1946.

The parties may agree to as little as a seven day notice for a month-to-month tenancy. If you reduce the notice period, be sure that your notice doesn't attempt to terminate the tenancy during a period for which rent has already been paid.

The law does not require the termination to coincide with the payment of rent. If a tenant who pays rent on the first of each month gives a thirty day notice to vacate on the tenth, the tenant may legally vacate thirty days later without liability for rent after that date. The rent is due and payable to, and including, the date of termination.

In most cases you do not have to give a good reason to terminate a tenancy. In fact you do not have to give any reason. However, you cannot terminate a tenancy for an illegal reason, such as retaliation or discrimination. In public housing and some rent controlled areas you must have a good reason. There are special rules which you must carefully follow.

To terminate a month-to-month tenancy use Form 26 in appendix D, THIRTY-DAY NOTICE OF TERMINATION OF TENANCY. For a weekly rental, or a rental where the tenant has agreed in writing to seven days notice, you can change the "30" to "7" on the notice.

You should personally attempt to hand the notice to the tenant at the property. If the tenant is not there, you should next try to serve him or her at work, if you know where the tenant works. If neither of these are successful, you can serve another adult at the property and mail a second copy to the tenant. If there is no other adult at the property, you can post a copy on the front door of the property and mail a second copy to the tenant. You can also send the notice by certified or registered mail, but you must add five additional days to the time given to the tenant.

EXPIRATION OF RENTAL OR LEASE TERM

When the term of a lease ends, the tenant is expected to vacate the property without notice. This is different from some states where a lease is presumed to be renewed unless the tenant gives the landlord notice that she is leaving. If you believe that a tenant may not be expecting to leave at the end of the lease, or if you would simply like to be sure it is understood, you can use Form 17.

If you accept rent after the lease terminates, it is presumed to convert to a periodic (month-to-month) tenancy. You will then need to give a thirty day notice to terminate the tenancy.

If your property is subject to local rent control, you will probably need good cause to terminate. Check your local ordinance regarding your right to terminate or to increase the rent.

Special requirements apply to public housing. For more information, see the section on "Special Rules for Public Housing" later in this chapter.

EARLY TERMINATION BY TENANT

There are several reasons for a tenant to terminate the tenancy early. Some of them are legally justified and some not.

DESTRUCTION OF PREMISES
If the premises are destroyed, such as by fire or earthquake, the tenant may immediately vacate the premises and terminate the rental. California Civil Code, section 1933.

PREMISES UNINHABITABLE
If the premises are damaged so that the premises become *uninhabitable* as defined in California Civil Code, section 1941.1, and the landlord has not improved (or cannot improve) the conditions within a reasonable time, the tenant may vacate the premises and terminate the rental.

REMEDIES FOR BREACH BY TENANT
If the tenant leaves the premises before the end of the lease agreement, and without the legal right to do so, the tenant has breached the agreement. The landlord then has two options:

1. The landlord may relet the property and sue the tenant for the unpaid rent during the time the property was vacant. The landlord's duty to mitigate is met if reasonable efforts are used to find another tenant.

2. The landlord may ignore the duty to mitigate, and hold the tenant liable for the unpaid rent until the lease expires. California

Civil Code, section 1951.4 allows this if the lease contained a notice to the tenant of the landlord's intent to do this, and the lease:

a.   allowed subletting or assignment, or

b.   allowed subletting or assignment with reasonable standards or conditions, or

c.   allowed subletting or assignment with the landlord's consent which will not unreasonably be withheld.

ABANDONMENT   If the tenant leaves early by abandoning the property, you must choose which of the following procedures to follow.

First, be certain that the tenant has in fact left with no intent to return. If you simply assume that the tenant has abandoned the property and rent it to another tenant, you will be liable if the original tenant returns. Check the obvious signs such as removal of furniture, clothing, and other personal items. Telephone the tenant's work place, references, and bank. Once you believe that the tenant has gone for good, you have two options.

1.   You may re-rent the property and take the chance that the tenant does not return. This saves the time and money of following the formal legal procedures, but may create liability if the tenant returns.

2.   You may follow either of two legal remedies:

a.   You may serve a THREE-DAY NOTICE TO PAY RENT OR QUIT (Form 23), followed by an unlawful detainer action. This is the more expensive of the two remedies.

b.   You may serve a NOTICE OF BELIEF OF ABANDONMENT pursuant to California Civil Code, section 1951.3. This is included as Form 27 in this book. The section requires that the rent be due and unpaid for at least fourteen days and that the landlord had sufficient reason to believe that the tenant had abandoned the property.

The law allows for service either personally or by first class mail. Since abandonment almost always involves not knowing the location of the tenant, service by mail will be used. The landlord should mail to the property address unless there is another address where the landlord believes the tenant can be reached. Again, this will seldom be the case. If the tenant does not reply in writing within eighteen days after the date of the mailing, stating that there is no intent to abandon and giving an address for legal service, the landlord may re-enter and take possession of the premises.

Check the rental application. If you make a few phone calls and are unable to find anyone who knows the whereabouts of the tenant, you will have reason to believe that the tenant has abandoned.

The landlord may enter the property at any time before taking possession for reasons of health and safety.

The following are a few examples of what could happen:

- In a Missouri case a landlord took the refrigerator, washing machine, and stove, and the tenant was awarded $10,000 in damages. *Smiley v. Cardin*, 655 S.W.2d 114 (Mo.Ct.App. 1983).

- In a District of Columbia case where purchasers of a tax deed to property kept changing the locks on the property, nailing the door shut and nailing "for sale" signs on the property when the occupant was away, a jury awarded the occupant $250,000 in punitive damages. They had used those tactics to try to force the occupant to sue them so that the government would have to defend their tax deed. The appeals court upheld the verdict. *Robinson v. Sarisky*, 535 A.2d 901 (D.C.App. 1988).

- In a Florida case a landlord posted a three-day notice and when the tenant was absent from the premises he entered and removed her possessions. In a lawsuit she testified that her possessions were all heirlooms and antiques and since the landlord had disposed of them he could not prove otherwise. She was awarded $31,000 in damages. *Reynolds v. Towne Mgt. of Fla., Inc.,* 426 So.2d 1011 (Fla. 2 DCA 1983).

EARLY TERMINATION BY LANDLORD

A landlord may terminate a tenancy before the end of the term for three reasons: failure to pay rent, failure to cure a curable breach of a covenant or condition of the lease, and committing an incurable breach of a covenant or condition.

FAILURE TO
PAY RENT

Failure to pay rent is the most common reason for eviction. The landlord serves a three day notice to pay rent or quit. The notice may be served any time after the rent is due. The unlawful detainer action may be brought on the forth day after the notice is served.

There is no grace period for rent payment unless the lease states one. However, allowing a tenant to continually pay rent late may modify your agreement or waive your right to rent on the agreed upon date. Many landlords routinely serve three day notices to pay rent or quit any time the rent is late. This preserves their right to insist on rent as agreed to in the lease or rental agreement.

A THREE-DAY NOTICE TO PAY RENT OR QUIT is included in appendix D as Form 23. This must be completed and served exactly as required by law or you can lose your eviction suit. The most important requirements are:

☞ *Calculating the three days.* This may sound simple, but many landlords have lost their case by making an error here. First, you must not serve the notice until the day after the rent is due. Even if the tenants tell you they cannot pay the rent on the day it is due, you must wait until the next day to serve the notice. Next, if the due date was a Saturday, Sunday, or legal holiday, you cannot serve the notice until the day after the next business day. Third, you do not count the day of service of the notice in the three days. Fourth, if the third day of the three day notice is a Saturday, Sunday or legal holiday you cannot file your eviction until the day after the next business day.

For example, suppose rent is due on the 25th of the month, and December 25th falls on a Friday. Since that day is a holiday, rent would not be due until Monday the 28th. You would serve the notice on the 29th, and since the 1st of January is a holiday followed by a weekend, the third day would be the 4th of January so you could not file your suit until the 5th!

☞ *Calculating the amount due.* On a three day notice you can only demand rent that is actually past due, not late fees or any other amounts due under the rental agreement.

☞ *Serving the notice.* You should personally attempt to hand the notice to the tenant at the property. If she is not there, you should next try to serve her at work, if you know where she works. If neither of these are successful, you can serve another adult at the property and mail a second copy to the tenant. If there is no other adult at the property, you can post a copy on the front door of the property and mail a second copy to the tenant. The three day period starts the day after both of these things have been accomplished.

In some areas it is possible to hire an off duty peace officer to deliver the notice in full uniform and possibly have a more serious effect on the tenant.

CURABLE BREACH

A curable, but uncured, breach of a covenant or condition is a situation when you want a tenant to stop doing something which violates the lease. Examples would include getting a pet or having a guest stay longer than permitted. A THREE-DAY NOTICE TO COMPLY OR QUIT is served. This is Form 24 in appendix D of this book. If the problem is not corrected, the unlawful detainer action may be filed on the fourth day after the notice is served. In using this notice you should calculate the three days and serve the notice as mentioned for the previous notice.

INCURABLE
BREACH

An incurable breach of a covenant or condition is a situation when the tenant has done something so bad that you simply want him out. Perhaps the tenant has left and moved someone in without your consent or has caused severe damage to the property or has assaulted another tenant. For this, you would use a THREE-DAY NOTICE TO QUIT (Form 25). This remedy may be difficult to use and an attorney is recommended. The biggest problem is knowing whether a court will consider the action of the tenant to be incurable, or if you will be told you should have sent the three day notice to cure. When in doubt it is best to use the notice to cure first, or if the tenancy is month-to-month, to use a thirty day notice of termination. In using this notice you should calculate the three days and serve the notice as mentioned for the previous notices.

DRUG DEALING
TENANTS

Knowingly allowing a drug dealing tenant to remain in possession may subject a landlord to liability for damage or injury to other tenants, tenant's guests, workers, neighbors and anyone else who could foreseeably be damaged or injured. In extreme cases forfeiture of the property could result.

The other side of the problem is that to accuse someone of dealing drugs could subject the landlord to liability. Use of a thirty day notice is recommended because no reason for the termination must be stated.

If you have a fixed term lease with your tenants or your property is subject to rent control or other limitations and you suspect a tenant of drug dealing, you should consult an attorney.

SPECIAL RULES FOR PUBLIC HOUSING

For non-payment of rent the landlord must give the tenant fourteen days notice rather than a three day notice, and it must be mailed or hand delivered, not posted. (24 CFR 866.4(1)(2).) The notice must inform the tenant of her right to a grievance procedure. At least one court has held that both a fourteen-day notice and a three-day notice must be given. *Stanton v. Housing Authority of Pittsburgh*, 469 F.Supp. 1013 (W.D.Pa.1977). But other courts have disagreed. *Ferguson v. Housing Authority of Middleboro*, 499 F.Supp. 334 (EDKy 1980).

📖 The public housing authority must prove both that the tenant did not pay the rent and that the tenant was at fault for not paying it. *Maxton Housing Authority v. McLean*, 328 S.E.2d (N.C. 1985).

📖 A Louisiana court held that a tenant was not at fault because her former husband did not pay the child support. *Housing Authority of City of New Iberia v. Austin*, 478 So.2d 1012 (La.App. 1986) writ denied, 481 So.2d 1334 (La. 1986).

📖 One Florida court held that posting both a fourteen day notice and a three day notice is too confusing. It suggested that the landlord only use a fourteen day notice or else deliver the three day notice so that the deadline was the same as for the fourteen day notice. *Broward Co. Housing Authority v. Simmons*, 4 F.L.W.Supp. 494 (Co.Ct. Broward 1996).

For breach of the terms of the lease other than payment of rent, a thirty-day notice must be given, except in emergencies, and it must inform the tenant of the reasons for termination, her right to reply, and her right to a grievance procedure. (24 CPR 366(4)(1).) If the tenant requests a grievance hearing a second notice must be given, even if she loses in the hearing. *Ferguson v. Housing Authority of Middleboro*, 499 F.Supp. 432 (EDKy 1980).

SECTION 236 APARTMENTS

For non-payment of rent, tenants must be given the three-day notice and be advised that if there is a judicial proceeding they can present a valid defense, if any. Service must be by first class mail and hand delivered or placed under the door. (24 CFR 450.4(a).)

For breach of the terms of the lease other than payment of rent, the tenant must first have been given notice that in the future such conduct would be grounds for terminating the lease. The notice of termination must state when the tenancy will be terminated, specifically why it is being terminated, and it must advise the tenant of the right to present a defense in the eviction suit. (24 CFR 450.)

The section of the law that states acceptance or payment of rent is a waiver of any past noncompliance, does not apply to the portion of the rent that is subsidized. (F.S. §83.56 (5).) However, waiver will occur if legal action is not taken within forty-five days.

SECTION 8
APARTMENTS

Under the Code of Federal Regulations, §882.215(c)(4) the landlord must notify the housing authority in writing at the commencement of the eviction proceedings. Also, the previous paragraph applies to Section 8 housing as well.

DEATH OF A TENANT

If a lease contains a clause binding the "heirs, successors and assigns" of the lessee, then the lease continues after the death of the tenant unless cancelled by the lessor and the heirs. Otherwise it is a personal contract which expires at death.

As a practical matter, you will probably want to rerent the property as soon as possible. However, you should make arrangements for the storage of the decedent's property or you may be liable for it. If you know the decedent's closest relative, you can probably be safe in turning over the property to him or her. (Be sure to get a signed receipt.) But if you think there is any chance there will be disputed claims to the property, give it only to a person who has been appointed executor of the estate.

OPTIONS TO CANCEL

Some landlords like to use a lease form giving them an option to cancel the lease. However, when a lease allows one party to cancel it at will, the lease is generally not considered binding and the courts will allow either party to cancel it at will. A lease will probably be held to be valid if the option to cancel is contingent upon some event. For example, a lease which gave the landlord the option to cancel if the property were condemned for road right of way purposes would probably be valid.

EVICTING A TENANT 10

This chapter explains the basic steps for filing an eviction case against a tenant. In most cases, service of the first notice or the filing of the complaint is enough to convince the tenant to move. Tenants rarely file an answer and these forms usually do the trick. However, an eviction case can get very complicated and may require complicated pleadings which are beyond the scope of this book. There are entire 300 page books on the market on the subject of evictions which explain in minute detail the more complicated procedures. If your eviction gets complicated you may want to consult one. We suggest: *The Eviction Book for California*, by Leigh Robinson published by ExPress, El Cerrito, CA, and *The Landlord's Law Book, Vol. 2: Evictions*, by David Brown, published by Nolo Press, Berkeley, CA.

SELF-HELP BY LANDLORD

The only way a landlord may recover possession of a dwelling unit is if the tenant voluntarily surrenders it to the landlord or abandons it, or if the landlord gets a court order giving the landlord possession.

Under California Civil Code, section 789.3, landlords are specifically forbidden to use self-help methods to evict tenants, such as interrupting utilities, changing locks, removing doors or windows, or removing the tenant's personal belongings from the unit. Violation of this law subjects the landlord to liability for a penalty of up to $100 per day, plus attorney's fees and any other actual damages suffered by the tenant.

When a tenant moves out and you "know" they have abandoned the property, it can be tempting to just take possession without bothering with any legal formalities. However, if the tenant does return, the landlord may incur liability as discussed on page 81.

SETTLING WITH THE TENANT

Although in a vast majority of evictions the tenants do not answer the complaint and the landlord wins quickly, some tenants can create nightmares for landlords. Clever tenants and legal aid lawyers can delay the case for months, and vindictive tenants can destroy the property with little worry of ever paying for it. Therefore, lawyers sometimes advise their clients to offer the tenant a cash settlement to leave. For example, a tenant may be offered $200 to be out of the premises and leave it clean within a week. Of course it hurts to give money to a tenant who already owes you money, but it could be cheaper than the court costs of an unlawful detainer action, vacancy time, and damage to the premises. Then again, an old American saying is, "Millions for defense but not one cent for tribute." You'll have to make your own decision based upon your tenant.

GROUNDS FOR EVICTION

A tenant can be evicted for one or more of the following reasons:

- ☞ violating one or more of the terms of the lease.

- ☞ failing to leave at the end of the term.

- ☞ violating California law regarding the duties of tenants.

VIOLATIONS OF THE LEASE | The most common violation of the lease by a tenant is the failure to pay the rent, but a tenant can also be evicted for violating other terms of the rental agreement, such as disturbing other tenants.

FAILURE TO LEAVE | A tenant may also be evicted for failing to leave after being served with a thirty day notice when there is a month-to-month tenancy. The tenant need not have done anything wrong, and the landlord need not state a reason for asking the tenant to leave.

As explained in chapter 4, there are certain requirements of the tenant regarding maintenance. If the tenant violates these, he or she can be evicted.

LIMITATIONS ON EVICTIONS | The reason for asking a tenant to leave cannot be for the purpose of retaliation or discrimination. Also, regulations on property subject to government control (e.g., public housing, subsidized housing, rent control property) may not only require that the landlord state a reason, but may have limitations on the reasons that justify an eviction.

TERMINATING THE TENANCY

It is an ancient rule of law that an eviction suit cannot be filed until the tenancy is legally terminated. There are cases from as far back as the 1500s in which evictions were dismissed because the landlord failed to properly terminate the tenancy, so if you make the same mistake, don't expect the judge to overlook it. What the judges often do in cases where the tenancy has not been properly terminated is order the landlord to pay the tenant's attorney fees.

TERMINATION FOR CAUSE | The tenancy may terminate by natural expiration or by action by the landlord. If you need to evict a tenant whose tenancy has not expired, you should carefully read the previous chapter and follow the procedures to properly terminate the tenancy.

TERMINATION BY EXPIRATION | If parties to a lease do not agree to renew or extend the agreement, then it automatically ends at its expiration date. (This is different from some areas in which the lease is automatically renewed unless notice is given that it is not being renewed.)

USING AN ATTORNEY

If your lease or rental agreement provides for the landlord to recover attorney's fees, the law allows the same for the tenant. There are also other situations in which you could be required by California law to pay your tenant's attorney's fees. Because of this it is important to do an eviction exactly as required. In some cases the tenant may just be waiting for the eviction notice before leaving the premises, and in such a case the landlord may regain the premises no matter what kind of papers he files. But in some cases tenants with no money and no defenses have gotten free lawyers, paid for by our tax dollars, who find technical defects in the case. This can cause a delay in the eviction and cause the landlord to be ordered to pay the tenant's attorney fees. A simple error in a landlord's court papers can cost him the case.

A landlord needing to do an eviction should consider the costs and benefits of using an attorney, compared to doing it without an attorney. One possibility is to file the case without an attorney and hope the tenant moves out. If the tenant stays and fights the case, an attorney can be hired to finish the case. Some landlords who prefer to do their evictions themselves start by paying a lawyer for a half-hour or hour of time to review the facts of the case and point out problems. You may also be able to find an attorney to give you advice as questions come up.

While a landlord has the right to evict a tenant without using an attorney, there are several instances where it is advisable to at least consult with a real estate attorney before proceeding. These include where:

☞   your tenant has a lawyer.

☞   your tenant contests the eviction.

☛ you are evicting based on the tenant's drug dealing or other misconduct, and are serving a notice that requires stating a reason for the eviction.

☛ you are serving a seven day notice when a thirty day notice would normally be used.

☛ your property is subject to rent control, or is public or subsidized housing.

☛ your tenant is also an employee of yours (i.e., manager). This may be avoided if you used an attorney when you hired the tenant as your manager.

☛ your tenant files bankruptcy.

☛ your tenant is in the military.

Whenever a tenant has an attorney, the landlord should also have one. Otherwise you risk the following types of problems:

📖 A winning tenant was awarded $8,675 in attorney fees that was figured at $150 an hour and then doubled.

📖 In a suit by a cooperative association against a tenant for $191.33 in maintenance fees and to enforce the association rules, the tenant won the suit and was awarded $87,375 in attorney's fees.

📖 An argument that a legal aid organization was not entitled to attorney fees did not win. The landlord had to pay $2,000 for twenty hours of the legal aid attorney's time in having the case dismissed.

It is, of course, important to find an attorney who both knows landlord/tenant law and charges reasonable fees. There are many subtleties of the law that can be missed by someone without experience. Some attorneys who specialize in landlord/tenant work charge very modest fees unless the case gets complicated. Others charge an hourly rate that can add up to thousands of dollars. You should check with other landlords or a local apartment association for names of good attorneys, or you might try calling the manager of a large apartment complex in the area.

The California Bar Association certifies specialists in the various areas of law. One becomes a specialist by proving experience and taking an examination. Consult your county association for a list.

If you get a security deposit at the beginning of the tenancy and start the eviction immediately upon a default, then the deposit should be nearly enough to cover the attorney's fee.

WHO CAN SUE?

A landlord can represent himself in court and does not need an attorney. A landlord's agent, such as the apartment manager can also represent the landlord. However, it is considered the unauthorized practice of law for any other person who is not an attorney to represent a party in court.

FORMS

Each county in the state makes its own rules regarding forms. Some have their own required forms. Some have optional forms. Some do not have forms. We have included forms in this book which should work in most areas. Before using them, you should ask your court clerk if they have any required or recommended forms. For guidance on how to fill out the forms, see appendix C. ***Note:*** Special forms have been authorized for Downey, El Cajon, and North Santa Barbara. Contact your court clerk to obtain them.

COURT PROCEDURES

COMPLAINT

An eviction is started by filing a *complaint* against the tenant. An eviction suit is called an *unlawful detainer* action. The complaint must be filed in municipal court (formerly called *justice court*), and a filing fee must be paid. Small claims court no longer hears eviction cases, and superior courts will only hear cases involving claims of damages in excess of $25,000. If your damages are over $25,000, you should consult an attorney.

Note: Before you may file a complaint, you must have given the tenant either a three day notice or a thirty day notice. See chapter 9 for information about which type of notice is required in your situation and how to calculate the three or thirty days correctly.

A COMPLAINT is included in this book as Form 29 in appendix D. You should go over it carefully and be sure to fill it out completely and accurately. A sample is included in appendix C.

CIVIL CASE
COVER SHEET

The next form you need to fill out is the CIVIL COVER SHEET which is Form 28 in appendix D. It is very straightforward and easy to fill out. It is primarily used for statistical purposes to let the courts keep track of what types of cases are being filed.

SUMMONS

The third form you need to file is the SUMMONS, included in appendix D as Form 30. This is an important form and must be completed correctly. It is the notice to the tenants that they are being sued. It should include the names of all adults living in the premises. If there are people living there whose named you do not know, you should list their names as John Doe, Jane Doe, etc.

PREJUDGMENT
CLAIM OF
RIGHT TO
POSSESSION

If there are any adults living at the premises whose names you do not know, or if you think someone other than your tenant may claim to be living there, you should prepare a PREJUDGMENT CLAIM OF RIGHT TO POSSESSION (Form 31). This is served with the summons and complaint and provides legal notice to everyone at the premises. The claimant then has ten days to file a Claim of Right to Possession. If this is not done, the claim cannot be made when the marshal or sheriff comes to actually evict the tenant. If you do not do this and someone you have not served claims to have a right to live there, it will delay your eviction.

COPIES

You will need to have an original of all of the above forms and a copy of the COMPLAINT for each defendant. You will need two copies of each PREJUDGMENT CLAIM OF RIGHT TO POSSESSION for each person you expect to serve. You do not need extra copies of the CIVIL CASE COVER SHEET. You should make a copy of everything for your own file. When making photocopies, be sure the backs of the forms are printed upside down as they are in this book. (The reason for this is so that they can be read when attached in the court file by a clip at the top.)

FILING

Once you have prepared the papers, you need to file them in the judicial district where the property is located. This is usually done personally, but you may have your process server do it or the clerk may let you file by mail. Call your clerk to find out if this is possible.

SERVICE OF PROCESS

A copy of the COMPLAINT and SUMMONS are *served* upon the tenants by the sheriff, a marshall, a private process server or any adult person other than the plaintiff. However, if you will be using the PREJUDGMENT CLAIM OF RIGHT TO POSSESSION, only a sheriff, a marshall, or private process server may serve them.

A process server may cost a few dollars more than the sheriff, but can often get service quicker and may be more likely to serve the papers personally, allowing you to get a money judgment. A process server will also make it more likely that the service and completion of the summons are done properly, than if you have a friend or relative do it.

The best way to serve the papers is to personally hand them to the parties, or to leave them in their presence if they refuse to take them. With this type of service the case will proceed more quickly and allow you to get a money judgment.

If the process server is unable to serve the tenant personally, the papers can be handed to another adult member of the household or they can be served by posting one copy on the property and mailing an additional copy to each tenant. However, these methods have strict rules that must be followed. If you decide to post and mail a copy, then you must petition for a judge's permission. If you need to use either of these methods, you should hire a process server or consult an attorney.

PUBLIC HOUSING

In Section 8 housing, under the Code of Federal Regulations §882.215(c)(4) the local housing authority must be notified in writing before the tenant can be served with the eviction.

The papers served on the tenants are the copy of the complaint with a copy of the summons stapled on top. If there are parties whose names you do not know, they are given the complaint, summons and the prejudgment claim of right to possession.

RETURN OF SERVICE

After service is made, the person performing the service must return the original summonses (the ones with the court seals on them) to the court with the backs filled out completely.

WAIT FIVE DAYS

After the complaint and summons have been served on the defendants, they have five days (excluding the day they are served and any legal holidays) to file an answer. Fortunately, at this point most tenants move out. If they have not filed an answer, you can request that a default be entered on the sixth day (unless it falls on a Saturday or Sunday, then it would be entered on Monday). If the tenants have filed any type of answer with the court, you cannot get a default. Skip the next section and move on to "Tenant's Answer."

DEFAULT

If the tenants have not answered, you have three options on how to proceed. The easiest and fastest procedure is to have the clerk enter the default and judgment for possession. The drawback is that you may not be able to get a money judgment, but since it probably wouldn't be collectable, you may not mind. To use this procedure you would need a REQUEST FOR ENTRY OF CLERK'S DEFAULT (Form 32), CLERK'S JUDGMENT FOR POSSESSION (Form 33), and WRIT OF EXECUTION (Form 34). In filling out Form 32 you would check the box for a "Clerk's Judgment" and check boxes "1. c." and "1. e.(1)." In forms 32 and 34 you would not fill in any of the areas regarding monetary amounts. On both of these forms be sure to fill in the sections about whether the PREJUDGMENT CLAIM OF RIGHT TO POSSESSION (Form 31) was served (1.e.(10 on form 32 and 9. on form 34). See appendix C. File these with the court clerk with the appropriate filing fee and they should issue your WRIT OF EXECUTION. Skip the next sections and move on to "Serving the Writ."

If you do wish to get a money judgment, at the same time you are requesting the default you can ask that a hearing be set before a judge for a money judgment. Unfortunately, not all counties are allowing this, even though the plain words of the statute allow it. To do this you complete a second set of Forms 32, 33, and 34, but on Form 32 you check boxes "1.c." and "1.d." and fill in the monetary amounts under lines 2. and 5. On Form 34, complete the monetary amounts on lines 11. through 18. See appendix C.

The second option is to set a hearing and get a judgment for possession and money damages from a judge. This may take much longer than getting a default through the clerk and if you want the tenants out quickly you may prefer to forego the money judgment. For this procedure you need Forms 32, 34 and either Form 35 or a judgment form provided by your clerk. To fill out Form 32 you would check the box for a court judgment and then check the boxes for 1. c. and d. and fill in the information under 2. Also, on both Forms 32 and 34, be sure to fill in the sections about whether the PREJUDGMENT CLAIM OF RIGHT TO POSSESSION was served (1.e.(10 on form 32 and 9. on form 34). See appendix C.

The third option is to apply for a judgment for possession and money damages from a judge by using a declaration instead of testimony at a hearing. For this you would prepare the forms the same as in the second option, except that you would check boxes under 1.e.(2) and 4.a., b., and c. You would need Form 36, or to type the information from

Form 36 on legal paper (with numbers down the left side). Ask your clerk what is required.

MILITARY PERSONNEL
Special rules apply to military personnel. There will not be a default entered unless the tenant has an attorney. Consult an attorney if your tenant is in the military and refuses to leave. If the tenant is in the military, but his or her spouse is not and the spouse is on the lease, you can proceed against the non-military spouse. Always contact the tenant's commanding officer before beginning eviction. This will usually resolve the matter.

TENANT'S MOTION
If the tenant files any type of legal motion, such as a Motion to Strike or a Motion to Quash, it is obvious that she either knows the law or is being helped by someone who does. Unless you have experience in a similar case, you should seek the advice of an attorney familiar with tenant evictions.

JURY DEMAND
If the tenant demands a jury trial, especially if he also has an attorney, you should consult an attorney because the case will be much more complicated than without a jury.

A request for discovery by a tenant is another sign that you need to consult an attorney. *Discovery* is a process in which parties can ask each other questions (either written ones called *interrogatories* or oral ones called a *deposition*) under oath. They can also subpoena each other's records, including bank statements and charge card receipts. Failure to respond can result in being held in contempt of court and giving false information can result in a criminal charge of perjury.

TENANT'S ANSWER
A tenant may file an answer to your complaint in the form of a letter to the court or he may use the court form answer in which boxes are checked to respond to your allegations. If the letter simply gives an excuse as to why the rent is unpaid or denies that your complaint is correct, you can move ahead to "Setting the Trial." If the tenant checked the "Affirmative Defenses" boxes on the form answer, or if the tenant includes affirmative defenses in his letter or files a counterclaim, you should seek the advice of an attorney. If you do not, the minimum you

should do is file a response to the tenant' defenses (denying they are true, if they are not) or an answer to the counterclaim (denying the allegations which are untrue).

SETTING THE
TRIAL

The next step will be setting a trial date. This is done by filing either a MEMORANDUM TO SET CIVIL CASE FOR TRIAL or a REQUEST FOR TRIAL SETTING depending on the county you are in. This form can be obtained from the court clerk. The trial date will be set and a trial will follow in approximately two or three weeks. If you win, the same steps to evict should be taken as with the default judgment. If you lose, you will have to begin again. Unless you know precisely how to win the next time, consult an attorney.

If no one shows up at the hearing except you, explain to the judge that you are ready to proceed. The judge may ask you questions or to read your complaint under oath. The judge may have a judgment form or may ask you for one. You can use Form 37 in appendix D unless your county has its own form.

TENANT'S
ATTORNEY

If the tenant shows up with an attorney and you were not told previously, you should ask the judge for a continuance to get your own attorney. If you make a mistake and lose, you may have to pay the tenant's attorney fees.

If the tenants do appear for the hearing, they will probably present one or more of the following defenses. The particular defenses may depend upon your reason for eviction. Common defenses include:

☛ If you are evicting for nonpayment of rent, the tenant may argue that you failed to keep the building habitable, which excuses the nonpayment of rent. If the tenant had notified you of repairs that you failed to make before you served your three day notice, this could be a winning argument. Even worse would be if you had been cited by a government inspector for health or safety violations.

- ☛ If you are not evicting for nonpayment of rent, the more common arguments are retaliation, discrimination, or violation of a rent control ordinance. These, as well as habitability, have been covered earlier.

- ☛ The tenant may always argue that you did not follow proper legal procedure in serving your notice or summons and complaint. Failing to properly fill out the forms may result in your having to start over.

STIPULATION

You should arrive for the trial early and if you see the tenant is present, try to discuss the matter and see if something can be worked out. Since there is no way of knowing how a trial will turn out, and even the best cases have been lost over a small mistake, most lawyers prefer to settle a case whenever possible. This will allow you to recover some back rent and avoid the hassle of cleaning and re-renting the unit. If you wish to settle with the tenant and come to an agreement where the rent will be paid over time, then you can enter into a *stipulation* to delay the case. A stipulation is a contract entered into a court record. If you can work out a satisfactory arrangement with the tenant, you may file a STIPULATION FOR ENTRY OF JUDGMENT (Form 38) in the case. A judgment will then be issued which reflects this agreement. A typical stipulation might allow the tenant to stay for a slightly longer time than if eviction procedures were followed and call for some periodic payments of past-due rent. If the arrangement you have worked out with the tenant does not fit this form, you can retype it to conform to your agreement.

Once the case is filed, you should never accept any rent from the tenant without signing a stipulation. If you do, your case can be dismissed and you will have to start over again with a new notice and complaint.

PRESENTING YOUR CASE

To win your case you will need to prove the claims in your complaint and rebut the defenses, answers and/or counterclaims of the tenant. Much of your proof will be your own testimony, but you can also use evidence, such as a copy of the lease and any notices, or photos of any damages. It is also helpful to have a witness who can verify what you have said.

The trial is usually held in the following manner, but ask your judge before you start because he or she may prefer a less formal procedure:

1. opening remarks by the judge,

2. landlord's opening statement,

3. tenant's opening statement,

4. landlord's testimony and evidence,

5. tenant's testimony and evidence,

6. landlord's rebuttal and closing argument,

7. tenant's closing argument, and

8. landlord's rebuttal to tenant's closing argument.

OPENING STATEMENT

In your opening statement, tell the judge what the case is about and what you plan to prove.

TESTIMONY AND EVIDENCE

In your testimony and evidence you go point by point through your complaint and state the facts of the case, presenting evidence wherever it is available.

REBUTTAL AND CLOSING ARGUMENT

In your rebuttal and closing argument you point out what parts of the tenant's evidence are untrue (if any) and argue that even if some points are true, you should win the case anyway because they do not constitute a legal defense.

REBUTTAL TO TENANT'S CLOSING ARGUMENT

In your rebuttal to the tenant's closing argument you point out the flaws in the tenant's argument, show any inconsistencies in his testimony, counter any of his legal arguments with your own and summarize why you are entitled to win in spite of his presentation of the case.

JUDGMENT

Once both sides have finished their presentation, the judge may announce a decision or say that the case will be taken under advisement. The reason for the latter may be that the judge wants to research the law, or perhaps thinks the parties are too emotional and might get upset. If a decision is made on the spot, you should present your proposed judgment (Form 37 in appendix D). If it is taken under advisement, you will receive the judgment in the mail within a few days. If it doesn't arrive within a few days, you can call the judge's secretary for the status of your case, but don't make a pest of yourself.

If you won the case, you will need to bring a prepared WRIT OF EXECUTION (Form 34 in appendix D) to the court clerk along with the fee.

The WRIT OF EXECUTION is then taken to the office of the sheriff or marshal, along with written authorization, instructions to carry out the writ and the sheriff's fee. The marshal or sheriff will prepare a five day notice to vacate and serve it or post it at the property.

After five days, the marshal or sheriff will physically remove the tenant from the property.

Once the tenant leaves, you may have to deal with personal property left behind. Abandoned personal property was discussed in chapter 8. California law does not allow you to claim the proceeds from auctioning off the tenant's personal property unless you have a judgment. This would apply to back rent that the tenant owes.

TENANT'S APPEAL

A tenant has thirty days to file a notice of appeal. The appeal from the municipal court is to the appellate department of the superior court.

The tenant's appeal does not necessarily delay eviction, unless the judge grants a stay and the tenant deposits rent with the court. If your tenant feels strongly enough to deposit rent with the court, consult an attorney. Since the WRIT OF POSSESSION gives the tenant twenty-four hours to vacate the property, the tenant will have to act immediately if she wants to stop the eviction.

TENANT'S BANKRUPTCY

If a tenant files bankruptcy, all legal actions against her must stop immediately. This provision is automatic from the moment the bankruptcy petition is filed (11 USC 362). If you take any action in court, seize the tenant's property, try to impose a landlord's lien, or use the security deposit for unpaid rent, you can be held in contempt of federal court. It is not necessary that you receive formal notice of the bankruptcy filing. Verbal notice is sufficient. If you do not believe the tenant, then you should call the bankruptcy court to confirm the filing.

The stay lasts until the debtor (the tenant) is discharged or the case is dismissed, or until the property is abandoned or voluntarily surrendered.

The landlord may ask for the right to continue with the eviction by filing a Motion for Relief from Stay and paying the filing fee. Within thirty days a hearing is held, and it may be held by telephone. The motion is governed by Bankruptcy Rule 9014 and the requirements of how the tenant must be served are contained in Rule 7004. However, for such a hearing the services of an attorney are usually necessary.

If the tenant filed bankruptcy after a judgment of eviction has been entered, there should be no problem lifting the automatic stay since the tenant has no interest in the property. *In re Cowboys, Inc.*, 24 B.R. (S.D. Fla. 1982).

The bankruptcy stay only applies to amounts owed to the landlord at the time of filing the bankruptcy. Therefore, the landlord can sue the tenant for eviction and rent owed for any time period *after* the filing of the bankruptcy petition, unless the bankruptcy trustee assumes the lease. The landlord can proceed during the bankruptcy without asking for relief from the automatic stay under three conditions. *In re Knight*, 8 B.R. 925 (D.C. Md. 1981):

1.   The landlord can only sue for rent due after the filing.

2. The landlord cannot sue until the trustee rejects the lease. (If the trustee does not accept the lease within sixty days of the Order for Relief, then §365(d)(1) provides that it is deemed rejected.)

3. The landlord must sue under the terms of the lease and may not treat the trustee's rejection as a breach.

In a Chapter 13 (reorganization) bankruptcy, the landlord should be paid the rent as it comes due.

If your tenant files bankruptcy and you decide it is worth hiring a lawyer, you should locate an attorney who is experienced in bankruptcy work. Prior to the meeting with the attorney you should gather as much information as possible (type of bankruptcy filed, assets, liabilities, case number, etc.).

LANDLORD'S APPEAL

Our legal system allows one chance to bring a case to court. If you didn't prepare for your trial, or thought you wouldn't need a witness and you lost, you don't have the right to try again. However, in certain limited circumstances you may be able to have your case reviewed.

- ☞ If the judge made a mistake in interpreting the law which applies to your case, then that is grounds for reversal.

- ☞ If new evidence is discovered after the trial which could not have been discovered before the trial, then a new trial might be granted, but this is not very common.

- ☞ If one party lied at trial and that party was believed by the judge or jury, there is usually not much that can be done.

- ☞ There are certain other grounds for rehearing such as misconduct of an attorney or errors during the trial, but these matters are beyond the scope of this book.

If you wish to appeal your case, you should consult with an attorney or review a book in the law library on California appellate practice. However, if you want to remove the tenant quickly, you should just file a new eviction action. It is much quicker than the appeals process.

SATISFACTION OF JUDGMENT

If, after a judgment has been entered against the tenant, the tenant pays the amount due, it is the landlord's responsibility to file a SATISFACTION OF JUDGMENT. (See Form 43.)

Note: Occasionally someone will write to the publisher and say that they followed this book but the judge gave the tenants extra time to move, or acted in some other manner that is contradictory to what is said in this book. Remember, most times a case will go smoothly, but judges may interpret the law differently and judges do sometimes make mistakes or make an exception when the case seems to warrant it. If your case gets complicated, you should invest in an experienced landlord/tenant attorney that can finish your case quickly.

MONEY DAMAGES AND BACK RENT 11

Trying to collect a judgment against a former tenant is usually not worth the time and expense. Most landlords are just glad to regain possession of the property. Tenants who don't pay rent usually don't own property that can be seized, and it is very difficult to garnish wages. However, former tenants occasionally come into money, and some landlords have been surprised many years later when called by a title insurance company wanting to pay off their judgment because it is a lien on property they bought. Therefore it is usually worthwhile to at least put a claim for back rent into an eviction complaint.

MAKING A CLAIM

If a tenant moved out owing rent or leaving damage to the property, you can file a suit in small claims court. Be sure you know where the tenant lives or works because you must have the papers served on the tenant in order to get a judgment.

To make a claim against a tenant for back rent in an eviction, you should check the boxes in the COMPLAINT (Form 29) that request past due rent and damages. If you have not checked these boxes you can later file a separate suit in small claims court for both back rent and damage to the premises. Also, you should instruct your process server to attempt personal service rather than posting. But keep in mind that if the tenant avoids the process server, it may take a lot longer to get him out.

UNCONTESTED EVICTION

In order to get a money judgement you must get a judgment signed by a judge rather than the clerk. If you used the clerk's default and judgment for your eviction, then you must file a separate small claims case for money damages. However, you have the following options to get a money judgment with your eviction suit:

☞ If your county allows it, you can request a money judgment from a judge at the same time as you request the clerk's judgment for possession.

☞ You can have a hearing before a judge for both a money judgment and possession.

☞ You can use a sworn declaration instead of a court hearing.

These procedures are explained in the previous chapter.

CONTESTED EVICTION

If the tenant files a response in the case and you are required to set a trial, the issue of rent owed can be brought up at the trial. If the tenant moves out prior to trial, you should still attend the trial both to obtain a judgment that you are entitled to possession and for a money judgment.

If the tenant does not attend the trial but is still in the unit, there will be rent owed for the time from the trial to the actual day the tenant moves out. Therefore, you should ask the judge to retain jurisdiction until those amounts can be ascertained. (Different judges may have different procedures for doing this.) Otherwise you may have to file a separate suit in small claims court.

AMOUNT

You are entitled to a judgment against the tenant for the rent due, damage to the premises and the costs of your lawsuit, if any.

RENT | Under California law in a month-to-month tenancy, you are entitled to rent for the entire month of the final month in which the tenant leaves even if he moved out early in the month.

If the tenant signed a lease, you are entitled to rent for the entire term of the lease less any rent you receive by renting to some one else, plus any costs of finding a new tenant. For this reason you should wait until the end of the lease term to be able to accurately assess your damages.

DAMAGE TO THE PREMISES | You may seek compensation from the tenant for damage to the premises, but this does not include "normal wear and tear." (See "Keeping the Deposit" in chapter 3.) These amounts cannot be awarded in your eviction suit, but you can deduct them from the security deposit or may sue for them in small claims court. For more information about small claims court, see *How to Win in Small Claims Court in California*, by Royce Orleans Hurst and Mark Warda, available from your local bookstore or directly from the publisher by calling 1-800-226-5291.

COSTS | The costs that you may collect are your filing fees, process server fees and sheriff fees in your eviction, small claims case, or both.

COLLECTING YOUR JUDGMENT

As mentioned earlier in this chapter, it is usually not worth the trouble to get a judgment against a tenant, and attempting to collect it may be futile, but in some cases you may be able to collect. Assuming that you have already applied the tenant's security deposit toward the judgment, you can also take the following actions to collect what you are owed.

FINDING ASSETS | You will need to know a tenant's assets. If you have a tenant application with bank account numbers, employer name and address, and automobile descriptions, you may be able to use those if they are still current. A common technique to find out a person's bank balance is to call the bank and say something like "Would a check for $1000 against account number 0123456789 be good today?" If not, call later (or another branch) and ask the same of a check for $500 and so on until you know the approximate balance. If there is enough to make it worth your while, you can begin garnishment as explained below.

If you don't have any information about the tenant's accounts or assets, you are allowed to order the tenant to appear in court and disclose this information under oath.

EXAMINATION OF THE DEBTOR

To schedule such an appearance you need to fill out and file an APPLICATION AND ORDER FOR APPEARANCE AND EXAMINATION (Form 40). Once this is signed by the judge, it will need to be personally served on the tenant. This is best done by the sheriff or a process server. This must be done at least ten days prior to the date of the examination.

At the examination the debtor will be required to answer under oath the questions that you ask. Failing to answer truthfully could subject the tenant to a fine or even jail time. You should use the DEBTOR QUESTIONNAIRE (Form 41) and ask each question on both pages.

Once you know what the debtor owns, you can garnish it, levy upon it, or put a lien on it.

GARNISHING PROPERTY

Garnishment is a legal procedure for seizing cash owed to a person, such as money in a bank or credit union, or earnings held by an employer. It is accomplished by using the same WRIT OF EXECUTION form used to get possession, but you check the "Execution (Money Judgment)" box.

Money in an account is easy to seize, but wages are not. Under federal law, you can only garnish 25% of the amount over $154.50 that a person earns per week. Also, under California law, a person may claim a higher exemption if the money is needed for support.

Before preparing the form, you should call the clerk to find out what the current fee is, then make four copies and file three of them and the original with the clerk.

LEVYING ON PROPERTY

A *levy* is a legal procedure where a sheriff takes control of an item of personal property, such as a vehicle or furniture or business equipment.

The problem with this is again the exemptions. The first $1,900 equity in a car is exempt, as are most household items, up to $5,000 in jewelry and antiques, and $5,000 in business tools. Also, the sheriff's fee for the levy is hundreds of dollars. Unless the tenant is quite wealthy, a levy will probably not be very useful.

FILING A LIEN

Even if the tenants have no property now, some time in the future they may inherit or buy real estate. A court judgment becomes a lien on all real property owned by the judgment debtor in every county where an ABSTRACT OF JUDGMENT (Form 46) is recorded. The judgment lien is valid for ten years, and is renewable for an additional ten years.

Even if you don't have much hope of collecting, it doesn't hurt to record your judgment in a few counties where the tenant may try to buy property in the future. The tenant who can't afford to pay rent today, may be in the market to buy property (or may inherit property) many years from now. Also, it will be a blot on his credit which he may later want to clear up.

SELF SERVICE STORAGE SPACE 12

APPLICABILITY

The rental of space in self-storage facilities is controlled by the California Business and Professional Code (C.B.P.C.), beginning with section 21700.

A self-storage facility is real property used to store personal property. It is not a warehouse nor a garage or other part of a private residence. It cannot be used as a residence.

If you rented out a garage separately, and not as part of a residence rental, it could qualify.

RENTAL AGREEMENT

In addition to the occupant's name and address, the rental agreement must also have a space for the occupant to provide an alternative address (although the occupant is not required to give one) (C.B.P.C. §21712). If the landlord wishes to have the ability to sell the stored property in order to satisfy unpaid rent, the agreement must so provide.

TERMINATION FOR UNPAID RENT

If the rent is unpaid for fourteen days, the landlord may terminate the agreement by sending a notice to the occupant's (tenant's) last known address and the alternative address, if any, given in the rental agreement.

LIENS

The owner of a self-storage facility has a lien for rent, labor, or other charges on the property stored in the unit (C.B.P.C. §21702). It does not matter whose property it is; the lien attaches to any property in the unit on the date it is brought to the facility.

The Business and Professional Code sets forth the instructions for how the lien sale is to be carried out, and even includes the forms that should be sent to the occupant. Copies of these forms are included in appendix D of this book.

Mobile Home Parks 13

Mobile homes in California require different eviction procedures, depending on several factors, such as the classification of the unit as a *mobile home* or a *recreational vehicle* (RV), and the ownership of the unit.

Let's start with an easy one: the landlord owns the unit. In such instances, the eviction procedures are the same as described earlier for houses or apartments.

The more difficult procedures come when the landlord owns the land (e.g., trailer park), but the landlord does not own the RV or mobile home. This is because the unit may be sold to pay for the back rent. You are evicting the *unit*—not just the *tenant*.

The distinction between an RV and a mobile home depends on two factors:

1. If the unit requires a moving permit to go onto public roads, it is a mobile home.

2. If the unit does not require a moving permit, it still may be considered a mobile home if it occupies a mobile home space or occupies an RV space for more than nine months.

Note: To add to the confusion, units such a motor coaches and camping trailers are always considered RVs. When in doubt, check California Civil Code, sections 798 and 799.

Once you have determined that you are dealing with a mobile home, you follow a procedure somewhat similar to an eviction from a house or apartment:

1. Serve a THREE DAY-SIXTY DAY NOTICE (Form 48). Three days is the time for payment of rent and the sixty days is the time to remove the mobile home before you can take further action.

2. File a COMPLAINT (Form 29), SUMMONS (Form 30), and (optional) PREJUDGMENT CLAIM OF RIGHTS TO POSSESSION (Form 31). These are the same as in house and apartment evictions, but you must wait the sixty days before you can file them.

3. File a REQUEST FOR ENTRY OF CLERK'S DEFAULT and a WRIT OF EXECUTION (Forms 32 and 34). In contested cases, follow the same rules as for houses or apartments. After you win, file for the writ. At this time, you will be given a date when the marshal will lock out the tenant.

After the lockout, you are not finished. You don't own the unit, so you can't take possession as you would your house or apartment. You must have the unit removed, sold, or take ownership yourself. The procedure depends on whether the tenant or a third party is the owner.

If the tenant is both the registered and the legal owner, you would return the WRIT OF POSSESSION to the court and obtain from the court a WRIT OF EXECUTION of the judgment. Deliver the WRIT OF EXECUTION and instructions to the marshal to sell the unit to pay the judgment. The unit would be sold at auction, a lien sale as in a foreclosure. You would become the owner if there was no one willing to pay enough to satisfy the judgment. The title you receive should then be taken to the Housing and Community Development Agency to clear title in your name.

If there is a different legal owner, you must give notice to the legal owner, wait the statutory period (minimum of ten days) for the owner to pay you, and publish a notice before holding the sale. You must also give notice to any other lienholders. The procedure is similar to fore-closure.

If a unit is abandoned, you have three options:

1. Follow the unlawful detainer procedures as described above.

2. Follow the procedure for abandonment (California Civil Code, section 798.61). The difference between the abandoned mobile home and an abandoned apartment is that the rent on the mobile home must be unpaid for more than sixty days before you may proceed.

3. If there are lienholders, contact them for payment or a lien-holder's sale to raise the money for payment.

APPENDIX A
CALIFORNIA STATUTES

California Civil Code section 1719 Bad Checks

California Civil Code sections 1940 through 1954.1 Landlord/Tenant

California Civil Code sections 1954.50 through 1954.53 Rent Control

California Civil Code sections 1980 through 1991 Abandoned Property

1719. (a) (1) Notwithstanding any penal sanctions that may apply, any person who passes a check on insufficient funds shall be liable to the payee for the amount of the check and a service charge payable to the payee for an amount not to exceed twenty-five dollars ($25) for the first check passed on insufficient funds and an amount not to exceed thirty-five dollars ($35) for each subsequent check to that payee passed on insufficient funds.

(2) Notwithstanding any penal sanctions that may apply, any person who passes a check on insufficient funds shall be liable to the payee for damages equal to treble the amount of the check if a written demand for payment is mailed by certified mail to the person who had passed a check on insufficient funds and the written demand informs this person of (A) the provisions of this section, (B) the amount of the check, and (C) the amount of the service charge payable to the payee. The person who had passed a check on insufficient funds shall have 30 days from the date the written demand was mailed to pay the amount of the check, the amount of the service charge payable to the payee, and the costs to mail the written demand for payment. If this person fails to pay in full the amount of the check, the service charge payable to the payee, and the costs to mail the written demand within this period, this person shall then be liable instead for the amount of the check, minus any partial payments made toward the amount of the check or the service charge within 30 days of the written demand, and damages equal to treble that amount, which shall not be less than one hundred dollars ($100) nor more than one thousand five hundred dollars ($1,500). When a person becomes liable for treble damages for a check that is the subject of a written demand, that person shall no longer be liable for any service charge for that check and any costs to mail the written demand.

(3) Notwithstanding paragraphs (1) and (2), a person shall not be liable for the service charge, costs to mail the written demand, or treble damages if he or she stops payment in order to resolve a good faith dispute with the payee. The payee is entitled to the service charge, costs to mail the written demand, or treble damages only upon proving by clear and convincing evidence that there was no good faith dispute, as defined in subdivision (b).

(4) Notwithstanding paragraph (1), a person shall not be liable under that paragraph for the service

charge if, at any time, he or she presents the payee with written confirmation by his or her financial institution that the check was returned to the payee by the financial institution due to an error on the part of the financial institution.

(5) Notwithstanding paragraph (1), a person shall not be liable under that paragraph for the service charge if the person presents the payee with written confirmation that his or her account had insufficient funds as a result of a delay in the regularly scheduled transfer of, or the posting of, a direct deposit of a social security or government benefit assistance payment.

(6) As used in this subdivision, to "pass a check on insufficient funds" means to make, utter, draw, or deliver any check, draft, or order for the payment of money upon any bank, depository, person, firm, or corporation that refuses to honor the check, draft, or order for any of the following reasons:

(A) Lack of funds or credit in the account to pay the check.

(B) The person who wrote the check does not have an account with the drawee.

(C) The person who wrote the check instructed the drawee to stop payment on the check.

(b) For purposes of this section, in the case of a stop payment, the existence of a "good faith dispute" shall be determined by the trier of fact. A "good faith dispute" is one in which the court finds that the drawer had a reasonable belief of his or her legal entitlement to withhold payment. Grounds for the entitlement include, but are not limited to, the following: services were not rendered, goods were not delivered, goods or services purchased are faulty, not as promised, or otherwise unsatisfactory, or there was an overcharge.

(c) n the case of a stop payment, the notice to the drawer required by this section shall be in substantially the following form:

NOTICE

To: _____
    (name of drawer)

_____ is the payee of
(name of payee)

a check you wrote for $ _____
                          (amount)

The check was not paid because you stopped payment, and the payee demands payment. You may have a good faith dispute as to whether you owe the full amount. If you do not have a good faith dispute with the payee and fail to pay the payee the full amount of the check in cash, a service charge of an amount not to exceed twenty-five dollars ($25) for the first check passed on insufficient funds and an amount not to exceed thirty-five dollars ($35) for each subsequent check passed on insufficient funds, and the costs to mail this notice within 30 days after this notice was mailed, you could be sued and held responsible to pay at least both of the following:

(1) The amount of the check.

(2) Damages of at least one hundred dollars ($100) or, if higher, three times the amount of the check up to one thousand five hundred dollars ($1,500).

If the court determines that you do have a good faith dispute with the payee, you will not have to pay the service charge, treble damages, or mailing cost.

If you stopped payment because you have a good faith dispute with the payee, you should try to work out your dispute with the payee.

You can contact the payee at:

_____
(name of payee)

_____
(street address)

_____
(telephone number)

You may wish to contact a lawyer to discuss your legal rights and responsibilities.

_____
(name of sender of notice)

(d) In the case of a stop payment, a court may not award damages or costs under this section unless the court receives into evidence a copy of the written demand which, in that case, shall have been sent to the drawer and a signed certified mail receipt showing delivery, or attempted delivery if refused, of the written demand to the drawer' s last known address.

(e) A cause of action under this section may be brought in small claims court by the original payee, if it does not exceed the jurisdiction of that court, or in any other appropriate court. The payee shall, in order to recover damages because the drawer instructed the drawee to stop payment, show to the satisfaction of the trier of fact that there was a reasonable effort on the part of the payee to reconcile and resolve the dispute prior to pursuing the dispute through the courts.

(f) A cause of action under this section may be brought in municipal court by a holder of the check or an assignee of the payee.

However, if the assignee is acting on behalf of the payee, for a flat fee or a percentage fee, the assignee may not charge the payee a greater flat fee or percentage fee for that portion of the amount collected that represents treble damages than is charged the payee for collecting the face amount of the check, draft, or order. This subdivision shall not apply to an action brought in small claims court.

(g) Notwithstanding subdivision (a), if the payee is a municipal court, the written demand for payment described in subdivision (a) may be mailed to the drawer by a municipal court clerk. Notwithstanding subdivision (d), in the case of a stop payment where the demand is mailed by a municipal court clerk, a court may not award damages or costs pursuant to subdivision (d), unless the court receives into evidence a copy of the written demand, and a certificate of mailing by a municipal court clerk in the form provided for in subdivision (4) of Section 1013a of the Code of Civil Procedure for service in civil actions. For purposes of this subdivision, in courts where a single court clerk serves more than one court, the clerk shall be deemed the court clerk of each court.

(h) The requirements of this section in regard to remedies are mandatory upon a court.

(i) The assignee of the payee or a holder of the check may demand, recover, or enforce the service charge, damages, and costs specified in this section to the same extent as the original payee.

(j) (1) A drawer is liable for damages and costs only if all of the requirements of this section have been satisfied.

(2) The drawer shall in no event be liable more than once under this section on each check for a service charge, damages, or costs.

(k) Nothing in this section is intended to condition, curtail, or otherwise prejudice the rights, claims, remedies, and defenses under Division 3 (commencing with Section 3101) of the Commercial Code of a drawer, payee, assignee, or holder, including a holder in due course as defined in Section 3302 of the Commercial Code, in connection with the enforcement of this section.

CIVIL CODE
SECTION 1940-1954.1

1940.(a) Except as provided in subdivision (b), this chapter shall apply to all persons who hire dwelling units located within this state including tenants, lessees, boarders, lodgers, and others, however denominated.

(b) The term "persons who hire" shall not include a person who maintains either of the following:

(1) Transient occupancy in a hotel, motel, residence club, or other facility when the transient occupancy is or would be subject to tax under Section 7280 of the Revenue and Taxation Code. The term "persons who hire" shall not include a person to whom this paragraph pertains if the person has not made valid payment for all room and other related charges owing as of the last day on which his or her occupancy is or would be subject to tax under Section 7280 of the Revenue and Taxation Code.

(2) Occupancy at a hotel or motel where the innkeeper retains a right of access to and control of the dwelling unit and the hotel or motel provides or offers all of the following services to all of the residents:

(A) Facilities for the safeguarding of personal property pursuant to Section 1860.

(B) Central telephone service subject to tariffs covering the same filed with the California Public Utilities Commission.

(C) Maid, mail, and room services.

(D) Occupancy for periods of less than seven days.

(E) Food service provided by a food establishment, as defined in Section 113780 of the Health and Safety Code, located on or adjacent to the premises of the hotel or motel and owned or operated by the innkeeper or owned or operated by a person or entity pursuant to a lease or similar relationship with the innkeeper or person or entity affiliated with the innkeeper.

(c) "Dwelling unit" means a structure or the part of a structure that is used as a home, residence, or sleeping place by one person who maintains a household or by two or more persons who maintain a common household.

(d) Nothing in this section shall be construed to limit the application of any provision of this chapter to tenancy in a dwelling unit unless the provision is so limited by its specific terms.

1940.1. (a) No person may require an occupant of a residential hotel, as defined in Section 50519 of the Health and Safety Code, to move, or to check out and reregister, before the expiration of 30 days occupancy if a purpose is to avoid application of this chapter pursuant to paragraph (1) of subdivision (b) of Section 1940.

(b) In addition to any remedies provided by local ordinance, any violation of subdivision (a) is punishable by a civil penalty of five hundred dollars ($500). In any action brought pursuant to this section, the prevailing party shall be entitled to reasonable attorney's fees.

1940.5. An owner or an owner's agent shall not refuse to rent a dwelling unit in a structure which received its valid certificate of occupancy after January 1, 1973, to an otherwise qualified prospective tenant or refuse to continue to rent to an existing tenant solely on the basis of that tenant's possession of a waterbed or other bedding with liquid filling material where all of the following requirements and conditions are met:

(a) A tenant or prospective tenant furnishes to the owner, prior to installation, a valid waterbed insurance policy or certificate of insurance for property damage. The policy shall be issued by a company licensed to do business in California and possessing a Best's Insurance Report rating of "B" or higher. The insurance policy shall be maintained in full force and effect until the bedding is permanently removed from the rental premises. The policy shall be written for no less than one hundred thousand dollars ($100,000) of coverage. The policy shall cover, up to the limits of the policy, replacement value of all property damage, including loss of use, incurred by the rental property owner or other caused by or arising out of the ownership, maintenance, use, or removal of the waterbed on the rental premises only, except for any damage caused intentionally or at the direction of the insured, or for any damage caused by or resulting from fire. The owner may require the tenant to produce evidence of insurance at any time. The carrier shall give the owner notice of cancellation or nonrenewal 10 days prior to this action. Every application for a policy shall contain the information as provided in subdivisions (a), (b), and (c) of Section 1962 and Section 1962.5.

(b) The bedding shall conform to the pounds-per-square foot weight limitation and placement as dictated by the floor load capacity of the residential structure. The weight shall be distributed on a pedestal or frame which is substantially the dimensions of the mattress itself.

(c) The tenant or prospective tenant shall install, maintain and remove the bedding, including, but not limited to, the mattress and frame, according to standard methods of installation, maintenance, and removal as prescribed by the manufacturer, retailer, or state law, whichever provides the higher degree of safety. The tenant shall notify the owner or owner's agent in writing of the intent to install, remove, or move the waterbed. The notice shall be delivered 24 hours prior to the installation, removal, or movement. The owner or the owner's agent may be present at the time of installation, removal, or movement at the owner's or the owner's agent's option. If the bedding is installed or moved by any person other than the tenant or prospective tenant, the tenant or prospective tenant shall deliver to the owner or to the owner's agent a written installation receipt stating the installer's name, address, and business affiliation where appropriate.

(d) Any new bedding installation shall conform to the owner's or the owner's agent's reasonable structural specifications for placement within the rental property and shall be consistent with floor capacity of the rental dwelling unit.

(e) The tenant or prospective tenant shall comply with the minimum component specification list prescribed by the manufacturer, retailer, or state law, whichever provides the higher degree of safety.

(f) Subject to the notice requirements of Section 1954, the owner, or the owner's agent, shall have the right to inspect the bedding installation upon completion, and periodically thereafter, to insure its conformity with this section. If installation or maintenance is not in conformity with this section, the owner may serve the tenant with a written notice of breach of the rental agreement. The owner may give the tenant three days either to bring the installation into conformity with those standards or to remove the bedding, unless there is an immediate danger to the structure, in which case there shall be immediate corrective action. If the bedding is installed by any person other than the tenant or prospective tenant, the tenant or prospective tenant shall deliver to the owner or to the owner's agent a written installation receipt stating the installer's name and business affiliation where appropriate.

(g) Notwithstanding Section 1950.5, an owner or owner's agent is entitled to increase the security deposit on the dwelling unit in an amount equal to one-half of one months' rent. The owner or owner's agent may charge a tenant, lessee, or sublessee a reasonable fee to cover administration costs. In no event does this section authorize the payment of a rebate of premium in violation of Article 5 (commencing with Section 750) of Chapter 1 of Part 2 of Division 1 of the Insurance Code. (h) Failure of the owner, or owner's agent, to exercise any of his or her rights pursuant to this section does not constitute grounds for denial of an insurance claim.

(i) As used in this section, "tenant" includes any lessee, and "rental" means any rental or lease.

1940.7. (a) The Legislature finds and declares that the December 10, 1983, tragedy in Tierra Santa, in which lives were lost as a result of a live munition exploding in a residential area that was formerly a military ordnance location, has demonstrated (1) the unique and heretofore unknown risk that there are other live munitions in former ordnance locations in California, (2) that these former ordnance locations need to be identified by the federal, state, or local authorities, and (3) that the people living in the neighborhood of these former ordnance locations should be notified of their existence. Therefore, it is the intent of the Legislature that the disclosure required by this section is solely warranted and limited by (1) the fact that these former ordnance locations cannot be readily observed or discovered by landlords and tenants, and (2) the ability of a landlord who has actual knowledge of a former ordnance location within the neighborhood of his or her rental property to disclose this information for the safety of the tenant.

(b) The landlord of a residential dwelling unit who has actual knowledge of any former federal or state ordnance locations in the neighborhood area shall give written notice to a prospective tenant of that knowledge prior to the execution of a rental agreement. In cases of tenancies in existence on January 1, 1990, this written notice shall be given to tenants as soon as practicable thereafter.

(c) For purposes of this section:

(1) "Former federal or state ordnance location" means an area identified by an agency or instrumentality of the federal or state government as an area once used for military training purposes and which may contain potentially explosive munitions.

(2) "Neighborhood area" means within one mile of the residential dwelling.

1940.9. (a) If the landlord does not provide separate gas and electric meters for each tenant's dwelling unit so that each tenant's meter measures only the electric or gas service to that tenant's dwelling unit and the landlord or his or her agent has knowledge that gas or electric service provided through a tenant's meter serves an area outside the tenant's dwelling unit, the landlord, prior to the inception of the tenancy or upon discovery, shall explicitly disclose that condition to the tenant and shall do either of the following:

(1) Execute a mutual written agreement with the tenant for payment by the tenant of the cost of the gas or electric service provided through the tenant's meter to serve areas outside the tenant's dwelling unit.

(2) Make other arrangements, as are mutually agreed in writing, for payment for the gas or electric service provided through the tenant's meter to serve areas outside the tenant's dwelling unit. These arrangements may include, but are not limited to, the landlord becoming the customer of record for the tenant's meter, or the landlord separately metering and becoming the customer of record for the area outside the tenant's dwelling unit.

(b) If a landlord fails to comply with subdivision (a), the aggrieved tenant may bring an action in a court of competent jurisdiction. The remedies the court may order shall include, but are not limited to, the following:

(1) Requiring the landlord to be made the customer of record with the utility for the tenant's meter.

(2) Ordering the landlord to reimburse the tenant for payments made by the tenant to the utility for service to areas outside of the tenant's dwelling unit. Payments to be reimbursed pursuant to this

paragraph shall commence from the date the obligation to disclose arose under subdivision (a).

(c) Nothing in this section limits any remedies available to a landlord or tenant under other provisions of this chapter, the rental agreement, or applicable statutory or common law.

(1941.) Section Nineteen Hundred and Forty-one. The lessor of a building intended for the occupation of human beings must, in the absence of an agreement to the contrary, put it into a condition fit for such occupation, and repair all subsequent dilapidations thereof, which render it untenantable, except such as are mentioned in section nineteen hundred and twenty-nine.

1941.1. A dwelling shall be deemed untenantable for purposes of Section 1941 if it substantially lacks any of the following affirmative standard characteristics:

(a) Effective waterproofing and weather protection of roof and exterior walls, including unbroken windows and doors.

(b) Plumbing or gas facilities which conformed to applicable law in effect at the time of installation, maintained in good working order.

(c) A water supply approved under applicable law, which is under the control of the tenant, capable of producing hot and cold running water, or a system which is under the control of the landlord, which produces hot and cold running water, furnished to appropriate fixtures, and connected to a sewage disposal system approved under applicable law.

(d) Heating facilities which conformed with applicable law at the time of installation, maintained in good working order.

(e) Electrical lighting, with wiring and electrical equipment which conformed with applicable law at the time of installation, maintained in good working order.

(f) Building, grounds and appurtenances at the time of the commencement of the lease or rental agreement in every part clean, sanitary, and free from all accumulations of debris, filth, rubbish, garbage, rodents and vermin, and all areas under control of the landlord kept in every part clean, sanitary, and free from all accumulations of debris, filth, rubbish, garbage, rodents, and vermin.

(g) An adequate number of appropriate receptacles for garbage and rubbish, in clean condition and good repair at the time of the commencement of the lease or rental agreement, with the landlord providing appropriate serviceable receptacles thereafter, and being responsible for the clean condition and good repair of such receptacles under his control.

(h) Floors, stairways, and railings maintained in good repair.

1941.2. (a) No duty on the part of the landlord to repair a dilapidation shall arise under Section 1941 or 1942 if the tenant is in substantial violation of any of the following affirmative obligations, provided the tenant's violation contributes substantially to the existence of the dilapidation or interferes substantially with the landlord's obligation under Section 1941 to effect the necessary repairs:

(1) To keep that part of the premises which he occupies and uses clean and sanitary as the condition of the premises permits.

(2) To dispose from his dwelling unit of all rubbish, garbage and other waste, in a clean and sanitary manner.

(3) To properly use and operate all electrical, gas and plumbing fixtures and keep them as clean and sanitary as their condition permits.

(4) Not to permit any person on the premises, with his permission, to willfully or wantonly destroy, deface, damage, impair or remove any part of the structure or dwelling unit or the facilities, equipment, or appurtenances thereto, nor himself do any such thing.

(5) To occupy the premises as his abode, utilizing portions thereof for living, sleeping, cooking or dining purposes only which were respectively designed or intended to be used for such occupancies.

(b) Paragraphs (1) and (2) of subdivision (a) shall not apply if the landlord has expressly agreed in writing to perform the act or acts mentioned therein.

1941.3. (a) On and after July 1, 1998, the landlord, or his or her agent, of a building intended for human habitation shall do all of the following:

(1) Install and maintain an operable dead bolt lock on each main swinging entry door of a dwelling unit. The dead bolt lock shall be installed in conformance with the manufacturer's specifications

and shall comply with applicable state and local codes including, but not limited to, those provisions relating to fire and life safety and accessibility for the disabled. When in the locked position, the bolt shall extend a minimum of 13/16 of an inch in length beyond the strike edge of the door and protrude into the doorjamb.

This section shall not apply to horizontal sliding doors. Existing dead bolts of at least one-half inch in length shall satisfy the requirements of this section. Existing locks with a thumb-turn deadlock that have a strike plate attached to the doorjamb and a latch bolt that is held in a vertical position by a guard bolt, a plunger, or an auxiliary mechanism shall also satisfy the requirements of this section. These locks, however, shall be replaced with a dead bolt at least 13/16 of an inch in length the first time after July 1, 1998, that the lock requires repair or replacement.

Existing doors which cannot be equipped with dead bolt locks shall satisfy the requirements of this section if the door is equipped with a metal strap affixed horizontally across the midsection of the door with a dead bolt which extends 13/16 of an inch in length beyond the strike edge of the door and protrudes into the doorjamb. Locks and security devices other than those described herein which are inspected and approved by an appropriate state or local government agency as providing adequate security shall satisfy the requirements of this section.

(2) Install and maintain operable window security or locking devices for windows that are designed to be opened. Louvered windows, casement windows, and all windows more than 12 feet vertically or six feet horizontally from the ground, a roof, or any other platform are excluded from this subdivision.

(3) Install locking mechanisms that comply with applicable fire and safety codes on the exterior doors that provide ingress or egress to common areas with access to dwelling units in multifamily developments. This paragraph does not require the installation of a door or gate where none exists on January 1, 1998.

(b) The tenant shall be responsible for notifying the owner or his or her authorized agent when the tenant becomes aware of an inoperable dead bolt lock or window security or locking device in the dwelling unit. The landlord, or his or her authorized agent, shall not be liable for a violation of subdivision (a) unless he or she fails to correct the violation within a reasonable time after he or she either has actual notice of a deficiency or receives notice of a deficiency.

(c) On and after July 1, 1998, the rights and remedies of tenant for a violation of this section by the landlord shall include those available pursuant to Sections 1942, 1942.4, and 1942.5, an action for breach of contract, and an action for injunctive relief pursuant to Section 526 of the Code of Civil Procedure. Additionally, in an unlawful detainer action, after a default in the payment of rent, a tenant may raise the violation of this section as an affirmative defense and shall have a right to the remedies provided by Section 1174.2 of the Code of Civil Procedure.

(d) A violation of this section shall not broaden, limit, or otherwise affect the duty of care owed by a landlord pursuant to existing law, including any duty that may exist pursuant to Section 1714. The delayed applicability of the requirements of subdivision (a) shall not affect a landlord's duty to maintain the premises in safe condition.

(e) Nothing in this section shall be construed to affect any authority of any public entity that may otherwise exist to impose any additional security requirements upon a landlord.

(f) This section shall not apply to any building which has been designated as historically significant by an appropriate local, state, or federal governmental jurisdiction.

(g) Subdivisions (a) and (b) shall not apply to any building intended for human habitation which is managed, directly or indirectly, and controlled by the Department of Transportation. This exemption shall not be construed to affect the duty of the Department of Transportation to maintain the premises of these buildings in a safe condition or abrogate any express or implied statement or promise of the Department of Transportation to provide secure premises. Additionally, this exemption shall not apply to residential dwellings acquired prior to July 1, 1997, by the Department of Transportation to complete construction of state highway routes 710 and 238 and related interchanges.

1941.4. The lessor of a building intended for the residential occupation of human beings shall be responsible for installing at least one usable telephone jack and for placing and maintaining the inside telephone wiring in good working order, shall ensure that the inside telephone wiring meets the applicable standards of the most recent National Electrical Code as adopted by the Electronic Industry Association, and shall make any required repairs. The lessor shall not restrict or interfere with access by the telephone utility to its telephone network facilities up to the demarcation point separating the inside wiring.

"Inside telephone wiring" for purposes of this section, means that portion of the telephone wire that connects the telephone equipment at the customer's premises to the telephone network at a demarcation point determined by the telephone corporation in accordance with orders of the Public Utilities Commission.

1942. (a) If within a reasonable time after written or oral notice to the landlord or his agent, as defined in subdivision (a) of Section 1962, of dilapidations rendering the premises untenantable which the landlord ought to repair, the landlord neglects to do so, the tenant may repair the same himself where the cost of such repairs does not require an expenditure more than one month's rent of the premises and deduct the expenses of such repairs from the rent when due, or the tenant may vacate the premises, in which case the tenant shall be discharged from further payment of rent, or performance of other conditions as of the date of vacating the premises. This remedy shall not be available to the tenant more than twice in any 12-month period.

(b) For the purposes of this section, if a tenant acts to repair and deduct after the 30th day following notice, he is presumed to have acted after a reasonable time. The presumption established by this subdivision is a rebuttable presumption affecting the burden of producing evidence and shall not be construed to prevent a tenant from repairing and deducting after a shorter notice if all the circumstances require shorter notice.

(c) The tenant's remedy under subdivision (a) shall not be available if the condition was caused by the violation of Section 1929 or 1941.2.

(d) The remedy provided by this section is in addition to any other remedy provided by this chapter, the rental agreement, or other applicable statutory or common law.

1942.1. Any agreement by a lessee of a dwelling waiving or modifying his rights under Section 1941 or 1942 shall be void as contrary to public policy with respect to any condition which renders the premises untenantable, except that the lessor and the lessee may agree that the lessee shall undertake to improve, repair or maintain all or stipulated portions of the dwelling as part of the consideration for rental.

The lessor and lessee may, if an agreement is in writing, set forth the provisions of Sections 1941 to 1942.1, inclusive, and provide that any controversy relating to a condition of the premises claimed to make them untenantable may by application of either party be submitted to arbitration, pursuant to the provisions of Title 9 (commencing with Section 1280), Part 3 of the Code of Civil Procedure, and that the costs of such arbitration shall be apportioned by the arbitrator between the parties.

1942.3. (a) In any unlawful detainer action by the landlord to recover possession from a tenant, a rebuttable presumption affecting the burden of producing evidence that the landlord has breached the habitability requirements in Section 1941 is created if all of the following conditions exist:

(1) The dwelling substantially lacks any of the affirmative standard characteristics listed in Section 1941.1.

(2) A public officer or employee who is responsible for the enforcement of any housing law has notified the landlord, or an agent of the landlord, in a written notice issued after inspection of the premises which informs the landlord of his or her obligations to abate the nuisance or repair the substandard conditions.

(3) The conditions have existed and have not been abated 60 days beyond the date of issuance of the notice specified in paragraph (2) and the delay is without good cause.

(4) The conditions were not caused by an act or omission of the tenant or lessee in violation of Section 1929 or 1941.2.

(b) The presumption specified in subdivision (a) does not arise unless all of the conditions set forth therein are proven, but failure to so establish the presumption shall not otherwise affect the right of the tenant to raise and pursue any defense based on the landlord's breach of the implied warranty of habitability.

(c) The presumption provided in this section shall apply only to rental agreements or leases entered into or renewed on or after January 1, 1986.

1942.4. (a) Any landlord who demands or collects rent when all of the following conditions exist is liable to the tenant or lessee for the actual damages sustained by the tenant or lessee and special damages in an amount not less than one hundred dollars ($100) nor more than one thousand dollars ($1,000):

(1) The rental dwelling substantially lacks any of the affirmative standard characteristics listed in Section 1941.1.

(2) A public officer or employee who is responsible for the enforcement of any housing law has notified the landlord, or an agent of the landlord, in a written notice issued after inspection of the premises that informs the landlord of his or her obligations to abate the nuisance or repair the substandard conditions.

(3) The conditions have existed and have not been abated 60 days beyond the date of issuance of the notice specified in paragraph (2) and the delay is without good cause.

(4) The conditions were not caused by an act or omission of the tenant or lessee in violation of Section 1929 or 1941.2.

(b) In addition to recovery of allowable costs of suit, the prevailing party shall be entitled to recovery of reasonable attorney's fees in an amount fixed by the court.

(c) Any court that awards damages under subdivision (a) may also order the landlord to abate any nuisance at the rental dwelling and to repair any substandard conditions of the rental dwelling, as defined in Section 1941.1, which significantly or materially affect the health or safety of the occupants of the rental dwelling and are uncorrected. If the court orders repairs or corrections, or both, the court's jurisdiction continues over the matter for the purpose of ensuring compliance.

(d) The tenant or lessee shall be under no obligation to undertake any other remedy prior to exercising his or her rights under this section.

(e) Any action under this section may be maintained in small claims court if the claim does not exceed the jurisdictional limit of that court.

(f) The remedy provided by this section applies only to rental agreements or leases entered into or renewed on or after January 1, 1986, and may be utilized in addition to any other remedy provided by this chapter, the rental agreement, lease, or other applicable statutory or common law. Nothing in this section shall require any landlord to comply with this section if he or she pursues his or her rights pursuant to Chapter 12.75 (commencing with Section 7060) of Division 7 of Title 1 of the Government Code.

1942.5. (a) If the lessor retaliates against the lessee because of the exercise by the lessee of his rights under this chapter or because of his complaint to an appropriate agency as to tenantability of a dwelling, and if the lessee of a dwelling is not in default as to the payment of his rent, the lessor may not recover possession of a dwelling in any action or proceeding, cause the lessee to quit involuntarily, increase the rent, or decrease any services within 180 days:

(1) After the date upon which the lessee, in good faith, has given notice pursuant to Section 1942, or has made an oral complaint to the lessor regarding tenantability; or

(2) After the date upon which the lessee, in good faith, has filed a written complaint, or an oral complaint which is registered or otherwise recorded in writing, with an appropriate agency, of which the lessor has notice, for the purpose of obtaining correction of a condition relating to tenantability; or

(3) After the date of an inspection or issuance of a citation, resulting from a complaint described in paragraph (2) of which the lessor did not have notice; or

(4) After the filing of appropriate documents commencing a judicial or arbitration proceeding involving the issue of tenantability; or

(5) After entry of judgment or the signing of an arbitration award, if any, when in the judicial proceeding or arbitration the issue of tenantability is determined adversely to the lessor.

In each instance, the 180-day period shall run from the latest applicable date referred to in paragraphs (1) to (5), inclusive.

(b) A lessee may not invoke the provisions of subdivision (a) more than once in any 12-month period.

(c) It shall be unlawful for a lessor to increase rent, decrease services, cause a lessee to quit involuntarily, bring an action to recover possession, or threaten to do any of such acts, for the purpose of retaliating against the lessee because he or she has lawfully organized or participated in a lessees' association or an organization advocating lessees' rights or has lawfully and peaceably exercised any rights under the law. In an action brought by or against the lessee pursuant to this subdivision, the lessee shall bear the burden of producing evidence that the lessor's conduct was, in fact, retaliatory.

(d) Nothing in this section shall be construed as limiting in any way the exercise by the lessor of his rights under any lease or agreement or any law pertaining to the hiring of property or his right to do any of the acts described in subdivision (a) or (c) for any lawful cause. Any waiver by a lessee of his rights under this section shall be void as contrary to public policy.

(e) Notwithstanding the provisions of subdivisions (a) to (d), inclusive, a lessor may recover possession of a dwelling and do any of the other acts described in subdivision (a) within the period or periods prescribed therein, or within subdivision (c), if the notice of termination, rent increase, or other act, and any pleading or statement of issues in an arbitration, if any, states the ground upon which the lessor, in good faith, seeks to recover possession, increase rent, or do any of the other acts described in subdivision (a) or (c). If such statement be controverted, the lessor shall establish its truth at the trial or other hearing.

(f) Any lessor or agent of a lessor who violates this section shall be liable to the lessee in a civil action for all of the following:

(1) The actual damages sustained by the lessee.

(2) Punitive damages in an amount of not less than one hundred dollars ($100) nor more than one thousand dollars ($1,000) for each retaliatory act where the lessor or agent has been guilty of fraud, oppression, or malice with respect to such act.

(g) In any action brought for damages for retaliatory eviction, the court shall award reasonable attorney's fees to the prevailing party if either party requests attorney's fees upon the initiation of the action.

(h) The remedies provided by this section shall be in addition to any other remedies provided by statutory or decisional law.

1943. A hiring of real property, other than lodgings and dwelling-houses, in places where there is no custom or usage on the subject, is presumed to be a month to month tenancy unless otherwise designated in writing; except that, in the case of real property used for agricultural or grazing purposes a hiring is presumed to be for one year from its commencement unless otherwise expressed in the hiring.

1944. A hiring of lodgings or a dwelling house for an unspecified term is presumed to have been made for such length of time as the parties adopt for the estimation of the rent. Thus a hiring at a monthly rate of rent is presumed to be for one month. In the absence of any agreement respecting the length of time or the rent, the hiring is presumed to be monthly.

1945. If a lessee of real property remains in possession thereof after the expiration of the hiring, and the lessor accepts rent from him, the parties are presumed to have renewed the hiring on the same terms and for the same time, not exceeding one month when the rent is payable monthly, nor in any case one year.

1945.5. Notwithstanding any other provision of law, any term of a lease executed after the effective date of this section for the hiring of residential real property which provides for the automatic renewal or extension of the lease for all or part of the full term of the lease if the lessee remains in possession after the expiration of the lease or fails to give notice of his intent not to renew or extend before the expiration of the lease shall be voidable by the party who did not prepare the lease unless such renewal or extension provision appears in at least eight-point boldface type, if the contract is printed, in the body of the lease agreement and a recital of the fact that such provision is contained in the body of the agreement appears in at least eight-point boldface type, if the contract is printed, immediately prior to the place where the lessee executes the agreement. In such case, the presumption in Section 1945 of this code shall apply.

Any waiver of the provisions of this section is void as against public policy.

1946. A hiring of real property, for a term not specified by the parties, is deemed to be renewed as stated in Section 1945, at the end of the term implied by law unless one of the parties gives written notice to the other of his intention to terminate the same, at least as long before the expiration thereof as the term of the hiring itself, not exceeding 30 days; provided, however, that as to tenancies from month to month either of the parties may terminate the same by giving at least 30 days' written notice thereof at any time and the rent shall be due and payable to and including the date of termination. It shall be competent for the parties to provide by an agreement at the time such tenancy is created that a notice of the intention to terminate the same may be given at any time not less than seven days before the expiration of the term thereof. The notice herein required shall be given in the manner prescribed in Section 1162 of the Code of Civil Procedure or by sending a copy by certified or registered mail addressed to the other party. In addition, the lessee may give such notice by sending a copy by certified or registered mail addressed to the agent of the lessor to whom the lessee has paid the rent for the month prior to the date of such notice or by delivering a copy to the agent personally.

1946.5. (a) The hiring of a room by a lodger on a periodic basis within a dwelling unit occupied by the owner may be terminated by either party giving written notice to the other of his or her intention to terminate the hiring, at least as long before the expiration of the term of the hiring as specified in Section 1946. The notice shall be given in a manner prescribed in Section 1162 of the Code of Civil Procedure or by certified or registered mail, restricted delivery, to the other party, with a return receipt requested.

(b) Upon expiration of the notice period provided in the notice of termination given pursuant to subdivision (a), any right of the lodger to remain in the dwelling unit or any part thereof is terminated by operation of law. The lodger's removal from the premises may thereafter be effected pursuant to the provisions of Section 602.3 of the Penal Code or other applicable provisions of law.

(c) As used in this section, "lodger" means a person contracting with the owner of a dwelling unit for a room or room and board within the dwelling unit personally occupied by the owner, where the owner retains a right of access to all areas of the dwelling unit occupied by the lodger and has overall control of the dwelling unit.

(d) This section applies only to owner-occupied dwellings where a single lodger resides. Nothing in this section shall be construed to determine or affect in any way the rights of persons residing as lodgers in an owner-occupied dwelling where more than one lodger resides.

1947. When there is no usage or contract to the contrary, rents are payable at the termination of the holding, when it does not exceed one year. If the holding is by the day, week, month, quarter, or year, rent is payable at the termination of the respective periods, as it successively becomes due.

1947.7. (a) The Legislature finds and declares that the operation of local rent stabilization programs can be complex and that disputes often arise with regard to standards of compliance with the regulatory processes of those programs. Therefore, it is the intent of the Legislature to limit the imposition of penalties and sanctions against an owner of residential rental units where that person has attempted in good faith to fully comply with the regulatory processes.

(b) An owner of a residential rental unit who is in substantial compliance with an ordinance or charter that controls or establishes a system of controls on the price at which residential rental units may be offered for rent or lease and which requires the registration of rents, or any regulation adopted pursuant thereto, shall not be assessed a penalty or any other sanction for noncompliance with the ordinance, charter, or regulation.

Restitution to the tenant or recovery of the registration or filing fees due to the local agency shall be the exclusive remedies which may be imposed against an owner of a residential rental unit who is in substantial compliance with the ordinance, charter, or regulation.

"Substantial compliance," as used in this subdivision, means that the owner of a residential rental unit has made a good faith attempt to comply with the ordinance, charter, or regulation sufficient to reasonably carry out the intent and purpose of the ordinance, charter, or regulation, but is not in full compliance, and has, after receiving notice of a deficiency from the local agency, cured the defect in a timely manner, as reasonably determined by the local agency.

"Local agency," as used in this subdivision, means the public entity responsible for the implementation of the ordinance, charter, or regulation.

(c) For any residential unit which has been registered and for which a base rent has been listed or for any residential unit which an owner can show, by a preponderance of the evidence, a good faith attempt to comply with the registration requirements or who was exempt from registration requirements in a previous version of the ordinance or charter and for which the owner of that residential unit has subsequently found not to have been in compliance with the ordinance, charter, or regulation, all annual rent adjustments which may have been denied during the period of the owner's noncompliance shall be restored prospectively once the owner is in compliance with the ordinance, charter, or regulation.

(d)   In those jurisdictions where, prior to January 1, 1990, the local ordinance did not allow the restoration of annual rent adjustment, once the owner is in compliance with this section the local agency may phase in any increase in rent caused by the restoration of the annual rent adjustments that is in excess of 20 percent over the rent previously paid by the tenant, in equal installments over three years, if the tenant demonstrates undue financial hardship due to the restoration of the full annual rent adjustments. This subdivision shall remain operative only until January 1, 1993, unless a later enacted statute which is chaptered by January 1, 1993, deletes or extends that date.

(e)   For purposes of this subdivision, an owner shall be deemed in compliance with the ordinance, charter, or regulation if he or she is in substantial compliance with the applicable local rental registration requirements and applicable local and state housing code provisions, has paid all fees and penalties owed to the local agency which have not otherwise been barred by the applicable statute of limitations, and has satisfied all claims for refunds of rental overcharges brought by tenants or by the local rent control board on behalf of tenants of the affected unit.

(f)   Nothing in this section shall be construed to grant to any public entity any power which it does not possess independent of this section to control or establish a system of control on the price at which accommodations may be offered for rent or lease, or to diminish any power to do so which that public entity may possess, except as specifically provided in this section.

(g)   In those jurisdictions where an ordinance or charter controls, or establishes a system of controls on, the price at which residential rental units may be offered for rent or lease and requires the periodic registration of rents, and where, for purposes of compliance with subdivision (e) of

Section 1954.53, the local agency requires an owner to provide the name of a present or former tenant, the tenant's name and any additional information provided concerning the tenant, is confidential and shall be treated as confidential information within the meaning of the Information Practices Act of 1977 (Chapter 1 (commencing with Section 1798) of Title 1.8 of this part). A local agency shall, to the extent required by this subdivision, be considered an "agency" as defined in subdivision (b) of Section 1798.3. For purposes of compliance with subdivision (e) of Section 1954.53, a local agency subject to this subdivision may request, but shall not compel, an owner to provide any information regarding a tenant other than the tenant's name.

1947.8. (a) If an ordinance or charter controls or establishes a system of controls on the price at which residential rental units may be offered for rent or lease and requires the registration of rents, the ordinance or charter, or any regulation adopted pursuant thereto, shall provide for the establishment and certification of permissible rent levels for the registered rental units, and any changes thereafter to those rent levels, by the local agency as provided in this section.

(b)   If the ordinance, charter, or regulation is in effect on January 1, 1987, the ordinance, charter, or regulation shall provide for the establishment and certification of permissible rent levels on or before January 1, 1988, including completion of all appeals and administrative proceedings connected therewith. After July 1, 1990, no local agency may maintain any action to recover excess rent against any property owner who has registered the unit with the local agency within the time limits set forth in this section if the initial certification of permissible rent levels affecting that particular property has not been completed, unless the delay is willfully and intentionally caused by the property owner or is a result of court proceedings or further administrative proceedings ordered by a court. If the ordinance, charter, or regulation is adopted on or after January 1, 1987, the ordinance, charter, or regulation shall provide for the establishment and certification of permissible rent levels within one year after it is adopted, including completion of all appeals and administrative proceedings connected therewith. Upon the request of the landlord or the tenant, the local agency shall provide the landlord and the tenant with a certificate or other documentation reflecting the permissible rent levels of the rental unit. A landlord may request a certificate of permissible rent levels for rental units which have a base rent established, but which are vacant and not exempt from registration under this section. The landlord or the tenant may appeal the determination of the permissible rent levels reflected in the certificate. The permissible rent levels reflected in the certificate or other documentation shall, in the absence of intentional misrepresentation or fraud, be binding and conclusive upon the local agency unless the determination of the permissible rent levels is being appealed.

(c) After the establishment and certification of permissible rent levels under subdivision (b), the local agency shall, upon the request of the landlord or the tenant, provide the landlord and the tenant with a certificate of the permissible rent levels of the rental unit. The certificate shall be issued within five business days from the date of request by the landlord or the tenant. The permissible rent levels reflected in the certificate shall, in the absence of intentional misrepresentation or fraud, be binding and conclusive upon the local agency unless the determination of the permissible rent levels is being appealed. The landlord or the tenant may appeal the determination of the permissible rent levels reflected in the certificate. Any appeal of a determination of permissible rent levels as reflected in the certificate, other than an appeal made pursuant to subdivision (b), shall be filed with the local agency within 15 days from issuance of the certificate. The local agency shall notify, in writing, the landlord and the tenant of its decision within 60 days following the filing of the appeal.

(d) The local agency may charge the person to whom a certificate is issued a fee in the amount necessary to cover the reasonable costs incurred by the local agency in issuing the certificate.

(e) The absence of a certification of permissible rent levels shall not impair, restrict, abridge, or otherwise interfere with either of the following:

(1) A judicial or administrative hearing.

(2) Any matter in connection with a conveyance of an interest in property.

(f) The record of permissible rent levels is a public record for purposes of the California Public Records Act, Chapter 3.5 (commencing with Section 6250) of Division 7 of Title 1 of the Government Code.

(g) Any notice specifying the rents applicable to residential rental units which is given by an owner to a public entity or tenant in order to comply with Chapter 12.75 (commencing with Section 7060) of Division 7 of Title 1 of the Government Code shall not be considered a registration of rents for purposes of this section.

(h) "Local agency," as used in this section, means the public entity responsible for the implementation of the ordinance, charter, or regulation.

(i) Nothing in this section shall be construed to grant to any public entity any power which it does not possess independent of this section to control or establish a system of control on the price at which accommodations may be offered for rent or lease, or to diminish any such power which that public entity may possess, except as specifically provided in this section.

1947.10. (a) After July 1, 1990, in any city, county, or city and county which administers a system of controls on the price at which residential rental units may be offered for rent or lease and which requires the registration of rents, any owner who evicts a tenant based upon the owner's or the owner's immediate relative's intention to occupy the tenant's unit, shall be required to maintain residence in the unit for at least six continuous months. If a court determines that the eviction was based upon fraud by the owner or the owner's immediate relative to not fulfill this six-month requirement, a court may order the owner to pay treble the cost of relocating the tenant from his or her existing unit back into the previous unit and may order the owner to pay treble the amount of any increase in rent which the tenant has paid. If the tenant decides not to relocate back into the previous unit, the court may order the owner to pay treble the amount of one month's rent paid by the tenant for the unit from which he or she was evicted and treble the amount of any costs incurred in relocating to a different unit. The prevailing party shall be awarded attorney's fees and court costs.

(b) The remedy provided by this section shall not be construed to prohibit any other remedies available to a any party affected by this section.

1947.11. (a) In any city, county, or city and county which administers a system of controls on the price at which residential rental units may be offered for rent or lease and which requires the registration of rents, upon the establishment of a certified rent level, any owner who charges rent to a tenant in excess of the certified lawful rent ceiling shall refund the excess rent to the tenant upon demand. If the owner refuses to refund the excess rent and if a court determines that the owner willfully or intentionally charged the tenant rent in excess of the certified lawful rent ceiling, the court shall award the tenant a judgment for the excess amount of rent and may treble that amount. The prevailing party shall be awarded attorney's fees and court costs.

(b) The remedy provided by this section shall not be construed to prohibit any other remedies available to any party affected by this section.

(c) This section shall not be construed to extend the time within which actions are required to be brought beyond the otherwise applicable limitation set forth in the Code of Civil Procedure.

1947.15. (a) The Legislature declares the purpose of this section is to:

(1) Ensure that owners of residential rental units that are subject to a system of controls on the price at which the units may be offered for rent or lease, or controls on the adjustment of the rent level, are not precluded or discouraged from obtaining a fair return on their properties as guaranteed by the United States Constitution and California Constitution because the professional expenses reasonably required in the course of the administrative proceedings, in order to obtain the rent increases necessary to provide a fair return, are not treated as a legitimate business expense.

(2) Encourage agencies which administer a system of controls on the price at which residential rental units may be offered for rent or lease, or controls the adjustment of the rent level, to enact streamlined administrative procedures governing rent adjustment petitions which minimize, to the extent possible, the cost and expense of these administrative proceedings.

(3) Ensure that the cost of professional services reasonably incurred and required by owners of residential rental units subject to a system of controls in the price at which the units may be offered for rent or lease, or controls on the adjustments of the rent level in the course of defending rights related to the rent control

system, be treated as a legitimate business expense.

(b) Any city, county, or city and county, including a charter city, which administers an ordinance, charter provision, rule, or regulation that controls or establishes a system of controls on the price at which all or any portion of the residential rental units located within the city, county, or city and county, may be offered for rent or lease, or controls the adjustment of the rent level, and which does not include a system of vacancy decontrol, as defined in subdivision (i), shall permit reasonable expenses, fees, and other costs for professional services, including, but not limited to, legal, accounting, appraisal, bookkeeping, consulting, property management, or architectural services, reasonably incurred in the course of successfully pursuing rights under or in relationship to, that ordinance, charter provision, rule, or regulation, or the right to a fair return on an owner's property as protected by the United States Constitution or California Constitution, to be included in any calculation of net operating income and operating expenses used to determine a fair return to the owner of the property. All expenses, fees, and other costs reasonably incurred by an owner of property in relation to administrative proceedings for purposes specified in this subdivision shall be included in the calculation specified in this subdivision.

(c) Reasonable fees that are incurred by the owner in successfully obtaining a judicial reversal of an adverse administrative decision regarding a petition for upward adjustment of rents shall be assessed against the respondent public agency which issued the adverse administrative decision, and shall not be included in the calculations specified in subdivisions (b) and (d).

(d) (1) Notwithstanding subdivision (b), the city, county, or city and county, on the basis of substantial evidence in the record that the expenses reasonably incurred in the underlying proceeding will not reoccur annually, may amortize the expenses for a period not to exceed five years, except that in extraordinary circumstances, the amortization period may be extended to a period of eight years. The extended amortization period shall not apply to vacant units and shall end if the unit becomes vacant during the period that the expense is being amortized. An amortization schedule shall include a reasonable rate of interest.

(2) Any determination of the reasonableness of the expenses claimed, of an appropriate amortization period, or of the award of an upward adjustment of rents to compensate the owner for expenses and costs incurred shall be made as part of, or immediately following, the decision in the underlying administrative proceeding.

(e) Any and all of the following factors shall be considered in the determination of the reasonableness of the expenses, fees, or other costs authorized by this section:

(1) The rate charged for those professional services in the relevant geographic area.

(2) The complexity of the matter.

(3) The degree of administrative burden or judicial burden, or both, imposed upon the property owner.

(4) The amount of adjustment sought or the significance of the rights defended and the results obtained.

(5) The relationship of the result obtained to the expenses, fees, and other costs incurred (that is, whether professional assistance was reasonably related to the result achieved).

(f) This section shall not be applicable to any ordinance, rule, regulation, or charter provision of any city, county, or city and county, including a charter city, to the extent that the ordinance, rule, or regulation, or charter provision places a limit on the amount of rent that an owner may charge a tenant of a mobilehome park.

(g) For purposes of this section, the rights of a property owner shall be deemed to be successfully pursued or defended if the owner obtains an upward adjustment in rents, successfully defends his or her rights in an administrative proceeding brought by the tenant or the local rent board, or prevails in a proceeding, brought pursuant to Section 1947.8 concerning certification of maximum lawful rents.

(h) (1) If it is determined that a landlord petition assisted by attorneys or consultants is wholly without merit, the tenant shall be awarded a reduction in rent to compensate for the reasonable costs of attorneys or consultants retained by the tenant to defend the petition brought by the landlord. The reasonableness of the costs of the tenant's defense of the action brought by the landlord shall be determined pursuant to the same provisions established by this section for

determining the reasonableness of the landlord's costs for the professional services. The determination of the reasonableness of the expenses claimed, an appropriate amortization period, and the award of a reduction in rents to compensate the tenant for costs incurred shall be made immediately following the decision in the underlying administrative proceeding.

(2) If it is determined that a landlord's appeal of an adverse administrative decision is frivolous or solely intended to cause unnecessary delay, the public agency which defended the action shall be awarded its reasonably incurred expenses, including attorney's fees, in defending the action. As used in this paragraph, "frivolous" means either (A) totally and completely without merit; or (B) for the sole purpose of harassing an opposing party.

(i) For purposes of this section, the following terms shall have the following meanings:

(1) "Vacancy decontrol" means a system of controls on the price at which residential rental units may be offered for rent or lease which permits the rent to be increased to its market level, without restriction, each time a vacancy occurs. "Vacancy decontrol" includes systems which reimpose controls on the price at which residential rental units may be offered for rent or lease upon rerental of the unit.

(2) "Vacancy decontrol" includes circumstances where the tenant vacates the unit of his or her own volition, or where the local jurisdiction permits the rent to be raised to market rate after an eviction for cause, as specified in the ordinance, charter provision, rule, or regulation.

(j) This section shall not be construed to affect in any way the ability of a local agency to set its own fair return standards or to limit other actions under its local rent control program other than those expressly set forth in this section.

1948. The attornment of a tenant to a stranger is void, unless it is made with the consent of the landlord, or in consequence of a judgment of a Court of competent jurisdiction.

1949. Every tenant who receives notice of any proceeding to recover the real property occupied by him or her, or the possession of the real property, shall immediately inform his or her landlord of the proceeding, and also deliver to the landlord the notice, if in writing, and is responsible to the landlord for all damages which he or she may sustain by reason of any omission to inform the landlord of the notice, or to deliver it to him or her if in writing.

1950. One who hires part of a room for a dwelling is entitled to the whole of the room, notwithstanding any agreement to the contrary; and if a landlord lets a room as a dwelling for more than one family, the person to whom he first lets any part of it is entitled to the possession of the whole room for the term agreed upon, and every tenant in the building, under the same landlord, is relieved from all obligation to pay rent to him while such double letting of any room continues.

1950.5. (a) This section applies to security for a rental agreement for residential property that is used as the dwelling of the tenant.

(b) As used in this section, "security" means any payment, fee, deposit or charge, including, but not limited to, an advance payment of rent, used or to be used for any purpose, including, but not limited to, any of the following:

(1) The compensation of a landlord for a tenant's default in the payment of rent.

(2) The repair of damages to the premises, exclusive of ordinary wear and tear, caused by the tenant or by a guest or licensee of the tenant.

(3) The cleaning of the premises upon termination of the tenancy.

(4) To remedy future defaults by the tenant in any obligation under the rental agreement to restore, replace, or return personal property or appurtenances, exclusive of ordinary wear and tear, if the security deposit is authorized to be applied thereto by the rental agreement.

(c) A landlord may not demand or receive security, however denominated, in an amount or value in excess of an amount equal to two months' rent, in the case of unfurnished residential property, and an amount equal to three months' rent, in the case of furnished residential property, in addition to any rent for the first month paid on or before initial occupancy.

This subdivision does not prohibit an advance payment of not less than six months' rent where the term of the lease is six months or longer.

This subdivision does not preclude a landlord and a tenant from entering into a mutual agreement for the landlord, at the request of the tenant and for a specified fee or charge, to make structural, decorative, furnishing, or other similar

alterations, if the alterations are other than cleaning or repairing for which the landlord may charge the previous tenant as provided by subdivision (e).

(d) Any security shall be held by the landlord for the tenant who is party to the lease or agreement. The claim of a tenant to the security shall be prior to the claim of any creditor of the landlord.

(e) The landlord may claim of the security only those amounts as are reasonably necessary for the purposes specified in subdivision (b). The landlord may not assert a claim against the tenant or the security for damages to the premises or any defective conditions that preexisted the tenancy, for ordinary wear and tear or the effects thereof, whether the wear and tear preexisted the tenancy or occurred during the tenancy, or for the cumulative effects of ordinary wear and tear occurring during any one or more tenancies.

(f) Within three weeks after the tenant has vacated the premises, the landlord shall furnish the tenant, by personal delivery or by first-class mail, postage prepaid, a copy of an itemized statement indicating the basis for, and the amount of, any security received and the disposition of the security and shall return any remaining portion of the security to the tenant.

(g) Upon termination of the landlord's interest in the dwelling unit in question, whether by sale, assignment, death, appointment of receiver or otherwise, the landlord or the landlord's agent shall, within a reasonable time, do one of the following acts, either of which shall relieve the landlord of further liability with respect to the security held:

(1) Transfer the portion of the security remaining after any lawful deductions made under subdivision (e) to the landlord's successor in interest. The landlord shall thereafter notify the tenant by personal delivery or by first-class mail, postage prepaid, of the transfer, of any claims made against the security, of the amount of the security deposited, and of the names of the successors in interest, their address, and their telephone number. If the notice to the tenant is made by personal delivery, the tenant shall acknowledge receipt of the notice and sign his or her name on the landlord's copy of the notice.

(2) Return the portion of the security remaining after any lawful deductions made under subdivision

(e) to the tenant, together with an accounting as provided in subdivision (f).

(h) Prior to the voluntary transfer of a landlord's interest in a dwelling unit, the landlord shall deliver to the landlord's successor in interest a written statement indicating the following:

(1) The security remaining after any lawful deductions are made.

(2) An itemization of any lawful deductions from any security received.

(3) His or her election under paragraph (1) or (2) of subdivision (g).

Nothing in this subdivision shall affect the validity of title to the real property transferred in violation of the provisions of this subdivision.

(i) In the event of noncompliance with subdivision (g), the landlord's successors in interest shall be jointly and severally liable with the landlord for repayment of the security, or that portion thereof to which the tenant is entitled, when and as provided in subdivisions (e) and (f). A successor in interest of a landlord may not require the tenant to post any security to replace that amount not transferred to the tenant or successors in interest as provided in subdivision (g), unless and until the successor in interest first makes restitution of the initial security as provided in paragraph (2) of subdivision (g) or provides the tenant with an accounting as provided in subdivision (f).

Nothing in this subdivision shall preclude a successor in interest from recovering from the tenant compensatory damages that are in excess of the security received from the landlord previously paid by the tenant to the landlord.

Notwithstanding the provisions of this subdivision, if, upon inquiry and reasonable investigation, a landlord's successor in interest has a good faith belief that the lawfully remaining security deposit is transferred to him or her or returned to the tenant pursuant to subdivision (g), he or she shall not be liable for damages as provided in subdivision (k), or any security not transferred pursuant to subdivision (g).

(j) Upon receipt of any portion of the security under paragraph (1) of subdivision (g), the landlord's successors in interest shall have all of the rights and obligations of a landlord holding the security with respect to the security.

(k) The bad faith claim or retention by a landlord or the landlord's successors in interest of the security or any portion thereof in violation of this section, or the bad faith demand of replacement security in violation of subdivision (i), may subject the landlord or the landlord's successors in interest to statutory damages of up to six hundred dollars ($600), in addition to actual damages. The court may award damages for bad faith whenever the facts warrant such an award, regardless of whether the injured party has specifically requested relief. In any action under this section, the landlord or the landlord's successors in interest shall have the burden of proof as to the reasonableness of the amounts claimed or the authority pursuant to this section to demand additional security deposits.

(l) No lease or rental agreement shall contain any provision characterizing any security as "nonrefundable."

(m) Any action under this section may be maintained in small claims court if the damages claimed, whether actual or statutory or both, are within the jurisdictional amount allowed by Section 116.220 of the Code of Civil Procedure.

(n) Proof of the existence of and the amount of a security deposit may be established by any credible evidence, including, but not limited to, a canceled check, a receipt, a lease indicating the requirement of a deposit as well as the amount, prior consistent statements or actions of the landlord or tenant, or a statement under penalty of perjury that satisfies the credibility requirements set forth in Section 780 of the Evidence Code.

(o) The amendments to this section made during the 1985 portion of the 1985-86 Regular Session of the Legislature that are set forth in subdivision (e) are declaratory of existing law.

1950.6. (a) Notwithstanding Section 1950.5, when a landlord or his or her agent receives a request to rent a residential property from an applicant, the landlord or his or her agent may charge that applicant an application screening fee to cover the costs of obtaining information about the applicant. The information requested and obtained by the landlord or his or her agent may include, but is not limited to, personal reference checks and consumer credit reports produced by consumer credit reporting agencies as defined in Section 1785.3. A landlord or his or her agent may, but is not required to, accept and rely upon a consumer credit report presented by an applicant.

(b) The amount of the application screening fee shall not be greater than the actual out-of-pocket costs of gathering information concerning the applicant, including, but not limited to, the cost of using a tenant screening service or a consumer credit reporting service, and the reasonable value of time spent by the landlord or his or her agent in obtaining information on the applicant. In no case shall the amount of the application screening fee charged by the landlord or his or her agent be greater than thirty dollars ($30) per applicant. The thirty dollar ($30) application screening fee may be adjusted annually by the landlord or his or her agent commensurate with an increase in the Consumer Price Index, beginning on January 1, 1998.

(c) Unless the applicant agrees in writing, a landlord or his or her agent may not charge an applicant an application screening fee when he or she knows or should have known that no rental unit is available at that time or will be available within a reasonable period of time.

(d) The landlord or his or her agent shall provide, personally, or by mail, the applicant with a receipt for the fee paid by the applicant, which receipt shall itemize the out-of-pocket expenses and time spent by the landlord or his or her agent to obtain and process the information about the applicant.

(e) If the landlord or his or her agent does not perform a personal reference check or does not obtain a consumer credit report, the landlord or his or her agent shall return any amount of the screening fee that is not used for the purposes authorized by this section to the applicant.

(f) If an application screening fee has been paid by the applicant and if requested by the applicant, the landlord or his or her agent shall provide a copy of the consumer credit report to the applicant who is the subject of that report.

(g) As used in this section, "landlord" means an owner of residential rental property.

(h) As used in this section, "application screening fee" means any nonrefundable payment of money charged by a landlord or his or her agent to an applicant, the purpose of which is to purchase a consumer credit report and to validate, review, or otherwise process an application for the rent or lease of residential rental property.

(i) As used in this section, "applicant" means any entity or individual who makes a request to a landlord or his or her agent to rent a residential housing unit, or an entity or individual who agrees to act as a guarantor or cosignor on a rental agreement.

(j) The application screening fee shall not be considered an "advance fee" as that term is used in Section 10026 of the Business and Professions Code, and shall not be considered "security" as that term is used in Section 1950.5.

(k) This section is not intended to preempt any provisions or regulations that govern the collection of deposits and fees under federal or state housing assistance programs.

1950.7. (a) Any payment or deposit of money the primary function of which is to secure the performance of a rental agreement for other than residential property or any part of the agreement, other than a payment or deposit, including an advance payment of rent, made to secure the execution of a rental agreement, shall be governed by the provisions of this section. With respect to residential property, the provisions of Section 1950.5 shall prevail.

(b) Any such payment or deposit of money shall be held by the landlord for the tenant who is party to the agreement. The claim of a tenant to the payment or deposit shall be prior to the claim of any creditor of the landlord, except a trustee in bankruptcy.

(c) The landlord may claim of the payment or deposit only those amounts as are reasonably necessary to remedy tenant defaults in the payment of rent, to repair damages to the premises caused by the tenant, or to clean the premises upon termination of the tenancy, if the payment or deposit is made for any or all of those specific purposes. Where the claim of the landlord upon the payment or deposit is only for defaults in the payment of rent, then any remaining portion of the payment or deposit shall be returned to the tenant no later than two weeks after the date the landlord receives possession of the premises. Where the claim of the landlord upon the payment or deposit includes amounts reasonably necessary to repair damages to the premises caused by the tenant or to clean the premises, then any remaining portion of the payment or deposit shall be returned to the tenant at a time as may be mutually agreed upon by landlord and tenant, but in no event later than 30 days from the date the landlord receives possession of the premises.

(d) Upon termination of the landlord's interest in the unit in question, whether by sale, assignment, death, appointment of receiver or otherwise, the landlord or the landlord's agent shall, within a reasonable time, do one of the following acts, either of which shall relieve the landlord of further liability with respect to the payment or deposit:

(1) Transfer the portion of the payment or deposit remaining after any lawful deductions made under subdivision (c) to the landlord's successor in interest, and thereafter notify the tenant by personal delivery or certified mail of the transfer, of any claims made against the payment or deposit, and of the transferee's name and address. If the notice to the tenant is made by personal delivery, the tenant shall acknowledge receipt of the notice and sign his or her name on the landlord's copy of the notice.

(2) Return the portion of the payment or deposit remaining after any lawful deductions made under subdivision (c) to the tenant.

(e) Upon receipt of any portion of the payment or deposit under paragraph (1) of subdivision (d), the transferee shall have all of the rights and obligations of a landlord holding the payment or deposit with respect to the payment or deposit.

(f) The bad faith retention by a landlord or transferee of a payment or deposit or any portion thereof, in violation of this section, may subject the landlord or the transferee to damages not to exceed two hundred dollars ($200), in addition to any actual damages.

(g) This section is declarative of existing law and therefore operative as to all tenancies, leases, or rental agreements for other than residential property created or renewed on or after January 1, 1971.

1951. As used in Sections 1951.2 to 1952.6, inclusive:

(a) "Rent" includes charges equivalent to rent.

(b) "Lease" includes a sublease.

1951.2. (a) Except as otherwise provided in Section 1951.4, if a lessee of real property breaches the lease and abandons the property before the end of the term or if his right to possession is terminated by the lessor because of a breach of the lease, the lease terminates. Upon such termination, the lessor may recover from the lessee:

(1) The worth at the time of award of the unpaid rent which had been earned at the time of termination;

(2) The worth at the time of award of the amount by which the unpaid rent which would have been earned after termination until the time of award exceeds the amount of such rental loss that the lessee proves could have been reasonably avoided;

(3) Subject to subdivision (c), the worth at the time of award of the amount by which the unpaid rent for the balance of the term after the time of award exceeds the amount of such rental loss that the lessee proves could be reasonably avoided; and

(4) Any other amount necessary to compensate the lessor for all the detriment proximately caused by the lessee's failure to perform his obligations under the lease or which in the ordinary course of things would be likely to result therefrom.

(b) The "worth at the time of award" of the amounts referred to in paragraphs (1) and (2) of subdivision (a) is computed by allowing interest at such lawful rate as may be specified in the lease or, if no such rate is specified in the lease, at the legal rate. The worth at the time of award of the amount referred to in paragraph (3) of subdivision (a) is computed by discounting such amount at the discount rate of the Federal Reserve Bank of San Francisco at the time of award plus 1 percent.

(c) The lessor may recover damages under paragraph (3) of subdivision (a) only if:

(1) The lease provides that the damages he may recover include the worth at the time of award of the amount by which the unpaid rent for the balance of the term after the time of award, or for any shorter period of time specified in the lease, exceeds the amount of such rental loss for the same period that the lessee proves could be reasonably avoided; or

(2) The lessor relet the property prior to the time of award and proves that in reletting the property he acted reasonably and in a good-faith effort to mitigate the damages, but the recovery of damages under this paragraph is subject to any limitations specified in the lease.

(d) Efforts by the lessor to mitigate the damages caused by the lessee's breach of the lease do not waive the lessor's right to recover damages under this section.

(e) Nothing in this section affects the right of the lessor under a lease of real property to indemnification for liability arising prior to the termination of the lease for personal injuries or property damage where the lease provides for such indemnification.

1951.3. (a) Real property shall be deemed abandoned by the lessee, within the meaning of Section 1951.2, and the lease shall terminate if the lessor gives written notice of his belief of abandonment as provided in this section and the lessee fails to give the lessor written notice, prior to the date of termination specified in the lessor's notice, stating that he does not intend to abandon the real property and stating an address at which the lessee may be served by certified mail in any action for unlawful detainer of the real property.

(b) The lessor may give a notice of belief of abandonment to the lessee pursuant to this section only where the rent on the property has been due and unpaid for at least 14 consecutive days and the lessor reasonably believes that the lessee has abandoned the property. The date of termination of the lease shall be specified in the lessor's notice and shall be not less than 15 days after the notice is served personally or, if mailed, not less than 18 days after the notice is deposited in the mail.

(c) The lessor's notice of belief of abandonment shall be personally delivered to the lessee or sent by first-class mail, postage prepaid, to the lessee at his last known address and, if there is reason to believe that the notice sent to that address will not be received by the lessee, also to such other address, if any, known to the lessor where the lessee may reasonably be expected to receive the notice.

(d) The notice of belief of abandonment shall be in substantially the following form:

Notice of Belief of Abandonment

To: _____

(Name of lessee/tenant)

_____

(Address of lessee/tenant)

This notice is given pursuant to Section 1951.3 of the Civil Code concerning the real property leased by you at _____ (state location of the property by address or other sufficient description). The rent on this property has been due and unpaid for 14 consecutive days

and the lessor/landlord believes that you have abandoned the property. The real property will be deemed abandoned within the meaning of Section 1951.2 of the Civil Code and your lease will terminate on _____ (here insert a date not less than 15 days after this notice is served personally or, if mailed, not less than 18 days after this notice is deposited in the mail) unless before such date the under-signed receives at the address indicated below a written notice from you stating both of the following:

(1) Your intent not to abandon the real property.

(2) An address at which you may be served by certified mail in any action for unlawful detainer of the real property. You are required to pay the rent due and unpaid on this real property as required by the lease, and your failure to do so can lead to a court proceeding against you.

Dated: _____

_____

(Signature of lessor/landlord)

_____

(Type or print name of lessor/landlord)

_____

(Address to which lessee/tenant is to send notice)

(e) The real property shall not be deemed to be abandoned pursuant to this section if the lessee proves any of the following:

(1) At the time the notice of belief of abandonment was given, the rent was not due and unpaid for 14 consecutive days.

(2) At the time the notice of belief of abandonment was given, it was not reasonable for the lessor to believe that the lessee had abandoned the real property. The fact that the lessor knew that the lessee left personal property on the real property does not, of itself, justify a finding that the lessor did not reasonably believe that the lessee had abandoned the real property.

(3) Prior to the date specified in the lessor's notice, the lessee gave written notice to the lessor stating his intent not to abandon the real property and stating an address at which he may be served by certified mail in any action for unlawful detainer of the real property.

(4) During the period commencing 14 days before the time the notice of belief of abandonment was given and ending on the date the lease would have terminated pursuant to the notice, the

lessee paid to the lessor all or a portion of the rent due and unpaid on the real property.

(f) Nothing in this section precludes the lessor or the lessee from otherwise proving that the real property has been abandoned by the lessee within the meaning of Section 1951.2.

(g) Nothing in this section precludes the lessor from serving a notice requiring the lessee to pay rent or quit as provided in Sections 1161 and 1162 of the Code of Civil Procedure at any time permitted by those sections, or affects the time and manner of giving any other notice required or permitted by law. The giving of the notice provided by this section does not satisfy the requirements of Sections 1161 and 1162 of the Code of Civil Procedure.

1951.4. (a) The remedy described in this section is available only if the lease provides for this remedy. In addition to any other type of provision used in a lease to provide for the remedy described in this section, a provision in the lease in substantially the following form satisfies this subdivision:

"The lessor has the remedy described in California Civil Code Section 1951.4 (lessor may continue lease in effect after lessee's breach and abandonment and recover rent as it becomes due, if lessee has right to sublet or assign, subject only to reasonable limitations)."

(b) Even though a lessee of real property has breached the lease and abandoned the property, the lease continues in effect for so long as the lessor does not terminate the lessee's right to possession, and the lessor may enforce all the lessor's rights and remedies under the lease, including the right to recover the rent as it becomes due under the lease, if any of the following conditions is satisfied:

(1) The lease permits the lessee, or does not prohibit or otherwise restrict the right of the lessee, to sublet the property, assign the lessee's interest in the lease, or both.

(2) The lease permits the lessee to sublet the property, assign the lessee's interest in the lease, or both, subject to express standards or conditions, provided the standards and conditions are reasonable at the time the lease is executed and the lessor does not require compliance with any standard or condition that has become unreasonable at the time the lessee seeks to sublet or assign. For purposes of this paragraph, an express standard or condition is presumed to be reasonable; this presumption is a presumption affecting the burden of proof.

(3) The lease permits the lessee to sublet the property, assign the lessee's interest in the lease, or both, with the consent of the lessor, and the lease provides that the consent shall not be unreasonably withheld or the lease includes a standard implied by law that consent shall not be unreasonably withheld.

(c) For the purposes of subdivision (b), the following do not constitute a termination of the lessee's right to possession:

(1) Acts of maintenance or preservation or efforts to relet the property.

(2) The appointment of a receiver upon initiative of the lessor to protect the lessor's interest under the lease.

(3) Withholding consent to a subletting or assignment, or terminating a subletting or assignment, if the withholding or termination does not violate the rights of the lessee specified in subdivision (b).

1951.5. Section 1671, relating to liquidated damages, applies to a lease of real property.

1951.7. (a) As used in this section, "advance payment" means moneys paid to the lessor of real property as prepayment of rent, or as a deposit to secure faithful performance of the terms of the lease, or any other payment which is the substantial equivalent of either of these. A payment that is not in excess of the amount of one month's rent is not an advance payment for the purposes of this section.

(b) The notice provided by subdivision (c) is required to be given only if:

(1) The lessee has made an advance payment;

(2) The lease is terminated pursuant to Section 1951.2; and

(3) The lessee has made a request, in writing, to the lessor that he be given notice under subdivision (c).

(c) Upon the initial reletting of the property, the lessor shall send a written notice to the lessee stating that the property has been relet, the name and address of the new lessee, and the length of the new lease and the amount of the rent. The notice shall be delivered to the lessee personally, or be sent by regular mail to the lessee at the address shown on the request, not later than 30 days after the new lessee takes possession of the property. No notice is required if the amount of the rent due and unpaid at the time of termination exceeds the amount of the advance payment.

1951.8. Nothing in Section 1951.2 or 1951.4 affects the right of the lessor under a lease of real property to equitable relief where such relief is appropriate.

1952. (a) Except as provided in subdivision (c), nothing in Sections 1951 to 1951.8, inclusive, affects the provisions of Chapter 4 (commencing with Section 1159) of Title 3 of Part 3 of the Code of Civil Procedure, relating to actions for unlawful detainer, forcible entry, and forcible detainer.

(b)   Unless the lessor amends the complaint as provided in paragraph (1) of subdivision (a) of Section 1952.3 to state a claim for damages not recoverable in the unlawful detainer proceeding, the bringing of an action under the provisions of Chapter 4 (commencing with Section 1159) of Title 3 of Part 3 of the Code of Civil Procedure does not affect the lessor's right to bring a separate action for relief under Sections 1951.2, 1951.5, and 1951.8, but no damages shall be recovered in the subsequent action for any detriment for which a claim for damages was made and determined on the merits in the previous action.

(c)   After the lessor obtains possession of the property under a judgment pursuant to Section 1174 of the Code of Civil Procedure, he is no longer entitled to the remedy provided under Section 1951.4 unless the lessee obtains relief under Section 1179 of the Code of Civil Procedure.

1952.2. Sections 1951 to 1952, inclusive, do not apply to:

(a)   Any lease executed before July 1, 1971.

(b)   Any lease executed on or after July 1, 1971, if the terms of the lease were fixed by a lease, option, or other agreement executed before July 1, 1971.

1952.3. (a) Except as provided in subdivisions (b) and (c), if the lessor brings an unlawful detainer proceeding and possession of the property is no longer in issue because possession of the property has been delivered to the lessor before trial or, if there is no trial, before judgment is entered, the case becomes an ordinary civil action in which:

(1)   The lessor may obtain any relief to which he is entitled, including, where applicable, relief authorized by Section 1951.2; but, if the lessor seeks to recover damages described in paragraph (3) of subdivision (a) of Section 1951.2 or any other damages not recoverable in the unlawful detainer proceeding, the lessor shall first amend the complaint pursuant to Section 472 or 473 of the Code of Civil Procedure so that possession of the property is no longer in issue and to state a claim for such damages and shall serve a copy of the amended complaint on the defendant in the same manner as a copy of a summons and original complaint is served.

(2)   The defendant may, by appropriate pleadings or amendments to pleadings, seek any affirmative relief, and assert all defenses, to which he is entitled, whether or not the lessor has amended the complaint; but subdivision (a) of Section 426.30 of the Code of Civil Procedure does not apply unless, after delivering possession of the property to the lessor, the defendant (i) files a cross-complaint or (ii) files an answer or an amended answer in response to an amended complaint filed pursuant to paragraph (1).

(b)   The defendant's time to respond to a complaint for unlawful detainer is not affected by the delivery of possession of the property to the lessor; but, if the complaint is amended as provided in paragraph (1) of subdivision (a), the defendant has the same time to respond to the amended complaint as in an ordinary civil action.

(c)   The case shall proceed as an unlawful detainer proceeding if the defendant's default (1) has been entered on the unlawful detainer complaint and (2) has not been opened by an amendment of the complaint or otherwise set aside.

(d)   Nothing in this section affects the pleadings that may be filed, relief that may be sought, or defenses that may be asserted in an unlawful detainer proceeding that has not become an ordinary civil action as provided in subdivision (a).

1952.4. An agreement for the exploration for or the removal of natural resources is not a lease of real property within the meaning of Sections 1951 to 1952.2, inclusive.

1952.6. (a) Sections 1951 to 1952.2, inclusive, shall not apply to any lease or agreement for a lease of real property between any public entity and any nonprofit corporation whose title or interest in the property is subject to reversion to or vesting in a public entity and which issues bonds or other evidences of indebtedness, the interest on which is exempt from federal income taxes for the purpose of acquiring, constructing, or improving the property or a building or other facility thereon, or between any public entity and any other public entity, unless the lease or the agreement shall specifically provide that Sections 1951 to 1952.2, inclusive, or any portions thereof, are applicable to the lease or the agreement.

(b) Except as provided in subdivision (a), a public entity lessee in a contract for a capital lease of real property involving the payment of rents of one million dollars ($1,000,000) or more may elect to waive any of the remedies for a breach of the lease provided in Sections 1951 to 1952.2, inclusive, and contract instead for any other remedy permitted by law. As used in this subdivision, "capital lease" refers to a lease entered into for the purpose of acquiring, constructing, or improving the property or a building or other facility thereon.

(c) As used in this section, "public entity" includes the state, a county, city and county, city, district, public authority, public agency, or any other political subdivision or public corporation.

1952.8. On and after the effective date of this section, no owner of a gasoline service station shall enter into a lease with any person for the leasing of the station for the purpose of operating a gasoline service station, unless (a) the station is equipped with a vapor control system for the control of gasoline vapor emissions during gasoline marketing operations, including storage, transport, and transfer operations, if such vapor control system is required by law or by any rule or regulation of the State Air Resources Board or of the air pollution control district in which the station is located or (b) no vapor control system has been certified by the board prior to the date of the lease.

A lease entered into in violation of this section shall be voidable at the option of the lessee.

1953. (a) Any provision of a lease or rental agreement of a dwelling by which the lessee agrees to modify or waive any of the following rights shall be void as contrary to public policy:

(1) His rights or remedies under Section 1950.5 or 1954.

(2) His right to assert a cause of action against the lessor which may arise in the future.

(3) His right to a notice or hearing required by law.

(4) His procedural rights in litigation in any action involving his rights and obligations as a tenant.

(5) His right to have the landlord exercise a duty of care to prevent personal injury or personal property damage where that duty is imposed by law.

(b) Any provision of a lease or rental agreement of a dwelling by which the lessee agrees to modify or waive a statutory right, where the modification or waiver is not void under subdivision (a) or under Section 1942.1, 1942.5, or 1954, shall be void as contrary to public policy unless the lease or rental agreement is presented to the lessee before he takes actual possession of the premises. This subdivision does not apply to any provisions modifying or waiving a statutory right in agreements renewing leases or rental agreements where the same provision was also contained in the lease or rental agreement which is being renewed.

(c) This section shall apply only to leases and rental agreements executed on or after January 1, 1976.

1954. A landlord may enter the dwelling unit only in the following cases:

(a) In case of emergency.

(b) To make necessary or agreed repairs, decorations, alterations or improvements, supply necessary or agreed services, or exhibit the dwelling unit to prospective or actual purchasers, mortgagees, tenants, workmen or contractors.

(c) When the tenant has abandoned or surrendered the premises.

(d) Pursuant to court order.

Except in cases of emergency or when the tenant has abandoned or surrendered the premises, entry may not be made during other than normal business hours unless the tenant consents at the time of entry.

The landlord shall not abuse the right of access or use it to harass the tenant. Except in cases of emergency, when the tenant has abandoned or surrendered the premises, or if it is impracticable to do so, the landlord shall give the tenant reasonable notice of his intent to enter and enter only during normal business hours. Twenty-four hours shall be presumed to be reasonable notice in absence of evidence to the contrary.

1954.1. In any general assignment for the benefit of creditors, as defined in Section 493.010 of the Code of Civil Procedure, the assignee shall have the right to occupy, for a period of up to 90 days after the date of the assignment, any business premises held under a lease by the assignor upon payment when due of the monthly rental reserved in the lease for the period of such occupancy, notwithstanding any provision in the lease (whether heretofore or hereafter entered into) for the termination thereof upon the making of the assignment or the insolvency of the lessee or other condition relating to the financial condition of the lessee. This section shall be construed as establishing the reasonable rental value of the premises recoverable by a landlord upon a holding-over by the tenant upon the termination of a lease under the circumstances specified herein.

SECTIONS 1954.50-1954.53

1954.50. This chapter shall be known and may be cited as the Costa-Hawkins Rental Housing Act.

1954.51. As used in this chapter, the following terms have the following meanings:

(a) "Comparable units" means rental units that have approximately the same living space, have the same number of bedrooms, are located in the same or similar neighborhoods, and feature the same, similar, or equal amenities and housing services.

(b) "Owner" includes any person, acting as principal or through an agent, having the right to offer residential real property for rent, and includes a predecessor in interest to the owner, except that this term does not include the owner or operator of a mobilehome park, or the owner of a mobilehome or his or her agent.

(c) "Prevailing market rent" means the rental rate that would be authorized pursuant to 42 U.S.C.A. 1437 (f), as calculated by the United States Department of Housing and Urban Development pursuant to Part 888 of Title 24 of the Code of Federal Regulations.

(d) "Public entity" has the same meaning as set forth in Section 811.2 of the Government Code.

(e) "Residential real property" includes any dwelling or unit that is intended for human habitation.

(f) "Tenancy" includes the lawful occupation of property and includes a lease or sublease.

1954.52. (a) Notwithstanding any other provision of law, an owner of residential real property may establish the initial and all subsequent rental rates for a dwelling or a unit about which any of the following is true:

(1) It has a certificate of occupancy issued after February 1, 1995.

(2) It has already been exempt from the residential rent control ordinance of a public entity on or before February 1, 1995, pursuant to a local exemption for newly constructed units.

(3) It is alienable separate from the title to any other dwelling unit or is a subdivided interest in a subdivision as specified in subdivision (b), (d), or (f) of Section 11004.5 of the Business and Professions Code. This paragraph shall not apply to a dwelling or unit where the preceding tenancy has been terminated by the owner by notice pursuant to Section 1946 or has been terminated upon a change in the terms of the tenancy noticed pursuant to Section 827.

Where a dwelling or unit whose initial or subsequent rental rates are controlled by an ordinance or charter provision in effect on January 1, 1995, the following shall apply:

(A) An owner of real property as described in this paragraph may establish the initial and all subsequent rental rates for all existing and new tenancies in effect on or after January 1, 1999, if the tenancy in effect on or after January 1, 1999, was created between January 1, 1996, and December 31, 1998.

(B) Commencing on January 1, 1999, an owner of real property as described in this paragraph may establish the initial and all subsequent rental rates for all new tenancies if the previous tenancy was in effect on December 31, 1995.

(C) The initial rental rate for a dwelling or unit as described in this paragraph whose initial rental rate is controlled by an ordinance or charter provision in effect on January 1, 1995 shall not, until January 1, 1999, exceed the amount calculated pursuant to subdivision (c) of Section 1954.53. An owner of residential real property as described in this paragraph may until January 1, 1999, establish the initial rental rate for a dwelling or unit only where the tenant has voluntarily vacated, abandoned, or been evicted pursuant to paragraph (2) of Section 1161 of the Code of Civil Procedure.

(b) Subdivision (a) shall not apply where the owner has otherwise agreed by contract with a public entity in consideration for a direct financial contribution or any other forms of assistance specified in Chapter 4.3 (commencing with Section 65915) of Division 1 of Title 7 of the Government Code.

(c) Nothing in this section shall be construed to affect any authority of a public entity that may otherwise exist to regulate or monitor the basis for eviction.

(d) This section shall not apply to any dwelling or unit which contains serious health, safety, fire, or building code violations, excluding those caused by disasters, for which a citation has been issued by the appropriate governmental agency and which has remained unabated for six months or longer preceding the vacancy.

1954.53. (a) Notwithstanding any other provision of law, an owner of residential real property may establish the initial rental rate for a dwelling or unit, except where any of the following applies:

(1) The previous tenancy has been terminated by the owner by notice pursuant to Section 1946 or has been terminated upon a change in the terms of the tenancy noticed pursuant to Section 827, except a change permitted by law in the amount of rent or fees.

(2) The owner has otherwise agreed by contract with a public entity in consideration for a direct financial contribution or any other forms of assistance specified in Chapter 4.3 (commencing with Section 65915) of Division 1 of Title 7 of the Government Code.

(3) The initial rental rate for a dwelling or unit whose initial rental rate is controlled by an ordinance or charter provision in effect on January 1, 1995, shall not until January 1, 1999, exceed the amount calculated pursuant to subdivision (c).

(b) Subdivision (a) applies to, and includes, renewal of the initial hiring by the same tenant, lessee, authorized subtenant, or authorized sublessee for the entire period of his or her occupancy at the rental rate established for the initial hiring.

(c) The rental rate of a dwelling or unit whose initial rental rate is controlled by ordinance or charter provision in effect on January 1, 1995, shall, until January 1, 1999, be established in accordance with this subdivision. Where the previous tenant has voluntarily vacated, abandoned, or been evicted pursuant to paragraph (2) of Section 1161 of Code of Civil Procedure, an owner of residential real property may, no more than twice, establish the initial rental rate for a dwelling or unit in an amount that is no greater than 15 percent more than the rental rate in effect for the immediately preceding tenancy or in an amount that is 70 percent of the prevailing market rent for comparable units, whichever amount is greater.

The initial rental rate established pursuant to this subdivision shall not be deemed to substitute for or replace increases in rental rates otherwise authorized pursuant to law.

(d) Nothing in this section or any other provision of law shall be construed to preclude express establishment in a lease or rental agreement of the rental rates to be applicable in the event the rental unit subject thereto is sublet, and nothing in this section shall be construed to impair the obligations of contracts entered into prior to January 1, 1996.

Where the original occupant or occupants who took possession of the dwelling or unit pursuant to the rental agreement with the owner no longer permanently reside there, an owner may increase the rent by any amount allowed by this section to a lawful sublessee or assignee who did not reside at the dwelling or unit prior to January 1, 1996.

This subdivision shall not apply to partial changes in occupancy of a dwelling or unit where one or more of the occupants of the premises, pursuant to the agreement with the owner provided for above, remains an occupant in lawful possession of the dwelling or unit, or where a lawful sublessee or assignee who resided at the dwelling or unit prior to January 1, 1996, remains in possession of the dwelling or unit. Nothing contained in this section shall be construed to enlarge or diminish an owner's right to withhold consent to a sublease or assignment.

Acceptance of rent by the owner shall not operate as a waiver or otherwise prevent enforcement of a covenant prohibiting sublease or assignment or as a waiver of an owner's rights to establish the initial rental rate unless the owner has received written notice from the tenant that is party to the agreement and thereafter accepted rent.

(e) Nothing in this section shall be construed to affect any authority of a public entity that may otherwise exist to regulate or monitor the grounds for eviction. (f) This section shall not apply to any dwelling or unit which contains serious health, safety, fire, or building code violations, excluding those caused by disasters, for which a citation has been issued by the appropriate governmental agency and which has remained unabated for six months or longer preceding the vacancy.

SECTIONS 1980-1991

1980. As used in this chapter:

(a) "Landlord" means any operator, keeper, lessor, or sublessor of any furnished or unfurnished premises for hire, or his agent or successor in interest.

(b) "Owner" means any person other than the landlord who has any right, title, or interest in personal property.

(c) "Premises" includes any common areas associated therewith.

(d) "Reasonable belief" means the actual knowledge or belief a prudent person would have without making an investigation (including any investigation of public records) except that, where the landlord has specific information indicating that such an investigation would more probably than not reveal pertinent information and the cost of such an investigation would be reasonable in relation to the probable value of the personal property involved, "reasonable belief" includes the actual knowledge or belief a prudent person would have if such an investigation were made.

(e) "Tenant" includes any paying guest, lessee, or sublessee of any premises for hire.

1981. (a) This chapter provides an optional procedure for the disposition of personal property that remains on the premises after a tenancy has terminated and the premises have been vacated by the tenant.

(b) This chapter does not apply whenever Section 1862.5, 2080.8, 2080.9, or 2081 to 2081.6, inclusive, applies. This chapter does not apply to property that exists for the purpose of providing utility services and is owned by a public utility, whether or not that property is actually in operation to provide those utility services.

(c) This chapter does not apply to any manufactured home as defined in Section 18007 of the Health and Safety Code, any mobilehome as defined in Section 18008 of the Health and Safety Code, or to any commercial coach as defined in Section 18001.8 of the Health and Safety Code, including attachments thereto or contents thereof, whether or not the manufactured home, mobilehome, or commercial coach is subject to registration under the Health and Safety Code.

(d) This chapter does not apply to the disposition of an animal to which Chapter 7 (commencing with Section 17001) of Part 1 of Division 9 of the Food and Agricultural Code applies, and those animals shall be disposed of in accordance with those provisions.

(e) If the requirements of this chapter are not satisfied, nothing in this chapter affects the rights and liabilities of the landlord, former tenant, or any other person.

1982. (a) Personal property which the landlord reasonably believes to have been lost shall be disposed of pursuant to Article 1 (commencing with Section 2080) of Chapter 4 of Title 6. The landlord is not liable to the owner of the property if he complies with this subdivision.

(b) If the appropriate police or sheriff's department refuses to accept property pursuant to subdivision (a), the landlord may dispose of the property pursuant to this chapter.

1983. (a) Where personal property remains on the premises after a tenancy has terminated and the premises have been vacated by the tenant, the landlord shall give written notice to such tenant and to any other person the landlord reasonably believes to be the owner of the property.

(b) The notice shall describe the property in a manner reasonably adequate to permit the owner of the property to identify it. The notice may describe all or a portion of the property, but the limitation of liability provided by Section 1989 does not protect the landlord from any liability arising from the disposition of property not described in the notice except that a trunk, valise, box, or other container which is locked, fastened, or tied in a manner which deters immediate access to its contents may be described as such without describing its contents. The notice shall advise the person to be notified that reasonable costs of storage may be charged before the property is returned, where the property may be claimed, and the date before which the claim must be made. The date specified in the notice shall be a date not less than 15 days after the notice is personally delivered or, if mailed, not less than 18 days after the notice is deposited in the mail.

(c) The notice shall be personally delivered to the person to be notified or sent by first-class mail, postage prepaid, to the person to be notified at his last known address and, if there is reason to believe that the notice sent to that address will not be received by that person, also to such other address, if any, known to the landlord where such person may reasonably be expected to receive the notice. If the notice is sent by mail to the former tenant, one copy shall be sent to the premises vacated by such tenant.

1984. (a) A notice given to the former tenant which is in substantially the following form satisfies the requirements of Section 1983:

Notice of Right to Reclaim Abandoned Property

To:_____

(Name of former tenant)

_____

(Address of former tenant)

When you vacated the premises at

_____

(Address of premises, including room or apartment number, if any)

the following personal property remained:

_____

(Insert description of the personal property)

You may claim this property at

_____.

(Address where property may be claimed)

Unless you pay the reasonable cost of storage for all the above-described property, and take possession of the property which you claim, not later than _____ (insert date not less than 15 days after notice is personally delivered or, if mailed, not less than 18 days after notice is deposited in the mail) this property may be disposed of pursuant to Civil Code Section 1988.

(Insert here the statement required by subdivision (b) of this section)

Dated: _____

_____

(Signature of landlord)

_____

(Type or print name of landlord)

_____

(Telephone number)

_____

(Address)

(b) The notice set forth in subdivision (a) shall also contain one of the following statements:

(1) "If you fail to reclaim the property, it will be sold at a public sale after notice of the sale has been given by publication. You have the right to bid on the property at this sale. After the property is sold and the cost of storage, advertising, and sale is deducted, the remaining money will be paid over to the county. You may claim the remaining money at any time within one year after the county receives the money."

(2) "Because this property is believed to be worth less than $300, it may be kept, sold, or destroyed without further notice if you fail to reclaim it within the time indicated above."

1985. A notice which is in substantially the following form given to a person (other than the former tenant) the landlord reasonably believes to be the owner of personal property satisfies the requirements of Section 1983:

Notice of Right to Reclaim Abandoned Property

To:_____

(Name)

_____

(Address)

When _____

(name of former tenant)

vacated the premises at_____

_____ ,

(address of premises, including room or apartment number, if any)

the following personal property remained:

_____

(insert description of the personal property)

If you own any of this property, you may claim it at

_____.

(address where property may be claimed)

Unless you pay the reasonable cost of storage and take possession of the property to which you are

entitled not later than _____
(insert date not less than 15 days after notice is personally delivered or, if mailed, not less than 18 days after notice is deposited in the mail) this property may be disposed of pursuant to Civil Code Section 1988.

Dated: _____

_____
(Signature of landlord)

_____
(Type or print name of landlord)

_____
(Telephone number)

_____
(Address)

1986. The personal property described in the notice shall either be left on the vacated premises or be stored by the landlord in a place of safekeeping until the landlord either releases the property pursuant to Section 1987 or disposes of the property pursuant to Section 1988. The landlord shall exercise reasonable care in storing the property, but he is not liable to the tenant or any other owner for any loss not caused by his deliberate or negligent act.

1987. (a) The personal property described in the notice shall be released by the landlord to the former tenant or, at the landlord's option, to any person reasonably believed by the landlord to be its owner if such tenant or other person pays the reasonable cost of storage and takes possession of the property not later than the date specified in the notice for taking possession.

(b) Where personal property is not released pursuant to subdivision (a) and the notice stated that the personal property would be sold at a public sale, the landlord shall release the personal property to the former tenant if he claims it prior to the time it is sold and pays the reasonable cost of storage, advertising, and sale incurred prior to the time the property is withdrawn from sale.

1988. (a) If the personal property described in the notice is not released pursuant to Section 1987, it shall be sold at public sale by competitive bidding. However, if the landlord reasonably believes that the total resale value of the property not released is less than three hundred dollars ($300), the landlord may retain such property for his or her own use or dispose of it in any

manner. Nothing in this section shall be construed to preclude the landlord or tenant from bidding on the property at the public sale.

(b) Notice of the time and place of the public sale shall be given by publication pursuant to Section 6066 of the Government Code in a newspaper of general circulation published in the county where the sale is to be held. The last publication shall be not less than five days before the sale is to be held. The notice of the sale shall not be published before the last of the dates specified for taking possession of the property in any notice given pursuant to Section 1983. The notice of the sale shall describe the property to be sold in a manner reasonably adequate to permit the owner of the property to identify it. The notice may describe all or a portion of the property, but the limitation of liability provided by Section 1989 does not protect the landlord from any liability arising from the disposition of property not described in the notice, except that a trunk, valise, box, or other container which is locked, fastened, or tied in a manner which deters immediate access to its contents may be described as such without describing its contents.

(c) After deduction of the costs of storage, advertising, and sale, any balance of the proceeds of the sale which is not claimed by the former tenant or an owner other than such tenant shall be paid into the treasury of the county in which the sale took place not later than 30 days after the date of sale. The former tenant or other owner may claim the balance within one year from the date of payment to the county by making application to the county treasurer or other official designated by the county. If the county pays the balance or any part thereof to a claimant, neither the county nor any officer or employee thereof is liable to any other claimant as to the amount paid.

1989. (a) Notwithstanding subdivision (c) of Section 1981, where the landlord releases to the former tenant property which remains on the premises after a tenancy is terminated, the landlord is not liable with respect to that property to any person.

(b) Where the landlord releases property pursuant to Section 1987 to a person (other than the former tenant) reasonably believed by the landlord to be the owner of the property, the landlord is not liable with respect to that property to:

(1) Any person to whom notice was given pursuant to Section 1983; or

(2) Any person to whom notice was not given pursuant to Section 1983 unless such person proves that, prior to releasing the property, the landlord believed or reasonably should have believed that such person had an interest in the property and also that the landlord knew or should have known upon reasonable investigation the address of such person.

(c) Where property is disposed of pursuant to Section 1988, the landlord is not liable with respect to that property to:

(1) Any person to whom notice was given pursuant to Section 1983; or

(2) Any person to whom notice was not given pursuant to Section 1983 unless such person proves that, prior to disposing of the property pursuant to Section 1988, the landlord believed or reasonably should have believed that such person had an interest in the property and also that the landlord knew or should have known upon reasonable investigation the address of such person.

1990. (a) Costs of storage which may be required to be paid under this chapter shall be assessed in the following manner:

(1) Where a former tenant claims property pursuant to Section 1987, he may be required to pay the reasonable costs of storage for all the personal property remaining on the premises at the termination of the tenancy which are unpaid at the time the claim is made.

(2) Where an owner other than the former tenant claims property pursuant to Section 1987, he may be required to pay the reasonable costs of storage for only the property in which he claims an interest.

(b) In determining the costs to be assessed under subdivision (a), the landlord shall not charge more than one person for the same costs.

(c) If the landlord stores the personal property on the premises, the cost of storage shall be the fair rental value of the space reasonably required for such storage for the term of the storage.

1991. Where a notice of belief of abandonment is given to a lessee pursuant to Section 1951.3, the notice to the former tenant given pursuant to Section 1983 may, but need not, be given at the same time as the notice of belief of abandonment even though the tenancy is not terminated until the end of the period specified in the notice of belief of abandonment. If the notices are so given, the notices may, but need not, be combined in one notice that contains all the information required by the sections under which the notices are given.

Appendix B
Eviction Flowcharts
and Legal Holidays

On the next two pages are flowcharts showing each step in the eviction process. The first one is for an eviction for nonpayment of rent. The second one is for evictions based on the tenant's breach of some clause of the lease other than payment of rent, or for a month-to-month tenancy which a landlord wishes to terminate for any reason.

On the final page of this appendix is a list of the legal holidays in California. It is important to keep these dates in mind when calculating the three day notices.

EVICTION FLOWCHART—NONPAYMENT OF RENT

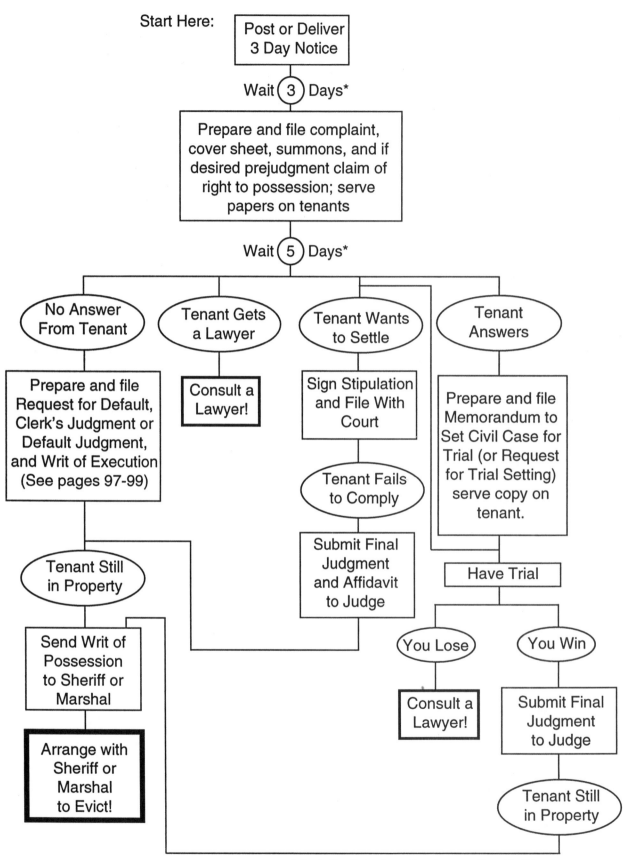

Start Here:

Post or Deliver 3 Day Notice

Wait (3) Days*

Prepare and file complaint, cover sheet, summons, and if desired prejudgment claim of right to possession; serve papers on tenants

Wait (5) Days*

No Answer From Tenant

Tenant Gets a Lawyer

Tenant Wants to Settle

Tenant Answers

Prepare and file Request for Default, Clerk's Judgment or Default Judgment, and Writ of Execution (See pages 97-99)

Consult a Lawyer!

Sign Stipulation and File With Court

Prepare and file Memorandum to Set Civil Case for Trial (or Request for Trial Setting) serve copy on tenant.

Tenant Fails to Comply

Tenant Still in Property

Submit Final Judgment and Affidavit to Judge

Have Trial

Send Writ of Possession to Sheriff or Marshal

You Lose

You Win

Arrange with Sheriff or Marshal to Evict!

Consult a Lawyer!

Submit Final Judgment to Judge

Tenant Still in Property

* Excluding Saturdays, Sundays and legal holidays

EVICTION FLOWCHART—BREACH OF LEASE OR 30 DAY TERMINATION

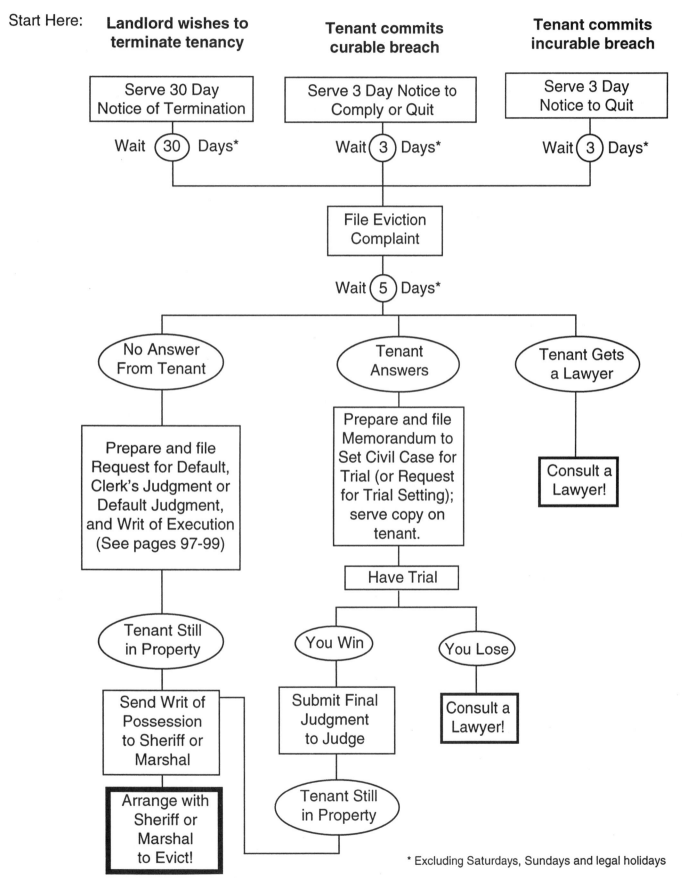

Start Here:

Landlord wishes to terminate tenancy

Serve 30 Day Notice of Termination

Wait (30) Days*

Tenant commits curable breach

Serve 3 Day Notice to Comply or Quit

Wait (3) Days*

Tenant commits incurable breach

Serve 3 Day Notice to Quit

Wait (3) Days*

File Eviction Complaint

Wait (5) Days*

No Answer From Tenant

Tenant Answers

Tenant Gets a Lawyer

Prepare and file Request for Default, Clerk's Judgment or Default Judgment, and Writ of Execution (See pages 97-99)

Prepare and file Memorandum to Set Civil Case for Trial (or Request for Trial Setting); serve copy on tenant.

Consult a Lawyer!

Tenant Still in Property

Have Trial

Send Writ of Possession to Sheriff or Marshal

You Win

You Lose

Arrange with Sheriff or Marshal to Evict!

Submit Final Judgment to Judge

Consult a Lawyer!

Tenant Still in Property

* Excluding Saturdays, Sundays and legal holidays

LEGAL HOLIDAYS IN CALIFORNIA

New Year's Day	Jan. 1
Martin Luther King, Jr.'s Birthday	Jan. 15
Abraham Lincoln's Birthday	Feb. 12
George Washington's Birthday	Third Mon. in Feb.
Good Friday	(varies)
Memorial Day	Last Mon. in May
Independence Day	July 4
Labor Day	First Mon. In Sept.
Admission's Day	Sept. 9
Columbus Day	Second Mon. in Oct.
Veterans' Day	Nov. 11
General Election Day	(varies)
Thanksgiving Day	Fourth Thurs. in Nov.
Christmas Day	Dec. 25

Note: When a legal holiday falls on a Sunday, the next day is considered a legal holiday. Not all California counties observe the same holidays, such as Good Friday, Admission's Day, and Columbus Day. Check your county to be sure you're not filing too soon after serving a notice.

Appendix C
Sample Filled-In Forms

This appendix includes sample filled-in copies of some of the more confusing forms in the book. These should help you in filling out your own forms. If you do not understand them, or are not sure if you have filled yours in right, you should ask the court clerk or consult an attorney.

The following sample forms are included in this appendix:

ATTORNEY OR PARTY WITHOUT ATTORNEY (*Name and Address*):

Louis Landlord
123 Home Circle
Anytown, CA 90000

TELEPHONE NO.: (555)555-5555

ATTORNEY FOR (*Name*):

FOR COURT USE ONLY

INSERT NAME OF COURT, JUDICIAL DISTRICT, AND BRANCH COURT, IF ANY:

Municipal Court of California
100 Justice Way
Eviction City, CA 90000

CASE NAME:

Louis Landlord v. Thomas Tenant

CIVIL CASE COVER SHEET
(Case Cover Sheets)

CASE NUMBER:

1. | 32 | Case category (*Insert code from list below for the ONE case type that best describes the case*):

01 Abuse of Process
02 Administrative Agency Review
03 Antitrust/Unfair Business Practices
04 Asbestos
05 Asset Forfeiture
06 Breach of Contract/Warranty
07 Business Tort
08 Civil Rights (*Discrimination, False Arrest*)
09 Collections (*Money Owed, Open Book Accounts*)
10 Construction Defect
11 Contractual Arbitration
12 Declaratory Relief
13 Defamation (*Slander, Libel*)
14 Eminent Domain/Inverse Condemnation
15 Employment (*Labor Commissioner Appeals, EDD Actions, Wrongful Termination*)
16 Fraud
17 Injunctive Relief

18 Insurance Coverage/Subrogation
19 Intellectual Property
20 Enforcement of Judgment (*Sister State, Foreign, Out-of-Country Abstracts*)
21 Partnership and Corporate Governance
22 PI/PD/WD—Auto (*Personal Injury/Property Damage/ Wrongful Death*)
23 PI/PD/WD—Nonauto
24 Product Liability
25 Professional Negligence (*Medical or Legal Malpractice, etc.*)
26 Real Property (*Quiet Title*)
27 RICO
28 Securities Litigation
29 Tax Judgment
30 Toxic Tort/Environmental
31 Unlawful Detainer—Commercial
32 Unlawful Detainer—Residential
33 Wrongful Eviction
34 Other: _____

2. Type of remedies sought (*check all that apply*): a. [X] Monetary b. [X] Nonmonetary c. [ ] Punitive
3. Number of causes of action: 1
4. Is this a class action suit? [ ] Yes [X] No

Date: June 1, 1998

Louis Landlord
....
(TYPE OR PRINT NAME)

▶ *Louis Landlord* (signature)
(SIGNATURE OF PARTY OR ATTORNEY FOR PARTY)

NOTE TO PLAINTIFF

- This cover sheet shall accompany each civil action or proceeding, except those filed in small claims court or filed under the Probate Code, Family Law Code, or Welfare and Institutions Code.
- File this cover sheet in addition to any cover sheet required by local court rule.
- Do not serve this cover sheet with the complaint.
- This cover sheet shall be used for statistical purposes only and shall have no effect on the assignment of the case.

Form Adopted by Rule 982.2
Judicial Council of California
982.2(b)(1) [New July 1, 1996]

CIVIL CASE COVER SHEET
(Case Cover Sheets)

155

ATTORNEY OR PARTY WITHOUT ATTORNEY *(Name and Address):*	TELEPHONE NO.:	FOR COURT USE ONLY
Louis Landlord 123 Home Circle Anytown, CA 90000	(555) 555-5555	

ATTORNEY FOR *(Name):*

NAME OF COURT:	Municipal Court of California
STREET ADDRESS:	100 Justice Way
MAILING ADDRESS:	Eviction City, CA 90000
CITY AND ZIP CODE:	Eviction City Branch
BRANCH NAME:	

PLAINTIFF: Louis Landlord

DEFENDANT: Thomas Tenant

[X] DOES 1 TO __10__

COMPLAINT—Unlawful Detainer*

CASE NUMBER:

1. a. Plaintiff is   (1) [X] an individual over the age of 18 years   (4) [ ] a partnership
      (2) [ ] a public agency   (5) [ ] a corporation
      (3) [ ] other *(specify):*

   b. [ ] Plaintiff has complied with the fictitious business name laws and is doing business under the fictitious **name of**
      (specify):

2. Defendants named above are in possession of the premises located at *(street address, apt. No., city, and county):*
   100 Renter Circle, Apt. 9
   Eviction City, CA 90000

3. Plaintiff's interest in the premises is   [x] as owner   [ ] other *(specify):*

4. The true names and capacities of defendants sued as Does are unknown to plaintiff.

5. a. On or about *(date):* 2/1/98   defendants *(names):* Thomas Tenant

     (1) agreed to rent the premises for a   [X] month-to-month tenancy   [ ] other tenancy *(specify):*
     (2) agreed to pay rent of $ 900.00   payable [X] monthly [ ] other *(specify frequency):*
       The rent is due on the   [X] first of the month   [ ] other day *(specify):*
   b. This [X] written [ ] oral agreement was made with
     (1) [X] plaintiff   (3) [ ] plaintiff's predecessor in interest
     (2) [ ] plaintiff's agent   (4) [ ] other *(specify):*
   c. [X] The defendants not named in item 5a are
       (1) [ ] subtenants   (2) [ ] assignees   (3) [X] other *(specify):* Status unknown
   d. [ ] The agreement was later changed as follows *(specify):*

   e. [X] A copy of the written agreement is attached and labeled Exhibit 1.

6. [X] a. Defendants *(names):* Thomas Tenant
       were served the following notice on the same date and in the same manner:
       (1) [X] 3-day notice to pay rent or quit   (4) [ ] 3-day notice to quit
       (2) [ ] 3-day notice to perform covenants or quit   (5) [ ] 30-day notice to quit
       (3) [X] other *(specify):* Prejudgment Claim of Right to Possession
   b. (1) On *(date):* May 14, 1998   the period stated in the notice expired at the end of the day.
     (2) Defendants failed to comply with the requirements of the notice by that date.
   c. All facts stated in the notice are true.
   d. [ ] The notice included an election of forfeiture.
   e. [X] A copy of the notice is attached and labeled Exhibit 2.
   f. [ ] One or more defendants was served (1) with a different notice, or (2) on a different date, or (3) in a different manner,
       as stated in attachment 6f. *(Check item 7c and attach a statement providing the information required by items 6a-e*
       and 7 for each defendant.)

*NOTE: Do not use this form for evictions after sale (Code Civ. Proc., § 1161a).
(Continued on reverse)

Form Approved by the Judicial Council of California 982.1(90) [Rev. July 1, 1996]	**COMPLAINT—Unlawful Detainer**	Civil Code, § 1940 et seq.; Code of Civil Procedure, § 425.12

PLAINTIFF (Name): Louis Landlord	CASE NUMBER:
DEFENDANT (Name): Thomas Tenant	

7. a. [X] The notice in item 6a was served on the defendants named in item 6a as follows:

    (1) [X] by personally handing a copy to defendant on *(date)*: 5/10/98

    (2) [ ] by leaving a copy with *(name or description)*:   , a person
        of suitable age and discretion, on *(date)*:   at defendant's [ ] residence [ ] business
        AND mailing a copy to defendant at defendant's place of residence on *(date)*:
        because defendant cannot be found at defendant's residence or usual place of business.

    (3) [ ] by posting a copy on the premises on *(date)*:   ([ ] and giving a copy to a person found
        residing at the premises) AND mailing a copy to defendant at the premises on *(date)*:
        (a) [ ] because defendant's residence and usual place of business cannot be ascertained OR
        (b) [ ] because no person of suitable age or discretion can be found there.

    (4) [ ] *(not for 3-day notice; see Civil Code section 1946 before using)* by sending a copy by certified or registered
        mail addressed to defendant on *(date)*:

    (5) [ ] *(not for residential tenancies; see Civil Code section 1953 before using)* in the manner specified in a written
        commercial lease between the parties.

  b. [X] *(Name)*: Thomas Tenant was served on behalf of all defendants who signed a joint written rental agreement.

  c. [ ] Information about service of notice on the defendants named in item 6f is stated in attachment 7c.

8. [ ] Plaintiff demands possession from each defendant because of expiration of a fixed-term lease.

9. [X] At the time the 3-day notice to pay rent or quit was served, the amount of **rent due** was $ 900

10. [X] The fair rental value of the premises is $ 30   per day.

11. [ ] Defendants' continued possession is malicious, and plaintiff is entitled to statutory damages under Code of Civil Procedure
    section 1174(b). *(State specific facts supporting a claim up to $600 in attachment 11.)*

12. [ ] A written agreement between the parties provides for attorney fees.

13. [ ] Defendants' tenancy is subject to the local rent control or eviction control ordinance of *(city or county, title of ordinance, and
    date of passage)*:

    Plaintiff has met all applicable requirements of the ordinances.

14. [ ] Other allegations are stated in attachment 14.

15. Plaintiff remits to the jurisdictional limit, if any, of the court.

16. PLAINTIFF REQUESTS

  a. possession of the premises.

  b. costs incurred in this proceeding.

  c. [X] past due rent of $ 900

  d. [ ] reasonable attorney fees.

  e. [X] forfeiture of the agreement.

  f. [X] damages at the rate stated in item 10 from
    (date): June 1, 1998   for each day
    defendants remain in possession through entry of judgment.

  g. [ ] statutory damages up to $600 for the conduct alleged in item 11.

  h. [ ] other *(specify)*:

17. [X] Number of pages attached *(specify)*: 5

UNLAWFUL DETAINER ASSISTANT (Business and Professions Code sections 6400-6415)

18. *(must be answered in all cases)* An unlawful detainer assistant [x] did **not** [ ] did for compensation give advice or
assistance with this form. *(If plaintiff has received any help or advice for pay from an unlawful detainer assistant, state)*:

  a. Assistant's name: b. Telephone No.:

  c. Street address, city, and ZIP:

  d. County of registration: e. Registration No.:   f. Expires on *(date)*:

Louis Landlord   ▶ *Louis Landlord*
....
    (TYPE OR PRINT NAME)   (SIGNATURE OF PLAINTIFF OR ATTORNEY)

VERIFICATION

(Use a different verification form if the verification is by an attorney or for a corporation or partnership.)

I am the plaintiff in this proceeding and have read this complaint. I declare under penalty of perjury under the laws of the State of
California that the foregoing is true and correct.

Date: June 1, 1998

Louis Landlord   ▶ *Louis Landlord*
....
    (TYPE OR PRINT NAME)   (SIGNATURE OF PLAINTIFF)

SUMMONS
(CITACION JUDICIAL)

UNLAWFUL DETAINER—EVICTION
(PROCESO DE DESAHUCIO—EVICCION)

NOTICE TO DEFENDANT: *(Aviso a acusado)*

Thomas Tenant

YOU ARE BEING SUED BY PLAINTIFF:
(A Ud. le está demandando)

Louis Landlord

FOR COURT USE ONLY
(SOLO PARA USO DE LA CORTE)

You have **5 DAYS** after this summons is served on you to file a typewritten response at this court. (To calculate the five days, count Saturday and Sunday, but do not count other court holidays.)	*Después de que le entreguen esta citación judicial usted tiene un plazo de 5 DIAS para presentar una respuesta escrita a máquina en esta corte. (Para calcular los cinco días, cuente el sábado y el domingo, pero no cuente ningún otro día feriado observado por la corte.)*
A letter or phone call will not protect you. Your typewritten response must be in proper legal form if you want the court to hear your case.	*Una carta o una llamada telefónica no le ofrecerá protección; su respuesta escrita a máquina tiene que cumplir con las formalidades legales apropiadas si usted quiere que la corte escuche su caso.*
If you do not file your response on time, you may lose the case, you may be evicted, and your wages, money, and property may be taken without further warning from the court.	*Si usted no presenta su respuesta a tiempo, puede perder el caso, le pueden obligar a desalojar su casa, y le pueden quitar su salario, su dinero y otras cosas de su propiedad sin aviso adicional por parte de la corte.*
There are other legal requirements. You may want to call an attorney right away. If you do not know an attorney, you may call an attorney referral service or a legal aid office *(listed in the phone book).*	*Existen otros requisitos legales. Puede que usted quiera llamar a un abogado inmediatamente. Si no conoce a un abogado, puede llamar a un servicio de referencia de abogados o a una oficina de ayuda legal (vea el directorio telefónico).*

The name and address of the court is: *(El nombre y dirección de la corte es)*

Municipal Court of California
100 Justice Way - Eviction City, CA 90000

CASE NUMBER: *(Número del caso)*

The name, address, and telephone number of plaintiff's attorney, or plaintiff without an attorney, is:
(El nombre, la dirección y el número de teléfono del abogado del demandante, o del demandante que no tiene abogado, es)

Louis Landlord
123 Home Circle
Anytown, CA 90000   Telephone: (555) 555-5555

(Must be answered in all cases) An **unlawful detainer assistant (B&P 6400-6415)** [X] did **not** [ ] did for compensation give advice or assistance with this form. *(If plaintiff has received **any** help or advice for pay from an unlawful detainer assistant, state):*

a. Assistant's name: b. Telephone No.:
c. Street address, city, and ZIP:

d. County of registration: e. Registration No.:   f. Expires on *(date)*:

Date: Clerk, by _____ , Deputy
(Fecha)   *(Actuario)*   *(Delegado)*

[SEAL]

NOTICE TO THE PERSON SERVED: You are served
1. [X] as an individual defendant.
2. [ ] as the person sued under the fictitious name of *(specify)*:

3. [ ] on behalf of *(specify)*:

   under: [ ] CCP 416.10 (corporation)   [ ] CCP 416.60 (minor)
          [ ] CCP 416.20 (defunct corporation)   [ ] CCP 416.70 (conservatee)
          [ ] CCP 416.40 (association or partnership) [ ] CCP 416.90 (individual)
          [ ] other:
4. [ ] by personal delivery on *(date)*:
       (See reverse for Proof of Service)

Form Adopted by Rule 982
Judicial Council of California
982(a)(11) [Rev. January 1, 1997]

SUMMONS—UNLAWFUL DETAINER

Code of Civil Procedure, §§ 412.20, 1167

158

PLAINTIFF: Louis Landlord	CASE NUMBER:
DEFENDANT: Thomas Tenant	

PROOF OF SERVICE

1. At the time of service I was at least 18 years of age and not a party to this action, and **I served copies** of the *(specify documents)*:

   3 day notice and prejudgment claim of right to possession

2. a. Party served *(specify name of party as shown on the documents served)*:

   Thomas Tenant

   b. Person served: [X] party in item 2a [ ] other *(specify name and title or relationship to the party named in item 2a)*:

   c. Address: 100 Renter Circle, Apt. 9
   Eviction City, CA 90000

3. I served the party named in item 2
   a. [X] **by personally delivering** the copies (1) on *(date)*: 5/10/98 (2) at *(time)*: 6:00 p.m.
   b. [ ] **by leaving** the copies with or in the presence of *(name and title or relationship to person indicated in item 2b)*:

      (1) [ ] **(business)** a person at least 18 years of age apparently in charge at the office or usual place of business of the person served. I informed him or her of the general nature of the papers.
      (2) [ ] **(home)** a competent member of the household (at least 18 years of age) at the dwelling house or usual place of abode of the person served. I informed him or her of the general nature of the papers.
      (3) on *(date)*: (4) at *(time)*:
      (5) [ ] A **declaration of diligence** is attached. *(Substituted service on natural person, minor, conservatee, or candidate.)*
   c. [ ] **by mailing** the copies to the person served, addressed as shown in item 2c, by first-class mail, postage prepaid,
      (1) on *(date)*: (2) from *(city)*:
      (3) [ ] with two copies of the *Notice and Acknowledgment of Receipt* and a postage-paid return envelope addressed to me.
      (4) [ ] to an address outside California with return receipt requested. ← *(Attach completed form.)* ↰
   d. [ ] **by** causing copies to be mailed. A declaration of mailing is attached.
   e. [ ] **other** *(specify other manner of service and authorizing code section)*:

4. The "Notice to the Person Served" (on the summons) was completed as follows:
   a. [X] as an individual defendant.
   b. [ ] as the person sued under the fictitious name of *(specify)*:
   c. [ ] on behalf of *(specify)*:
      under: [ ] CCP 416.10 (corporation) [ ] CCP 416.60 (minor) [ ] other:
             [ ] CCP 416.20 (defunct corporation) [ ] CCP 416.70 (conservatee)
             [ ] CCP 416.40 (association or partnership) [ ] CCP 416.90 (individual)

5. **Person serving** *(name, address, and telephone number)*:

   Sally Server
   28 Main St.
   Eviction City, CA 90000
   (555)555-5555

   a. **Fee** for service: $ 100
   b. [ ] Not a registered California process server
   c. [ ] Exempt from registration under B&P § 22350(b)
   d. [X] Registered California process server
      (1) [ ] Employee or independent contractor
      (2) Registration No.: 1234
      (3) County: Lemon
      (4) Expiration *(date)*: 6-2-99

6. [X] **I declare** under penalty of perjury under the laws of the State of California that the foregoing is true and correct.

7. [ ] **I am a California sheriff, marshal, or constable and** I certify that the foregoing is true and correct.

Date: ▶ _____
(SIGNATURE)

982(a)(11) [Rev. January 1, 1997]   **PROOF OF SERVICE**
(Summons—Unlawful Detainer)   Page two
Code of Civil Procedure, § 417.10(f)

159

NOTICE: EVERYONE WHO LIVES IN THIS RENTAL UNIT MAY BE EVICTED BY COURT ORDER. READ THIS FORM IF YOU LIVE HERE AND IF YOUR NAME IS NOT ON THE ATTACHED SUMMONS AND COMPLAINT.

1. If you live here and you do not complete and submit this form within 5 days of the date of service shown on this form, you will be evicted without further hearing by the court along with the persons named in the Summons and Complaint.
2. If you file this form, your claim will be determined in the eviction action against the persons named in the Complaint.
3. If you do not file this form, you will be evicted without further hearing.

CLAIMANT OR CLAIMANT'S ATTORNEY *(Name and Address):*	TELEPHONE NO.:	FOR COURT USE ONLY

Louis Landlord   (555)555-5555
123 Home Circle
Anytown, CA 90000

ATTORNEY FOR *(Name)*:

NAME OF COURT: Municipal Court of California
STREET ADDRESS: 100 Justice Way
MAILING ADDRESS: Eviction City, CA 90000
CITY AND ZIP CODE:
BRANCH NAME: Eviction City Branch
PLAINTIFF: Louis Landlord

DEFENDANT: Thomas Tenant

PREJUDGMENT CLAIM OF RIGHT TO POSSESSION— Unlawful Detainer (Pilot Project—C.C.P. §§ 1167.2, 1167.25) Riverside Consolidated/Coordinated Courts and the Downey, El Cajon, and North Santa Barbara County Municipal Courts	CASE NUMBER: 1212

Complete this form only if ALL of these statements are true:	*(To be completed by the process server)*
1. You are NOT named in the accompanying Summons and Complaint. **2. You occupied the premises on or before the date the unlawful detainer (eviction) Complaint was filed.** **3. You still occupy the premises.**	**DATE OF SERVICE:** *(Date that this form is served or delivered, and posted, and mailed by the officer or process server)*

I DECLARE THE FOLLOWING UNDER PENALTY OF PERJURY:

1. My name is *(specify)*:

2. I reside at *(street address, unit No., city and ZIP code)*:

3. The address of "the premises" subject to this claim is *(address)*:

4. On *(insert date)*: [   ], the landlord or the landlord's authorized agent filed a complaint to recover possession of the premises. *(This date is the court filing date on the accompanying Summons and Complaint.)*

5. I occupied the premises on the date the complaint was filed *(the date in item 4)*. I have continued to occupy the premises ever since.

6. I was at least 18 years of age on the date the complaint was filed *(the date in item 4)*.

7. I claim a right to possession of the premises because I occupied the premises on the date the complaint was filed *(the date in item 4)*.

8. I was not named in the Summons and Complaint.

9. I understand that if I make this claim of right to possession, I will be added as a defendant to the unlawful detainer (eviction) action.

(Continued on reverse)

PREJUDGMENT CLAIM OF RIGHT TO POSSESSION—
Unlawful Detainer (Pilot Project—C.C.P. §§ 1167.2, 1167.25)
Code of Civil Procedure, §§ 415.46
715.010, 715.020, 1167.25, 1174.25

PLAINTIFF (Name): Louis Landlord	CASE NUMBER:
DEFENDANT (Name): Thomas Tenant	

NOTICE: If you fail to file this claim, you will be evicted without further hearing.

10. I understand that I must file this form with the court within five (5) days from the date of service shown on this form. I may file this form by taking it to the Court or mailing it by registered or certified mail, return-receipt requested, and post-marked within five (5) days from the date of service shown on this form. I understand that if I fail to file this form, as described above, I will not be entitled to make a claim of right to possession.

11. I understand that in addition to filing this form, at the same time, I may also file a completed Reply Form.

12. **Rental agreement.** I have (check all that apply to you):
   a. ☐ an oral rental agreement with the landlord.
   b. ☐ a written rental agreement with the landlord.
   c. ☐ an oral rental agreement with a person other than the landlord.
   d. ☐ a written rental agreement with a person other than the landlord.
   e. ☐ other (explain):

I declare under penalty of perjury under the laws of the State of California that the foregoing is true and correct.

WARNING: Perjury is a felony punishable by imprisonment in the state prison.

Date:

....   ▶ _____
(TYPE OR PRINT NAME)   (SIGNATURE OF CLAIMANT)

NOTICE: This case will be scheduled for a pretrial hearing. If you file this claim-of-right-to-possession, you will be notified by the Court of the hearing date. At that hearing the Court will determine whether there is a substantial conflict as to a material fact or facts relevant to the unlawful detainer. At the end of the hearing the Court may order you to make a rent deposit with the Court, as requested by the landlord. At the pretrial hearing you will be allowed to verbally answer the complaint and present your testimony, the written declarations of others, and documentary or physical evidence as to material facts relevant to the unlawful detainer. If the court determines that a pretrial rent deposit is required, it will be no greater than an amount equal to 15 days' rent or $500, whichever is less.

Should the court order you to make a pretrial rent deposit and you have timely returned the "reply form," you will have two court days from the date of the hearing to make the deposit. If you fail to timely return the "reply form" and the Court orders a pretrial rent deposit, you must make the deposit that same day to preserve your right to a trial. Failure to make a court-ordered pretrial rent deposit will result in judgment being entered against you for possession of your residence. If the case proceeds to trial, you may be found liable for rent, costs, and, in some cases, treble damages.

— NOTICE TO OCCUPANTS —

YOU MUST ACT AT ONCE if all the following are true:
   1. You are NOT named in the accompanying Summons and Complaint.
   2. You occupied the premises on or before the date the unlawful detainer (eviction) complaint was filed. (The date is the court filing date on the accompanying Summons and Complaint.)
   3. You still occupy the premises.

(Where to file this form)   You can complete and SUBMIT THIS CLAIM FORM WITHIN 5 DAYS from the date of service (on the reverse of this form) at the court where the unlawful detainer (eviction) complaint was filed.

(What will happen if you do not file this form)   If you do not complete and submit this form (and pay a filing fee or file the form for proceeding in forma pauperis if you cannot pay the fee), YOU WILL BE EVICTED.

After this form is properly filed, you will be added as a defendant in the unlawful detainer (eviction) action and your right to occupy the premises will be decided by the court. If you do not file this claim, you will be evicted without a hearing.

CP10. 6 (New August 1, 1995]   **PREJUDGMENT CLAIM OF RIGHT TO POSSESSION—**   Page two

Unlawful Detainer (Pilot Project—C.C.P. §§ 1167.2, 1167.25)

ATTORNEY OR PARTY WITHOUT ATTORNEY *(Name and Address)*:	TELEPHONE NO.:	FOR COURT USE ONLY
Louis Landlord 123 Home Circle Anytown, CA 90000	(555) 555-5555	
ATTORNEY FOR *(Name)*:		

Insert name of court and name of judicial district and branch court, if any:

Municipal Court of California-Eviction City

PLAINTIFF:

    Louis Landlord

DEFENDANT:

    Thomas Tenant

REQUEST FOR **(Application)**	[X] **ENTRY OF DEFAULT** [X] **CLERK'S JUDGMENT** [ ] **COURT JUDGMENT**	CASE NUMBER: 1212

1. TO THE CLERK: On the complaint or cross-complaint filed
   a. On *(date)*:
   b. By *(name)*:
   c. [X] Enter default of defendant *(names)*:

       Thomas Tenant

   d. [ ] I request a court judgment under CCP 585(b), (c), 989, etc. *(Testimony required. Apply to the clerk for a hearing date, unless the court will enter a judgment on an affidavit under CCP 585(d).)*
   e. [X] Enter clerk's judgment
       (1) [X] For restitution of the premises only and issue a writ of execution on the judgment. CCP 1174(c) does not apply. (CCP 1169)   [X] Include in the judgment all tenants, subtenants, named claimants, and other occupants of the premises. The Prejudgment Claim of Right to Possession was served in compliance with CCP 415.46.
       (2) [ ] Under CCP 585(a). *(Complete the declaration under CCP 585.5 on the reverse (item 4).)*
       (3) [ ] For default previously entered on *(date)*:

2. **Judgment to be entered**

	Amount	Credits Acknowledged	Balance
a. Demand of complaint . . . . $		$	$
b. Statement of damages (CCP 425.11)			
(superior court only)†			
(1) Special · · · · · · · · · · · · · · · · · $Possession	$	$	
(2) General · · · · · · · · · · · · · · · · · $Only	$	$	
c. Interest . . . . $		$	$
d. Costs *(see reverse)* . . . . $		$	$
e. Attorney fees . . . . $		$	$
f. **TOTALS** . . . . $		$	$

    g. **Daily damages** were demanded in complaint at the rate of: $ per day beginning *(date)*:

3. [X] *(check if filed in an unlawful detainer case)* **UNLAWFUL DETAINER ASSISTANT** information is on the reverse *(complete item 3).*

Date: June 1, 1998

Louis Landlord . . . .   ▶   *Louis Landlord*
(TYPE OR PRINT NAME)   (SIGNATURE OF PLAINTIFF OR ATTORNEY FOR PLAINTIFF)
† *Personal injury or wrongful death actions only.*

FOR COURT USE ONLY	(1) [ ] Default entered as requested on *(date)*:
	(2) [ ] Default NOT entered as requested
	    (state reason):
	
	    Clerk, by: _____

(Continued on reverse)

Form Adopted by the Judicial
Council of California
982(a)(6) [Rev. July 1, 1996*]

REQUEST FOR ENTRY OF DEFAULT
(Application to Enter Default)

Code of Civil Procedure, §§ 585-587, 1169

*See note on reverse.

162

3. **UNLAWFUL DETAINER ASSISTANT** *(Business and Professions Code sections 6400-6415)* An **unlawful detainer assistant**
   [X] **did not** [ ] did for compensation give advice or assistance with this form. *(If declarant has received **any** help or advice for pay from an unlawful detainer assistant, state)*:
   a. Assistant's name:
                                                               b. Telephone No.:
   c. Street address, city, and ZIP:

   d. County of registration: e. Registration No.:   f. Expires on *(date)*

4. [X] **DECLARATION UNDER CCP 585.5** *(Required for clerk's judgment under CCP 585(a))* This action
   a. [ ] is [X] is not on a contract or installment sale for goods or services subject to CC 1801, etc. (Unruh Act).
   b. [ ] is [X] is not on a conditional sales contract subject to CC 2981, etc. (Rees-Levering Motor Vehicle Sales and Finance
   c. [ ] is [X] Act).
             is not on an obligation for goods, services, loans, or extensions of credit subject to CCP 395(b).

5. **DECLARATION OF MAILING (CCP 587)** A copy of this Request for Entry of Default was
   a. [ ] **not mailed** to the following defendants whose addresses are **unknown** to plaintiff or plaintiff's attorney *(names)*:

   b. [X] **mailed** first-class, postage prepaid, in a sealed envelope addressed to each defendant's attorney of record or, if none, to each defendant's last known address as follows:
       (1) Mailed on *(date)*:   (2) To *(specify names and addresses shown on the envelopes)*:

                                                                          Thomas Tenant
                                                                          100 Renter Circle, Ap.9
                                                                          Eviction City, CA 90000

I declare under penalty of perjury under the laws of the State of California that the foregoing items 3, 4, and 5 are true and correct.
Date:

Louis Landlord ....
           (TYPE OR PRINT NAME)   ▶   *Louis Landlord*
                                                                    (SIGNATURE OF DECLARANT)

6. **MEMORANDUM OF COSTS** *(Required if judgment requested)* **Costs and Disbursements** are as follows (CCP 1033.5):
   a. Clerk's filing fees · · · · · · · · · · · · · · · · · · · $
   b. Process server's fees · · · · · · · · · · · · · · · · $
   c. Other *(specify)*: · $
   d · $
   e. **TOTAL** · $
   f. [X] Costs and disbursements are waived.

   I am the attorney, agent, or party who claims these costs. To the best of my knowledge and belief this memorandum of costs is correct and these costs were necessarily incurred in this case.

   I declare under penalty of perjury under the laws of the State of California that the foregoing is true and correct.
   Date: June 1, 1998
   Louis Landlord ....
              (TYPE OR PRINT NAME)   ▶   *Louis Landlord*
                                                                    (SIGNATURE OF DECLARANT)

7. [X] **DECLARATION OF NONMILITARY STATUS** *(Required for a judgment)* No defendant named in item 1c of the application is in the military service so as to be entitled to the benefits of the Soldiers' and Sailors' Civil Relief Act of 1940 (50 U.S.C.appen. § 501 et seq.).

   I declare under penalty of perjury under the laws of the State of California that the foregoing is true and correct.
   Date: June 1, 1998
   Louis Landlord ....
              (TYPE OR PRINT NAME)   ▶   *Louis Landlord*
                                                                    (SIGNATURE OF DECLARANT)

NOTE: Continued use of form 982(a)(6) (Rev. Sept. 30, 1991) is authorized until June 30, 1997, *except* in unlawful detainer proceedings.

982(a)(6) [Rev. July 1, 1996*]   **REQUEST FOR ENTRY OF DEFAULT**   Page two
                                        (Application to Enter Default)

ATTORNEY OR PARTY WITHOUT ATTORNEY (Name and Address):	TELEPHONE NO.:	FOR RECORDER'S USE ONLY

☐ Recording requested by and return to:

Louis Landord
123 Home Circle
Anytown, CA 90000

TELEPHONE NO.: (555) 555-5555

☐ ATTORNEY FOR ☐ JUDGMENT CREDITOR ☐ ASSIGNEE OF RECORD

NAME OF COURT: Municipal Court of California
STREET ADDRESS: 100 Justice Way
MAILING ADDRESS: 100 Justice Way
CITY AND ZIP CODE: Eviction City, CA 90000
BRANCH NAME: Eviction City Branch

PLAINTIFF: Louis Landlord

DEFENDANT: Thomas Tenant

WRIT OF

☐ EXECUTION (Money Judgment)
☒ POSSESSION OF ☐ Personal Property
☒ Real Property
☐ SALE

CASE NUMBER: 1212

FOR COURT USE ONLY

1. **To the Sheriff or any Marshal or Constable of the County of:**

You are directed to enforce the judgment described below with daily interest and your costs as provided by law.

2. **To any registered process server:** You are authorized to serve this writ only in accord with CCP 699.080 or CCP 715.040.

3. (Name): Louis Landlord
is the ☒ judgment creditor ☐ assignee of record
whose address is shown on this form above the court's name.

4. **Judgment debtor** (name and last known address):

Thomas Tenant
100 Renter Circle, Apt. 9
Eviction City, CA 90000

☐ additional judgment debtors on reverse

5. **Judgment entered** on (date): June 29, 1998
6. ☐ **Judgment renewed** on (dates):

7. **Notice of sale** under this writ
   a. ☒ has not been requested.
   b. ☐ has been requested (see reverse).
8. ☐ Joint debtor information on reverse.

[SEAL]

9. ☒ See reverse for information on real or personal property to be delivered under a writ of possession or sold under a writ of sale.
10. ☐ This writ is issued on a sister-state judgment.
11. Total judgment . . . . $ Possession only
12. Costs after judgment (per filed order or memo CCP 685.090) . . . . $
13. Subtotal (add 11 and 12) . . . . $ _____
14. Credits . . . . $ _____
15. Subtotal (subtract 14 from 13) . . . . . . $ _____
16. Interest after judgment (per filed affidavit CCP 685.050) . . . . $
17. Fee for issuance of writ . . . . $
18. **Total** (add 15, 16, and 17) . . . . $ _____
19. Levying officer:
    (a) Add daily interest from date of writ (at the legal rate on 15) of. . . . . . $
    (b) Pay directly to court costs included in 11 and 17 (GC 6103.5, 68511.3; CCP 699.520(i)) . . . . $
20. ☐ The amounts called for in items 11-19 are different for each debtor. These amounts are stated for each debtor on Attachment 20.

Issued on (date): _____

Clerk, by _____, Deputy

— **NOTICE TO PERSON SERVED: SEE REVERSE FOR IMPORTANT INFORMATION.** —

(Continued on reverse)

Form Approved by the
Judicial Council of California
EJ-130 [Rev. January 1, 1997*]

WRIT OF EXECUTION

Code of Civil Procedure, §§ 699.520, 712.010, 715.010

* See note on reverse.

SHORT TITLE:	CASE NUMBER:
Landlord v. Tenant	1212

— Items continued from the first page —

4. ☐ **Additional judgment debtor** (*name and last known address*):

7. ☐ **Notice of sale** has been requested by (*name and address*):

8. ☐ **Joint debtor** was declared bound by the judgment (CCP 989-994)
   a. on (*date*):
   b. name and address of joint debtor:

   a. on (*date*):
   b. name and address of joint debtor:

   c. ☐ additional costs against certain joint debtors (*itemize*):

9. ☒ *(Writ of Possession or Writ of Sale)* **Judgment** was entered for the following:
   a. ☒ Possession of real property: The complaint was filed on (*date*): May 10, 1998   *(Check (1) or (2)):*
       (1) ☒ The Prejudgment Claim of Right to Possession was served in compliance with CCP 415.46.
              The judgment includes all tenants, subtenants, named claimants, and other occupants of the premises.
       (2) ☐ The Prejudgment Claim of Right to Possession was NOT served in compliance with CCP 415.46.
              (a) $ was the daily rental value on the date the complaint was filed.
              (b) The court will hear objections to enforcement of the judgment under CCP 1174.3 on the following
                  dates (*specify*):
   b. ☐ Possession of personal property
       ☐ If delivery cannot be had, then for the value (*itemize in 9e*) specified in the judgment or supplemental order.
   c. ☐ Sale of personal property
   d. ☐ Sale of real property
   e. Description of property:
       100 Renter Circle, Apt. 9
       Eviction City, CA 90000

— NOTICE TO PERSON SERVED —

WRIT OF EXECUTION OR SALE. Your rights and duties are indicated on the accompanying Notice of Levy.
WRIT OF POSSESSION OF PERSONAL PROPERTY. If the levying officer is not able to take custody of the property, the levying officer will make a demand upon you for the property. If custody is not obtained following demand, the judgment may be enforced as a money judgment for the value of the property specified in the judgment or in a supplemental order.
WRIT OF POSSESSION OF REAL PROPERTY. If the premises are not vacated within five days after the date of service on the occupant or, if service is by posting, within five days after service on you, the levying officer will remove the occupants from the real property and place the judgment creditor in possession of the property. Except for a mobile home, personal property remaining on the premises will be sold or otherwise disposed of in accordance with CCP 1174 unless you or the owner of the property pays the judgment creditor the reasonable cost of storage and takes possession of the personal property not later than 15 days after the time the judgment creditor takes possession of the premises.
► *A Claim of Right to Possession form accompanies this writ (unless the Summons was served in compliance with CCP 415.46).*

---

* NOTE: Continued use of form EJ-130 (Rev. July 1, 1996) is authorized through December 31, 1997.

EJ-130 [Rev. January 1, 1997*]   **WRIT OF EXECUTION**   Page two

ATTORNEY OR PARTY WITHOUT ATTORNEY *(Name and Address)*:	TELEPHONE NO.:	FOR COURT USE ONLY
Louis Landlord 123 Home Circle Anytown, CA 90000 ATTORNEY FOR *(Name)*:	(555) 555-5555	

Insert name of court and name of judicial district and branch court, if any:

Municipal Court of California- Eviction City

PLAINTIFF:

Louis Landlord

DEFENDANT:

Thomas Tenant

REQUEST FOR [X] **ENTRY OF DEFAULT** [ ] **CLERK'S JUDGMENT** **(Application)** [X] **COURT JUDGMENT**	CASE NUMBER: 1212

1. TO THE CLERK: On the complaint or cross-complaint filed
   a. On *(date)*: June 29, 1998
   b. By *(name)*: Louis Landlord
   c. [X] Enter default of defendant *(names)*:

   Thomas Tenant

   d. [X] I request a court judgment under CCP 585(b), (c), 989, etc. *(Testimony required. Apply to the clerk for a hearing date, unless the court will enter a judgment on an affidavit under CCP 585(d).)*
   e. [ ] Enter clerk's judgment
      (1) [ ] For restitution of the premises only and issue a writ of execution on the judgment. CCP 1174(c) does not apply. (CCP 1169) [ ] Include in the judgment all tenants, subtenants, named claimants, and other occupants of the premises. The Prejudgment Claim of Right to Possession was served in compliance with CCP 415.46.
      (2) [ ] Under CCP 585(a). *(Complete the declaration under CCP 585.5 on the reverse (item 4).)*
      (3) [ ] For default previously entered on *(date)*:

2. **Judgment to be entered**

	Amount	Credits Acknowledged	Balance
a. Demand of complaint	$ 900	$ 0	$ 900
b. Statement of damages (CCP 425.11) *(superior court only)*†			
(1) Special	$	$	$
(2) General	$	$	$
c. Interest	$	$	$
d. Costs *(see reverse)*	$ 112	$ 0	$ 112
e. Attorney fees	$	$	$
f. **TOTALS**	$ 1012	$ 0	$ 1012

   g. **Daily damages** were demanded in complaint at the rate of: $ 30   per day beginning *(date)* June 1, 1998

3. [X] *(check if filed in an unlawful detainer case)* **UNLAWFUL DETAINER ASSISTANT** information is on the reverse *(complete item 3).*

Date: June 1, 1998

Louis Landlord
    (TYPE OR PRINT NAME)

► *Louis Landlord*
   (SIGNATURE OF PLAINTIFF OR ATTORNEY FOR PLAINTIFF)

† *Personal injury or wrongful death actions only.*

FOR COURT USE ONLY	(1) [ ] Default entered as requested on *(date)*:
	(2) [ ] Default NOT entered as requested
	   (state reason):
	
	                   Clerk, by: _____

(Continued on reverse)

Form Adopted by the Judicial
Council of California
982(a)(6) [Rev. July 1, 1996*]

REQUEST FOR ENTRY OF DEFAULT
(Application to Enter Default)

Code of Civil Procedure, §§ 585-587, 1169

*See note on reverse.

SHORT TITLE:	CASE NUMBER:
Landlord v. Tenant	1212

3. **UNLAWFUL DETAINER ASSISTANT** (*Business and Professions Code sections 6400-6415*) An **unlawful detainer assistant**
[X] did **not** [ ] did for compensation give advice or assistance with this form. (*If declarant has received any help or advice for pay from an unlawful detainer assistant, state*):

   a. Assistant's name: b. Telephone No.:

   c. Street address, city, and ZIP:

   d. County of registration: e. Registration No.:   f. Expires on (*date*)

4. [X]   **DECLARATION UNDER CCP 585.5** (*Required for clerk's judgment under CCP 585(a)*) This action
   a. [ ] is [X] is not on a contract or installment sale for goods or services subject to CC 1801, etc. (Unruh Act).
   b. [ ] is [X] is not on a conditional sales contract subject to CC 2981, etc. (Rees-Levering Motor Vehicle Sales and Finance
   c. [ ] is [X] is Act).
                is not on an obligation for goods, services, loans, or extensions of credit subject to CCP 395(b).

5. **DECLARATION OF MAILING (CCP 587)** A copy of this Request for Entry of Default was
   a. [ ] **not mailed** to the following defendants whose addresses are **unknown** to plaintiff or plaintiff's attorney (*names*):

   b. [X] **mailed** first-class, postage prepaid, in a sealed envelope addressed to each defendant's attorney of record or, if none, to each defendant's last known address as follows:
     (1) Mailed on (*date*):   (2) To (*specify names and addresses shown on the envelopes*):
                                                      Thomas Tenant
                                                          100 Renter Circle, Apt. 9
                                                          Eviction City, CA 90000

    I declare under penalty of perjury under the laws of the State of California that the foregoing items 3, 4, and 5 are true and correct.

Date: June 1, 1998

..Louis..Landlord..   ▶   *Louis Landlord*
      (TYPE OR PRINT NAME)   (SIGNATURE OF DECLARANT)

---

6. **MEMORANDUM OF COSTS** (*Required if judgment requested*) **Costs and Disbursements** are as follows (CCP 1033.5):
   a. Clerk's filing fees · $ 12
   b. Process server's fees · · · · · · · · · · · · · · · · · $ 100
   c. Other (*specify*): · $
   d · $
   e. **TOTAL** · $ 112
   f. [ ] Costs and disbursements are waived.

    I am the attorney, agent, or party who claims these costs. To the best of my knowledge and belief this memorandum of costs is correct and these costs were necessarily incurred in this case.

    I declare under penalty of perjury under the laws of the State of California that the foregoing is true and correct.

Date: June 1, 1998

Louis Landlord
....   ▶   *Louis Landlord*
      (TYPE OR PRINT NAME)   (SIGNATURE OF DECLARANT)

---

7. [X] **DECLARATION OF NONMILITARY STATUS** (*Required for a judgment*) No defendant named in item 1c of the application is in the military service so as to be entitled to the benefits of the Soldiers' and Sailors' Civil Relief Act of 1940 (50 U.S.C.appen. § 501 et seq.).

    I declare under penalty of perjury under the laws of the State of California that the foregoing is true and correct.

Date:

Louis Landlord
....   ▶   *Louis Landlord*
      (TYPE OR PRINT NAME)   (SIGNATURE OF DECLARANT)

*NOTE: Continued use of form 982(a)(6) (Rev. Sept. 30, 1991) is authorized until June 30, 1997, *except* in unlawful detainer proceedings.

982(a)(6) [Rev. July 1, 1996*]   **REQUEST FOR ENTRY OF DEFAULT**   Page two
                               (Application to Enter Default)
                                                                  167

ATTORNEY OR PARTY WITHOUT ATTORNEY *(Name and Address):*		TELEPHONE NO.:	FOR RECORDER'S USE ONLY

☐ Recording requested by and return to:

```
Louis Landlord                    (555)555-5555
123 Home Circle
Anytown, CA 90000
```

☐ ATTORNEY FOR   ☑ JUDGMENT CREDITOR   ☐ ASSIGNEE OF RECORD

NAME OF COURT: Municipal Court of California
STREET ADDRESS: 100 Justice Way
MAILING ADDRESS: 100 Justice Way
CITY AND ZIP CODE: Eviction City, CA 90000
BRANCH NAME: Eviction City Branch

PLAINTIFF:
   Louis Landlord
DEFENDANT:
   Thomas Tenant

WRIT OF
☑ **EXECUTION (Money Judgment)**
☑ **POSSESSION OF** ☐ **Personal Property**
                 ☑ **Real Property**
☐ **SALE**

CASE NUMBER: 1212

FOR COURT USE ONLY

1. **To the Sheriff or any Marshal or Constable of the County of:**

   You are directed to enforce the judgment described below with daily interest and your costs as provided by law.

2. **To any registered process server:** You are authorized to serve this writ only in accord with CCP 699.080 or CCP 715.040.

3. *(Name):* Louis Landlord
   is the ☑ judgment creditor ☐ assignee of record
   whose address is shown on this form above the court's name.

4. **Judgment debtor** *(name and last known address):*

   ```
   Thomas Tenant
   100 Renter Circle, Apt. 9
   Eviction City, CA 90000
   ```

   ☐ additional judgment debtors on reverse

5. **Judgment entered** on *(date):* June 29, 1998
6. ☐ **Judgment renewed** on *(dates):*

7. **Notice of sale** under this writ
   a. ☑ has not been requested.
   b. ☐ has been requested *(see reverse).*
8. ☐ Joint debtor information on reverse.

[SEAL]

9. ☑ See reverse for information on real or personal property to be delivered under a writ of possession or sold under a writ of sale.
10. ☐ This writ is issued on a sister-state judgment.
11. Total judgment $1882
12. Costs after judgment (per filed order or memo CCP 685.090) . . . . $
13. Subtotal *(add 11 and 12)* $1882
14. Credits . . . . $ 0
15. Subtotal *(subtract 14 from 13)* $1882
16. Interest after judgment (per filed affidavit CCP 685.050) . . . . $
17. Fee for issuance of writ . . . . $
18. **Total** *(add 15, 16, and 17)* . . . . . . $ 1882
19. Levying officer:
    (a) Add daily interest from date of writ (at the legal rate on 15) of . . . . . . $
    (b) Pay directly to court costs included in 11 and 17 (GC 6103.5, 68511.3; CCP 699.520(i)) . . . . $
20. ☐ The amounts called for in items 11-19 are different for each debtor. These amounts are stated for each debtor on Attachment 20.

Issued on *(date):*	Clerk, by _____, Deputy

— NOTICE TO PERSON SERVED: SEE REVERSE FOR IMPORTANT INFORMATION. —

(Continued on reverse)

Form Approved by the
Judicial Council of California
EJ-130 [Rev. January 1, 1997*]

WRIT OF EXECUTION

Code of Civil Procedure, §§ 699.520, 712.010, 715.010
* See note on reverse.

168

— Items continued from the first page —

4. ☐ **Additional judgment debtor** *(name and last known address)*:

```
┌                          ┐   ┌                          ┐



└                          ┘   └                          ┘
```

7. ☐ **Notice of sale** has been requested by *(name and address)*:

```
┌                          ┐   ┌                          ┐



└                          ┘   └                          ┘
```

8. ☐ **Joint debtor** was declared bound by the judgment (CCP 989-994)
    a. on *(date)*:   a. on *(date)*:
    b. name and address of joint debtor: b. name and address of joint debtor:

```
┌                          ┐   ┌                          ┐



└                          ┘   └                          ┘
```

    c. ☐ additional costs against certain joint debtors *(itemize)*:

9. ☒ *(Writ of Possession or Writ of Sale)* **Judgment** was entered for the following:
    a. ☒ Possession of real property: The complaint was filed on *(date)*: June 1, 1998   **(Check (1) or (2))**:
        (1) ☒ The Prejudgment Claim of Right to Possession was served in compliance with CCP 415.46.
                The judgment includes all tenants, subtenants, named claimants, and other occupants of the premises.
        (2) ☐ The Prejudgment Claim of Right to Possession was NOT served in compliance with CCP 415.46.
            (a) $ was the daily rental value on the date the complaint was filed.
            (b) The court will hear objections to enforcement of the judgment under CCP 1174.3 on the following
                dates *(specify)*:
    b. ☐ Possession of personal property
        ☐ If delivery cannot be had, then for the value *(itemize in 9e)* specified in the judgment or supplemental order.
    c. ☐ Sale of personal property
    d. ☐ Sale of real property
    e. Description of property: 100 Renter Circle
                            Eviction City, CA 90000

— NOTICE TO PERSON SERVED —

WRIT OF EXECUTION OR SALE. Your rights and duties are indicated on the accompanying Notice of Levy.
WRIT OF POSSESSION OF PERSONAL PROPERTY. If the levying officer is not able to take custody of the property, the levying officer will make a demand upon you for the property. If custody is not obtained following demand, the judgment may be enforced as a money judgment for the value of the property specified in the judgment or in a supplemental order.
WRIT OF POSSESSION OF REAL PROPERTY. If the premises are not vacated within five days after the date of service on the occupant or, if service is by posting, within five days after service on you, the levying officer will remove the occupants from the real property and place the judgment creditor in possession of the property. Except for a mobile home, personal property remaining on the premises will be sold or otherwise disposed of in accordance with CCP 1174 unless you or the owner of the property pays the judgment creditor the reasonable cost of storage and takes possession of the personal property not later than 15 days after the time the judgment creditor takes possession of the premises.
► *A Claim of Right to Possession form accompanies this writ (unless the Summons was served in compliance with CCP 415.46).*

---

* NOTE: Continued use of form EJ-130 (Rev. July 1, 1996) is authorized through December 31, 1997.

EJ-130 [Rev. January 1, 1997*]   **WRIT OF EXECUTION**   Page two

169

Sample form G

ATTORNEY FOR *(Name):*

Insert name of court and name of judicial district and branch court, if any:
Municipal Court of California - Eviction City

PLAINTIFF:

  Louis Landlord

DEFENDANT:

  Thomas Tenant

REQUEST FOR (Application)	[X] ENTRY OF DEFAULT [ ] COURT JUDGMENT [X] CLERK'S JUDGMENT	CASE NUMBER: 1212

1. TO THE CLERK: On the complaint or cross-complaint filed
   a. On *(date):*
   b. By *(name):* Louis Landlord
   c. [X] Enter default of defendant *(names):*
      Thomas Tenant

   d. [ ] I request a court judgment under CCP 585(b), (c), 989, etc. *(Testimony required. Apply to the clerk for a hearing date, unless the court will enter a judgment on an affidavit under CCP 585(d).)*

   e. [X] Enter clerk's judgment
      (1) [ ] For restitution of the premises only and issue a writ of execution on the judgment. CCP 1174(c) does not apply. (CCP 1169) [ ] Include in the judgment all tenants, subtenants, named claimants, and other occupants of the premises. The Prejudgment Claim of Right to Possession was served in compliance with CCP 415.46.
      (2) [X] Under CCP 585(a). *(Complete the declaration under CCP 585.5 on the reverse (item 4).)*
      (3) [ ] For default previously entered on *(date):*

2. **Judgment to be entered**

	Amount	Credits Acknowledged	Balance
a. Demand of complaint	$ 900	$ 0	$900
b. Statement of damages (CCP 425.11) *(superior court only)*†			
(1) Special · · · · · · · · · · · · · · · ·	$	$	$
(2) General · · · · · · · · · · · · · · · ·	$	$	$
c. Interest · · · · · · · · · · · · · · · ·	$	$	$
d. Costs *(see reverse)*	$ 112	$ 0	$112
e. Attorney fees	$	$	$
f. **TOTALS**	$ 1012	$ 0	$1012

   g. **Daily damages** were demanded in complaint at the rate of: $ 30   per day beginning *(date):* June 1, 1998

3. [X] *(check if filed in an unlawful detainer case)* **UNLAWFUL DETAINER ASSISTANT** information is on the reverse *(complete item 3).*

Date: June 1, 1998

Louis Landlord . . . .   ▶ *Louis Landlord*
(TYPE OR PRINT NAME)   (SIGNATURE OF PLAINTIFF OR ATTORNEY FOR PLAINTIFF)
† *Personal injury or wrongful death actions only.*

FOR COURT USE ONLY	(1) [ ] Default entered as requested on *(date):* (2) [ ] Default NOT entered as requested *(state reason):*
	Clerk, by: _____

(Continued on reverse)

Form Adopted by the Judicial
Council of California
982(a)(6) [Rev. July 1, 1996*]

REQUEST FOR ENTRY OF DEFAULT
(Application to Enter Default)

Code of Civil Procedure, §§ 585-587, 1169

*See note on reverse.

170

3. **UNLAWFUL DETAINER ASSISTANT** *(Business and Professions Code sections 6400-6415)* An **unlawful detainer assistant**
   ☐ did **not**   ☒ did   for compensation give advice or assistance with this form. *(If declarant has received **any** help or advice for pay from an unlawful detainer assistant, state):*

   a. Assistant's name: b. Telephone No.:

   c. Street address, city, and ZIP:

   d. County of registration: e. Registration No.:   f. Expires on *(date)*

4. ☒   **DECLARATION UNDER CCP 585.5** *(Required for clerk's judgment under CCP 585(a))* This action
   a. ☐ is ☒ is not on a contract or installment sale for goods or services subject to CC 1801, etc. (Unruh Act).
   b. ☐ is ☒ is not on a conditional sales contract subject to CC 2981, etc. (Rees-Levering Motor Vehicle Sales and Finance
   c. ☐ is ☒ Act).
            is not on an obligation for goods, services, loans, or extensions of credit subject to CCP 395(b).

5. **DECLARATION OF MAILING (CCP 587)** A copy of this Request for Entry of Default was
   a. ☐ **not mailed** to the following defendants whose addresses are **unknown** to plaintiff or plaintiff's attorney *(names)*:

   b. ☒ **mailed** first-class, postage prepaid, in a sealed envelope addressed to each defendant's attorney of record or, if none, to each defendant's last known address as follows:

     (1) Mailed on *(date)*:   (2) To *(specify names and addresses shown on the envelopes)*:
                                                    Thomas Tenant
                                                    100 Renter Circle, Apt.9
                                                    Eviction City, CA 90000

   I declare under penalty of perjury under the laws of the State of California that the foregoing items 3, 4, and 5 are true and correct.

Date: June 1, 1998

Louis Landlord   ▶   *Louis Landlord*
....   _____
       (TYPE OR PRINT NAME)   (SIGNATURE OF DECLARANT)

6. **MEMORANDUM OF COSTS** *(Required if judgment requested)* **Costs and Disbursements** are as follows (CCP 1033.5):
   a. Clerk's filing fees · · · · · · · · · · · · · · · · · · $12
   b. Process server's fees · · · · · · · · · · · · · · · · $100
   c. Other *(specify)*: · · · · · · · · · · · · · · · · · · · $
   d · $
   e. **TOTAL** · $112
   f. ☐   Costs and disbursements are waived.

   I am the attorney, agent, or party who claims these costs. To the best of my knowledge and belief this memorandum of costs is correct and these costs were necessarily incurred in this case.

   I declare under penalty of perjury under the laws of the State of California that the foregoing is true and correct.

Date:

Louis Landlord   ▶   *Louis Landlord*
....   _____
       (TYPE OR PRINT NAME)   (SIGNATURE OF DECLARANT)

7. ☒   **DECLARATION OF NONMILITARY STATUS** *(Required for a judgment)* No defendant named in item 1c of the application is in the military service so as to be entitled to the benefits of the Soldiers' and Sailors' Civil Relief Act of 1940 (50 U.S.C.appen. § 501 et seq.).

   I declare under penalty of perjury under the laws of the State of California that the foregoing is true and correct.

Date: June 1, 1998

...Louis..Landlord.............................   ▶   *Louis Landlord*
       (TYPE OR PRINT NAME)   (SIGNATURE OF DECLARANT)

NOTE: Continued use of form 982(a)(6) (Rev. Sept. 30, 1991) is authorized until June 30, 1997, *except* in unlawful detainer proceedings.

ATTORNEY OR PARTY WITHOUT ATTORNEY (Name and Address):	TELEPHONE NO.:	FOR RECORDER'S USE ONLY

Recording requested by and return to:

Louis Landlord
123 Home Circle
Anytown, CA 90000   (555)555-5555

☐ ATTORNEY FOR   ☐ JUDGMENT CREDITOR   ☐ ASSIGNEE OF RECORD

NAME OF COURT: Municipal Court of California
STREET ADDRESS: 100 Justice Way
MAILING ADDRESS: 100 Justice Way
CITY AND ZIP CODE: Eviction City, CA 90000
BRANCH NAME: Eviction City Branch

PLAINTIFF:
Louis Landlord
DEFENDANT:
Thomas Tenant

WRIT OF	☒ EXECUTION (Money Judgment)	CASE NUMBER:
	☒ POSSESSION OF ☐ Personal Property ☒ Real Property	1212
	☐ SALE	FOR COURT USE ONLY

1. **To the Sheriff or any Marshal or Constable of the County of:**

You are directed to enforce the judgment described below with daily interest and your costs as provided by law.

2. **To any registered process server:** You are authorized to serve this writ only in accord with CCP 699.080 or CCP 715.040.

3. *(Name):* Louis Landlord
   is the ☒ judgment creditor ☐ assignee of record
   whose address is shown on this form above the court's name.

4. **Judgment debtor** *(name and last known address):*

Thomas Tenant
100 Renter Circle
Eviction City, CA 90000

☐ additional judgment debtors on reverse

5. **Judgment entered** on *(date):* June 29, 1998
6. ☐ **Judgment renewed** on *(dates):*

7. **Notice of sale** under this writ
   a. ☒ has not been requested.
   b. ☐ has been requested *(see reverse).*
8. ☐ Joint debtor information on reverse.

[SEAL]

9. ☒ See reverse for information on real or personal property to be delivered under a writ of possession or sold under a writ of sale.
10. ☐ This writ is issued on a sister-state judgment.
11. Total judgment . . . . $ 1882
12. Costs after judgment (per filed order or memo CCP 685.090) . . . . $
13. Subtotal *(add 11 and 12)* . . . . $ 1882
14. Credits . . . . $ 0
15. Subtotal *(subtract 14 from 13)* . . . . . $ 1882
16. Interest after judgment (per filed affidavit CCP 685.050) . . . . $
17. Fee for issuance of writ . . . . $
18. **Total** *(add 15, 16, and 17)* . . . . . . $ 1882
19. Levying officer:
    (a) Add daily interest from date of writ (at the legal rate on 15) of . . . . . . $
    (b) Pay directly to court costs included in 11 and 17 (GC 6103.5, 68511.3; CCP 699.520(i)) . . . . $
20. ☐ The amounts called for in items 11-19 are different for each debtor. These amounts are stated for each debtor on Attachment 20.

Issued on *(date):*	Clerk, by _____, Deputy

— NOTICE TO PERSON SERVED: SEE REVERSE FOR IMPORTANT INFORMATION. —

(Continued on reverse)

Form Approved by the
Judicial Council of California
EJ-130 [Rev. January 1, 1997*]

WRIT OF EXECUTION

Code of Civil Procedure, §§ 699.520, 712.010, 715.010
* See note on reverse.

172

— Items continued from the first page —

4. ☐ **Additional judgment debtor** *(name and last known address)*:

7. ☐ **Notice of sale** has been requested by *(name and address)*:

8. ☐ **Joint debtor** was declared bound by the judgment (CCP 989-994)

    a. on *(date)*:   a. on *(date)*:

    b. name and address of joint debtor: b. name and address of joint debtor:

    c. ☐ additional costs against certain joint debtors *(itemize)*:

9. ☒ *(Writ of Possession or Writ of Sale)* **Judgment** was entered for the following:

    a. ☒ Possession of real property: The complaint was filed on *(date)*:   **(Check (1) or (2))**:

        (1) ☒ The Prejudgment Claim of Right to Possession was served in compliance with CCP 415.46.

             The judgment includes all tenants, subtenants, named claimants, and other occupants of the premises.

        (2) ☐ The Prejudgment Claim of Right to Possession was NOT served in compliance with CCP 415.46.

            (a) $ was the daily rental value on the date the complaint was filed.

            (b) The court will hear objections to enforcement of the judgment under CCP 1174.3 on the following

                 dates *(specify)*:

    b. ☐ Possession of personal property

        ☐ If delivery cannot be had, then for the value *(itemize in 9e)* specified in the judgment or supplemental order.

    c. ☐ Sale of personal property

    d. ☐ Sale of real property

    e. Description of property: 100 Renter Circel, Apt. 9
                              Eviction City, CA 90000

— NOTICE TO PERSON SERVED —

WRIT OF EXECUTION OR SALE. Your rights and duties are indicated on the accompanying Notice of Levy.

WRIT OF POSSESSION OF PERSONAL PROPERTY. If the levying officer is not able to take custody of the property, the levying officer will make a demand upon you for the property. If custody is not obtained following demand, the judgment may be enforced as a money judgment for the value of the property specified in the judgment or in a supplemental order.

WRIT OF POSSESSION OF REAL PROPERTY. If the premises are not vacated within five days after the date of service on the occupant or, if service is by posting, within five days after service on you, the levying officer will remove the occupants from the real property and place the judgment creditor in possession of the property. Except for a mobile home, personal property remaining on the premises will be sold or otherwise disposed of in accordance with CCP 1174 unless you or the owner of the property pays the judgment creditor the reasonable cost of storage and takes possession of the personal property not later than 15 days after the time the judgment creditor takes possession of the premises.

▶ *A Claim of Right to Possession form accompanies this writ (unless the Summons was served in compliance with CCP 415.46).*

---

* NOTE: Continued use of form EJ-130 (Rev. July 1, 1996) is authorized through December 31, 1997.

EJ-130 [Rev. January 1, 1997*]   **WRIT OF EXECUTION**   Page two

ATTORNEY OR PARTY WITHOUT ATTORNEY *(Name and Address)*:	FOR COURT USE ONLY
Louis Landlord 123 Home Circle Anytown, CA 90000 ATTORNEY FOR *(Name)*:	

Insert name of court and name of judicial district and branch court, if any:

Municipal Court of California — Eviction City

PLAINTIFF:

Louis Landlord

DEFENDANT:

Thomas Tenant

CLERK'S JUDGMENT FOR POSSESSION UNLAWFUL DETAINER	CASE NUMBER 1212

The defendant(s) in this cause having been served with a summons and complaint, having failed to appear and answer the complaint within the time allowed by law, and default having been entered against them, upon application having been filed pursuant to Code of Civil procedure §1169, the Clerk hereby enters the following judgment:

ADJUDGED that plaintiff(s) __Louis Landlord_____
have and recover from defendant(s) __Thomas Tenant_____
the restitution and possession of those premises situated in the county of __Lemon_____ ,
state of California, more particularly described as follows: __100 Renter Circle, Apt. 9,__
__Eviction City, CA 90000_____

This judgment was entered on

_____

in _____Book _____
at Page _____

_____
                         Clerk

By:

_____
                    Deputy Clerk

CLERK'S JUDGMENT FOR POSSESSION
UNLAWFUL DETAINER

Code of Civil Procedure §1169

ATTORNEY OR PARTY WITHOUT ATTORNEY *(Name and Address)*: Louis Landlord 123 Home Circle Anytown, CA 90000	FOR COURT USE ONLY
ATTORNEY FOR *(Name)*:	

Insert name of court and name of judicial district and branch court, if any:
Municipal Court of California – Eviction City

PLAINTIFF:
    Louis Landlord

DEFENDANT:
    Thomas Tenant

DEFAULTJUDGMENT **UNLAWFUL DETAINER**	CASE NUMBER 1212

The defendant(s) in this cause having been served with a summons and complaint, having failed to appear and answer the complaint within the time allowed by law, and default having been entered against them, upon application having been filed by plaintiff(s), and the Court having ☐ heard the testimony and considered the evidence
      ☐ received the declaration submitted by plaintiff(s)   it is,

ORDERED AND ADJUDGED that plaintiff(s) Louis Landlord _____
_____ have and recover from defendant(s) Thomas Tenant _____
_____ the restitution and possession of those premises situated in the county of
Lemon _____, state of California, more particularly described as follows: 100 Renter
Circle, Apt. 9 – Eviction City, CA 90000 _____

for costs in the amount of $ 112 _____ and rent/damages in the amount of $ 1770 _____
for a total of $1882 _____.

Date: June 29, 1998 _____

_____
Judge David Decision

This judgment was entered on

_____
in _____ Book _____
at Page _____
_____
                            Clerk
By:
_____
                    Deputy Clerk

DEFAULT JUDGMENT
UNLAWFUL DETAINER

Code of Civil Procedure §1169 § 1174

ATTORNEY OR PARTY WITHOUT ATTORNEY *(Name and Address)*:	FOR COURT USE ONLY
Louis Landlord 123 Home Circle Anytown, CA 90000	

ATTORNEY FOR *(Name)*:

Insert name of court and name of judicial district and branch court, if any:

Municipal Court of California – Eviction City

PLAINTIFF:

    Louis Landlord

DEFENDANT:

    Thomas Tenant

DECLARATION IN SUPPORT OF DEFAULT JUDGMENT IN LIUE OF TESTIMONY	CASE NUMBER 1212

The undersigned, after first being sworn, deposes and says:

1. I am the plaintiff in the above styles case and the owner of the premises at 100 Renter Circle, Apt. 9 , in the city of Eviction City , County of Lemon , state of California.

2. Defendant(s) rented the premises from me on Feb. 1, 1998 by written agreement to pay $ 900 per month , payable in advance on the 1st of each month .

3. The current rent on the premises is ☒ the same ☐ $_____, having been raised:
       ☐ by agreement and subsequent payment
       ☐ by 30 days written notice

4. The daily rental value on the date of filing the complaint was $ 30 .

5. Defendant went into possession of the premises pursuant to the aforementioned agreement and remains in possession.

6. On May 2, 1998 defendant(s) were in default in payment of rent in the amount of $ 900 and I caused defendants to be served with written notice to pay the amount due or surrender possession of the premises within three days after service of the notice.

7. After Defendant(s) failed to pay said rent within said three days, I caused to be filed and served upon defendant(s) complaint(s) and summon(es) for unlawful detainer in the cause, in compliance with any applicable local rent control or eviction protection ordinance.

8. Defendant(s) have failed to answer or respond to said complaint as allowed by law.

9. Defendant(s)   ☐ vacated the premises on _____
               ☒ have not yet vacated the premises.

10. Rent remains unpaid for the period of from May 1, 1998 to June 1, 1998 in the total amount of $ 900 plus $ 30 per day until defendant(s) vacate the premises.

I declare under penalty of perjury under the laws of the state of California that the above statements are true and correct. and that if sworn as a witness I could swear to the above facts.

WHEREFORE I pray that judgment be entered against defendant(s) for possession of said premises, filing fees, service or process fees and other costs in this action of $ 112 , and past due rent of $ 900 .

Dated this 1st day of June , 1998 , at Eviction City , county of Lemon , state of California.

Louis Landlord

Plaintiff Louis Landlord

**DECLARATION IN SUPPORT OF DEFAULT JUDGMENT
IN LIEU OF TESTIMONY**

Code of Civil Procedure §§585(d), §1169

ATTORNEY OR PARTY WITHOUT ATTORNEY *(Name and Address)*:	FOR COURT USE ONLY
Louis Landlord 123 Home Circle Anytown, CA 90000	

ATTORNEY FOR *(Name)*:

Insert name of court and name of judicial district and branch court, if any:
Municipal Court of California - Eviction City

PLAINTIFF:
Louis Landlord

DEFENDANT:
Thomas Tenant

JUDGMENT AFTER TRIAL UNLAWFUL DETAINER	CASE NUMBER 1212

This cause came on for hearing on this date at the request of plaintiff(s) in courtroom __2__
before the Honorable _David Decision_ ,
with plaintiff(s) _Louis Landlord_
appearing in pro per and defendant(s) _Thomas Tenant_
_____ having

☒ not appeared
☐ appeared in pro per
☐ appeared through counsel _____

and the court having heard the testimony and considered the evidence, it is

ORDERED AND ADJUDGED that plaintiff(s)
Louis Landlord have and recover from defendant(s)
Thomas Tenant the restitution and possession of
those premises situated in the county of _Lemon_ , state of California, more particularly described as follows: _100 Renter Circle, Apt. 9 - Eviction City_
_____ ,

costs in the amount of $ _112_ and damages in the amount of $ _1870_ .

Date: _June 29, 1998_

Judge David Decision

This judgment was entered on

_____
in _____ Book _____
at Page _____

_____
Clerk

By:

_____
Deputy Clerk

ATTORNEY OR PARTY WITHOUT ATTORNEY *(Name and Address)*: Louis Landlord 123 Home Circle Anytown, CA 90000	FOR COURT USE ONLY

ATTORNEY FOR *(Name)*:

Insert name of court and name of judicial district and branch court, if any:
Municipal Court of California - Eviction City

PLAINTIFF:
   Louis Landlord

DEFENDANT:
   Thomas Tenant

STIPULATION FOR ENTRY OF JUDGMENT	CASE NUMBER 1212

The parties to this action hereby stipulate as follows:

1. The defendant(s) acknowledge the sum of $ 1812 to be due and owing to the plaintiff(s).

2. In partial payment of the above debt, the defendant(s) agree(s) to immediately pay to the plaintiff(s) the amount of $ 500 , and the balance of the above debt will be paid as follows:
$ 500 due on August 1, 1998 $ 500 due on September 1, 1998
$ 500 due on October 1, 1998 $ 312 due on November 1, 1998

In addition to the above-stated amounts, the defendant, as a further condition hereof, agrees to pay to the plaintiffs the sum of $ 900 on the 1st day of each month, in cash, representing periodic installments payable under the rental agreement between the parties for rent of the subject residential premises.

3. If all of the foregoing sums are paid as set out above, in full, and when due, this action shall be dismissed with prejudice, and each party does hereby release the other by a general release as if set out here in full.

4. If any of the above sums are not paid as set out above, the plaintiff(s) shall be entitled to a Judgment Pursuant to Stipulation for possession and or amounts due under this Stipulation. Defendant(s) hereby consent to the entry of said Judgment upon filing by Plaintiff(s) of an affidavit stating that the Stipulation has not been complied with and the amounts due. Defendant(s) hereby waive the right to notice or hearing before entry of said judgment.

Dated: June 29 , 1998 .

Louis Landlord   _Thomas Tenant_
Plaintiff Louis Landlord   Defendant Thomas Tenant

_____   _____
Plaintiff   Defendant

STIPULATION FOR ENTRY OF JUDGMENT

ATTORNEY OR PARTY WITHOUT ATTORNEY *(Name and Address)*:	FOR COURT USE ONLY
Louis Landlord 123 Home Circle Anytown, CA 90000	

ATTORNEY FOR *(Name)*:

Insert name of court and name of judicial district and branch court, if any:

Municipal Court of California - Eviction City

PLAINTIFF:

    Louis Landlord

DEFENDANT:

    Thomas Tenant

JUDGMENT PURSUANT TO STIPULATION	CASE NUMBER 1212

Pursuant to the stipulation entered into between the plaintiff(s) and defendant(s) in this cause, it is

ORDERED AND ADJUDGED that plaintiff(s) Louis Landlord
have and recover from defendant(s) Thomas Tenant
the restitution and possession of those premises situated in the county of Lemon,
state of California, more particularly described as follows: 100 Renter Circle, Apt. 9, Eviction City, CA 90000,

costs in the amount of $ 112 and damages in the amount of $ 1770.

Date: June 29, 1998

_____

Judge David Decision

This judgment was entered on

_____

in _____ Book _____
at Page _____

_____
                           Clerk

By:

_____
                    Deputy Clerk

Appendix D
Forms

Use of the following forms is described in the text or should be self-explanatory. If you do not understand any aspect of a form you should seek advice from an attorney.

LICENSE: Although this book is copyrighted, purchasers of the book are granted a license to copy the forms created by the author for their own personal use or use in their law practice.

Table of Forms

TENANT APPLICATION

Name: _____
      First   *Last*   *Middle*
Date of Birth _____ Soc.Sec. No. _____ Dr. Lic. No. _____

Name: _____
      First   *Last*   *Middle*
Date of Birth _____ Soc.Sec. No. _____ Dr. Lic. No. _____

Names of all other occupants (all adult occupants must sign the lease). Include ages of any minor children.
Names: _____   _____

_____   _____

Name(s) of anyone who will stay with you more than one week.
1. _____   2. _____

Your present address _____ _____
                          street   *city*   *state*   *zip*   *how long?*
Reason for leaving? _____
Present landlord _____ phone: _____
Address _____

Second previous landlord _____ phone: _____
Address _____ how long? _____

Have you ever been evicted? _____

Employer _____ phone: _____

Address _____ how long? _____

Job title _____ Supervisor _____

Current gross monthly income (before deductions) $_____

Other incomes $_____ Sources _____

Checking account: _____
                     bank   *branch*   *account no.*

Savings account: _____
                     bank   *branch*   *account no.*

Major credit card _____

Credit reference _____ Acct. no. _____

Balance owed _____ Monthly payment _____

Number of vehicles to kept at rental property? _____

_____
   make   *model*   *year*   *license no.*

_____
   make   *model*   *year*   *license no.*

Any pet? _____ Describe _____

Waterbed(s) or water filled furniture? _____ Describe _____

Emergency contact _____ _____
                              name   *phone*

_____
                          address

The undersigned hereby attest(s) that the above information is true and authorize(s) verification of any and all information given, as well as authorizing the obtaining of a credit report.

Application fee $_____   Deposit $ _____

Property to be rented is _____ Unit. _____

The rental amount is $ _____ per month plus a security deposit of $ _____.

Signature(s) of applicant(s)

_____ Date _____

_____ Date _____

Denial of Application to Rent

Your application to rent the property located at _____

_____

has been denied based in whole or in part on information supplied by the following credit reporting companies:

Company Name: _____
Address: _____
Phone: _____

Company Name: _____
Address: _____
Phone: _____

Company Name: _____
Address: _____
Phone: _____

You have the right to obtain a free copy of this report by contacting, within 60 days, the credit reporting agency indicated above and from any other consumer credit reporting agency that compiles and maintains files on a national basis.

You have the right to dispute the accuracy and completeness of any information in a consumer credit report furnished by a consumer credit reporting agency.

Date: _____

INSPECTION REPORT

Date: _____

Unit: _____

AREA	CONDITION			
	Move-In		Move-Out	
	Good	Poor	Good	Poor
Yard/garden				
Driveway				
Patio/porch				
Exterior				
Entry light/bell				
Living room/Dining room/Halls:				
Floors/carpets				
Walls/ceiling				
Doors/locks				
Fixtures/lights				
Outlets/switches				
Other				
Bedrooms:				
Floors/carpets				
Walls/ceiling				
Doors/locks				
Fixtures/lights				
Outlets/switches				
Other				
Bathrooms:				
Faucets				
Toilet				
Sink/tub				
Floors/carpets				
Walls/ceiling				
Doors/locks				
Fixtures/lights				
Outlets/switches				
Other				
Kitchen:				
Refrigerator				
Range				
Oven				
Dishwasher				
Sink/disposal				
Cabinets/counters				
Floors/carpets				
Walls/ceiling				
Doors/locks				
Fixtures/lights				
Outlets/switches				
Other				
Misc.				
Closets/pantry				
Garage				
Keys				
Other				

PET AGREEMENT

THIS AGREEMENT is made pursuant to that certain Lease dated _____
between _____ as
Landlord and _____as Tenant,
for rental of the property located at _____.

In consideration of $_____ as non-refundable cleaning payment and $_____
as additional security deposit paid by Tenant to Landlord, Tenant is allowed to keep the following pet(s): _____ on the
premises _____ under the
following conditions:

1. ❑ If the pet is a dog or cat, it is spayed or neutered.

   ❑ In the event the pet produces a litter, Tenant may keep them at the premises no
   longer than one month past weaning.

2. Tenant shall not engage in any commercial pet-raising activities.

3. No pets other than those listed above shall be kept on the premises without the further
   written permission of the Landlord.

4. Tenant agrees at all times to keep the pet from becoming a nuisance to neighbors and/or
   other tenants. This includes controlling the barking of the pet, if necessary and cleaning
   any animal waste on and about the premises.

5. In the event the pet causes destruction of the property, becomes a nuisance, or Tenant
   otherwise violates this agreement, Landlord may terminate the Lease according to
   California law.

6. An additional security deposit of $_____ shall be deposited with Landlord.

Date: _____

Landlord: Tenant:

_____   _____

_____   _____

AGREEMENT FOR USE OF WATERBED

The property received a valid Certificate of Occupancy after January 1, 1973, and water filled furniture (herein called bedding) is permitted as provided by California Civil Code 1940.5

Landlord and Tenant agree as follows:

1.   Tenant shall provide owner with a valid waterbed insurance policy or certificate or insurance for property damage in the amount of $_____ (not less than $100,000) prior to installation of the bedding. The policy shall remain in effect until the bedding is permanently removed from the rental property.

2.   The bedding must have been constructed after January 1, 1973, and must conform to the rules and regulations of the Bureau of Home Furnishings pursuant to Section 19155 of the Business and Professional Code and shall display a label declaring said compliance.

3.   The bedding must not exceed the pounds-per-square-foot limitation of the rental property.

4.   Tenant shall give Landlord at least 24 hours written notice of installation, moving, or removal of the bedding and Landlord may be present at these times.

5.   Landlord may increase the security deposit by an additional one-half month's rent.

6.   All other provisions of Civil Code 1940.5 are incorporated into this agreement

_____   _____
Landlord/Agent   Date

_____   _____
Tenant   Date

_____   _____
Tenant   Date

LEASE

LANDLORD:_____   TENANT:_____

_____   _____

PROPERTY:_____

IN CONSIDERATION of the mutual covenants and agreements herein contained, Landlord hereby leases to Tenant and Tenant hereby leases from Landlord the above-described property under the following terms:

1. TERM. This lease shall be for a term of _____ beginning _____, _____ and ending _____, _____.

2. RENT. The rent shall be $_____ per month and shall be due on or before the _____ day of each month. If rent is received more than three days late, a late charge of $_____ shall be paid.

3. PAYMENT. Payment must be received by Landlord on or before the due date at the following address: _____ or such place as designated by Landlord in writing. Tenant understands that this may require early mailing. If a check bounces, Tenant agrees to pay a late charge of $_____, and Landlord may require future payments in cash, money order, or certified funds. Tenant is hereby notified that default of financial obligations under this agreement may be reported to credit reporting companies and may result in derogatory information on Tenant's credit report.

4. DEFAULT. In the event Tenant defaults under any terms of this agreement, Landlord may recover possession as provided by Law and seek monetary damages.

5. SECURITY. Landlord acknowledges receipt of the sum of $_____ as security deposit. This deposit may not be used as last month's rent. Landlord may withhold from the security deposit amounts necessary to cover unpaid rent, damages to the premises caused by the Tenant beyond ordinary wear and tear and cleaning of the premises, if necessary.

Within three weeks after Landlord retakes possession of the premises, Landlord shall furnish Tenant with a written statement itemizing the amounts withheld with explanation and returning any unused portion of the deposit to Tenant.

6. UTILITIES. Tenant agrees to pay all utility charges on the property except: _____ _____.

7. MAINTENANCE. Tenant has examined the premises and has found them to be clean, safe, and in good repair and condition with the exception of the following:_____ _____

Tenant agrees to return the premises to Landlord at the termination of the tenancy in the same clean, safe, good repair and condition, except for normal wear and tear.

8. LOCKS. If Tenant adds or changes locks on the premises, Landlord shall be given copies of the keys. Landlord shall at all times have keys for access to the premises in case of emergencies.

9. ASSIGNMENT AND SUBLETTING. Tenant may not sublet the premises nor any portion of the premises, nor may Tenant assign this agreement without written permission of Landlord.

10. USE. Tenant shall not use the premises for any illegal purpose or any purpose which will increase the rate of insurance and shall not cause a nuisance for Landlord or neighbors. Tenant shall not create any environmental hazards on the premises.

11. LAWN (CHECK AND INITIAL): Tenant agrees to maintain the lawn and other landscaping on the premises at Tenant's expense.   Yes _____   No _____   Initials _____

12. LIABILITY. Tenant shall be responsible for insurance on his own property and agrees not to hold Landlord liable for any damages to Tenant's property on the premises.

13. ACCESS. Landlord reserves the right to enter the premises in an emergency and also to inspect the premises as well as show the premises to prospective purchasers, tenants, and workers. Except in emergency, Landlord shall give Tenant at least 24 hours notice and shall enter only between 8am and 6pm, Monday through Saturday, except holidays.

14. PETS. No pets shall be allowed on the premises except: _____.

15. WATERBEDS: No waterbeds or liquid filled furniture shall be allowed on the premises without Landlord's written permission.

16. OCCUPANCY. The premises shall be occupied as a residence only, and shall be occupied only by the following persons. (List all occupants, both adults and minors) _____ _____.

17. TENANT'S APPLIANCES. Tenant agrees not to use any heaters, fixtures or appliances drawing excessive current without consent of the Landlord.

18. PARKING. Tenant agrees that no parking is allowed on the premises except: _____ _____. No boats, recreation vehicles or disassembled automobiles may be stored on the premises.

19. FURNISHINGS. Any articles provided to tenant and listed on attached schedule are to be returned in good condition at the termination of this agreement.

20. ALTERATIONS AND IMPROVEMENTS. Tenant shall make no alterations to the property without the written consent of the Landlord and any such alterations or improvements shall become the property of the Landlord.

21. SMOKE DETECTORS. Tenant shall be responsible for keeping smoke detectors operational and for changing battery when needed.

22. LIENS. The estate of Landlord shall not be subject to any liens for improvements contracted by Tenant.

23. HARASSMENT. Tenant shall not do any acts to intentionally harass the Landlord or other tenants.

24. ATTORNEYS FEES. In the event of legal action, the prevailing party (shall) (shall not) recover reasonable attorney's fees in addition to any other recovery.

25. SEVERABILITY. In the event any section of this agreement shall be held to be invalid, all remaining provisions shall remain in full force and effect.

26. RECORDING. This agreement shall not be recorded in any public records.

27. WAIVER. Any failure by Landlord to exercise any rights under this agreement shall not constitute a waiver of Landlord's rights.

28. SUBORDINATION. Tenants interest in the premises shall be subordinate to any encumbrances now or hereafter placed on the premises, to any advances made under such encumbrances, and to any extensions or renewals thereof. Tenant agrees to sign any documents indicating such subordination which may be required by lenders.

29. ATTACHMENTS: The following attachments are incorporated and made a part of this agreement. (Tenant should initial) A. _____ B. _____ C. _____ D. _____

30. ENTIRE AGREEMENT. This rental agreement, including the above initialed attachments, constitutes the entire agreement between the parties and may not be modified except in writing signed by all parties.

31. OWNER OR MANAGER. The owner or manager for service of legal notices is: _____ _____.

WITNESS the hands and seals of the parties hereto as of this _____ day of _____, _____.

LANDLORD: TENANT:

_____   _____

_____   _____

CONDOMINIUM LEASE

LANDLORD:_____   TENANT:_____

_____   _____

PROPERTY:_____

IN CONSIDERATION of the mutual covenants and agreements herein contained, Landlord hereby leases to Tenant and Tenant hereby leases from Landlord the above-described property under the following terms:

1. TERM. This lease shall be for a term of _____ beginning _____, _____ and ending _____, _____.

2. RENT. The rent shall be $_____ per month and shall be due on or before the _____ day of each month. If rent is received more than three days late, a late charge of $_____ shall be paid.

3. PAYMENT. Payment must be received by Landlord on or before the due date at the following address: _____ or such place as designated by Landlord in writing. Tenant understands that this may require early mailing. If a check bounces, Tenant agrees to pay a late charge of $_____, and Landlord may require future payments in cash, money order, or certified funds. Tenant is hereby notified that default of financial obligations under this agreement may be reported to credit reporting companies and may result in derogatory information on Tenant's credit report.

4. DEFAULT. In the event Tenant defaults under any terms of this agreement, Landlord may recover possession as provided by Law and seek monetary damages.

5. SECURITY. Landlord acknowledges receipt of the sum of $_____ as security deposit. This deposit may not be used as last month's rent. Landlord may withhold from the security deposit amounts necessary to cover unpaid rent, damages to the premises caused by the Tenant beyond ordinary wear and tear and cleaning of the premises, if necessary. Within three weeks after Landlord retakes possession of the premises, Landlord shall furnish Tenant with a written statement itemizing the amounts withheld with explanation and returning any unused portion of the deposit to Tenant.

6. UTILITIES. Tenant agrees to pay all utility charges on the property except: _____ _____.

7. MAINTENANCE. Tenant has examined the premises and has found them to be clean, safe, and in good repair and condition with the exception of the following:_____ _____

Tenant agrees to return the premises to Landlord at the termination of the tenancy in the same clean, safe, good repair and condition, except for normal wear and tear.

8. LOCKS. If Tenant adds or changes locks on the premises, Landlord shall be given copies of the keys. Landlord shall at all times have keys for access to the premises in case of emergencies.

9. ASSIGNMENT AND SUBLETTING. Tenant may not sublet the premises nor any portion of the premises, nor may Tenant assign this agreement without written permission of Landlord.

10. COMMON INTEREST PROPERTY. Tenant acknowledges that the premises are subject to a Declaration of Covenants, Conditions and Restrictions and Association Rules and Regulations. Copies of these documents are attached to and made part of this agreement. Tenant agrees to comply with the requirements of these documents and to reimburse Landlord for any fines or charges levied against Landlord for Tenant's failure to comply with these requirements.

11. USE. Tenant shall not use the premises for any illegal purpose or any purpose which will increase the rate of insurance and shall not cause a nuisance for Landlord or neighbors. Tenant shall not create any environmental hazards on the premises.

12. LAWN (CHECK AND INITIAL): Tenant agrees to maintain the lawn and other landscaping on the premises at Tenant's expense.   Yes _____   No _____   Initials _____

13. LIABILITY. Tenant shall be responsible for insurance on his own property and agrees not to hold Landlord liable for any damages to Tenant's property on the premises.

14. ACCESS. Landlord reserves the right to enter the premises in an emergency and also to inspect the premises as well as show the premises to prospective purchasers, tenants, and workers. Except in emergency,

Landlord shall give Tenant at least 24 hours notice and shall enter only between 8am and 6pm, Monday through Saturday, except holidays.

15. PETS. No pets shall be allowed on the premises except: _____.

16. WATERBEDS: No waterbeds or liquid filled furniture shall be allowed on the premises without Landlord's written permission.

17. OCCUPANCY. The premises shall be occupied as a residence only, and shall be occupied only by the following persons. (List all occupants, both adults and minors) _____
_____.

18. TENANT'S APPLIANCES. Tenant agrees not to use any heaters, fixtures or appliances drawing excessive current without consent of the Landlord.

19. PARKING. Tenant agrees that no parking is allowed on the premises except: _____
_____. No boats, recreation vehicles or disassembled automobiles may be stored on the premises.

20. FURNISHINGS. Any articles provided to tenant and listed on attached schedule are to be returned in good condition at the termination of this agreement.

21. ALTERATIONS AND IMPROVEMENTS. Tenant shall make no alterations to the property without the written consent of the Landlord and any such alterations or improvements shall become the property of the Landlord.

22. SMOKE DETECTORS. Tenant shall be responsible for keeping smoke detectors operational and for changing battery when needed.

23. LIENS. The estate of Landlord shall not be subject to any liens for improvements contracted by Tenant.

24. HARASSMENT. Tenant shall not do any acts to intentionally harass the Landlord or other tenants.

25. ATTORNEYS FEES. In the event of legal action, the prevailing party (shall) (shall not) recover reasonable attorney's fees in addition to any other recovery.

26. SEVERABILITY. In the event any section of this agreement shall be held to be invalid, all remaining provisions shall remain in full force and effect.

27. RECORDING. This agreement shall not be recorded in any public records.

28. WAIVER. Any failure by Landlord to exercise any rights under this agreement shall not constitute a waiver of Landlord's rights.

29. SUBORDINATION. Tenants interest in the premises shall be subordinate to any encumbrances now or hereafter placed on the premises, to any advances made under such encumbrances, and to any extensions or renewals thereof. Tenant agrees to sign any documents indicating such subordination which may be required by lenders.

30. ATTACHMENTS: The following attachments are incorporated and made a part of this agreement. (Tenant should initial) A. _____ B. _____
C. _____ D. _____

32. ENTIRE AGREEMENT. This rental agreement, including the above initialed attachments, constitutes the entire agreement between the parties and may not be modified except in writing signed by all parties.

32. OWNER OR MANAGER. The owner or manager for service of legal notices is: _____
_____.

WITNESS the hands and seals of the parties hereto as of this _____ day of _____, _____.

LANDLORD: TENANT:

_____   _____

_____   _____

RENTAL AGREEMENT

LANDLORD:_____   TENANT:_____

_____   _____

PROPERTY:_____

IN CONSIDERATION of the mutual covenants and agreements herein contained, Landlord hereby rents to Tenant and Tenant hereby rents from Landlord the above-described property under the following terms:

1. TERM. This Rental Agreement shall be for a month-to-month tenancy. Unless prohibited by law, this agreement may be terminated by either party or modified by Landlord upon service of 30 days written notice.

2. RENT. The rent shall be $_____ per month and shall be due on or before the _____ day of each month. If rent is received more than three days late, a late charge of $_____ shall be paid.

3. PAYMENT. Payment must be received by Landlord on or before the due date at the following address: _____ or such place as designated by Landlord in writing. Tenant understands that this may require early mailing. If a check bounces, Tenant agrees to pay a late charge of $_____, and Landlord may require future payments in cash, money order, or certified funds. Tenant is hereby notified that default of financial obligations under this agreement may be reported to credit reporting companies and may result in derogatory information on Tenant's credit report.

4. DEFAULT. In the event Tenant defaults under any terms of this agreement, Landlord may recover possession as provided by Law and seek monetary damages.

5. SECURITY. Landlord acknowledges receipt of the sum of $_____ as security deposit. This deposit may not be used as last month's rent. Landlord may withhold from the security deposit amounts necessary to cover unpaid rent, damages to the premises caused by the Tenant beyond ordinary wear and tear and cleaning of the premises, if necessary

Within three weeks after Landlord retakes possession of the premises, Landlord shall furnish Tenant with a written statement itemizing the amounts withheld with explanation and returning any unused portion of the deposit to Tenant.

6. UTILITIES. Tenant agrees to pay all utility charges on the property except: _____
_____.

7. MAINTENANCE. Tenant has examined the premises and has found them to be clean, safe, and in good repair and condition with the exception of the following:_____
_____

Tenant agrees to return the premises to Landlord at the termination of the tenancy in the same clean, safe, good repair and condition, except for normal wear and tear.

8. LOCKS. If Tenant adds or changes locks on the premises, Landlord shall be given copies of the keys. Landlord shall at all times have keys for access to the premises in case of emergencies.

9. ASSIGNMENT AND SUBLETTING. Tenant may not sublet the premises nor any portion of the premises, nor may Tenant assign this agreement without written permission of Landlord.

10. USE. Tenant shall not use the premises for any illegal purpose or any purpose which will increase the rate of insurance and shall not cause a nuisance for Landlord or neighbors. Tenant shall not create any environmental hazards on the premises.

11. LAWN (CHECK AND INITIAL): Tenant agrees to maintain the lawn and other landscaping on the premises at Tenant's expense.   Yes _____   No _____   Initials _____

12. LIABILITY. Tenant shall be responsible for insurance on his own property and agrees not to hold Landlord liable for any damages to Tenant's property on the premises.

13. ACCESS. Landlord reserves the right to enter the premises in an emergency and also to inspect the premises as well as show the premises to prospective purchasers, tenants, and workers. Except in emergency, Landlord shall give Tenant at least 24 hours notice and shall enter only between 8am and 6pm, Monday through Saturday, except holidays.

14. PETS. No pets shall be allowed on the premises except: _____.

15. WATERBEDS: No waterbeds or liquid filled furniture shall be allowed on the premises without Landlord's written permission.

16. OCCUPANCY. The premises shall be occupied as a residence only, and shall be occupied only by the following persons. (List all occupants, both adults and minors) _____.

17. TENANT'S APPLIANCES. Tenant agrees not to use any heaters, fixtures or appliances drawing excessive current without consent of the Landlord.

18. PARKING. Tenant agrees that no parking is allowed on the premises except: _____ _____. No boats, recreation vehicles or disassembled automobiles may be stored on the premises.

19. FURNISHINGS. Any articles provided to tenant and listed on attached schedule are to be returned in good condition at the termination of this agreement.

20. ALTERATIONS AND IMPROVEMENTS. Tenant shall make no alterations to the property without the written consent of the Landlord and any such alterations or improvements shall become the property of the Landlord.

21. SMOKE DETECTORS. Tenant shall be responsible for keeping smoke detectors operational and for changing battery when needed.

22. LIENS. The estate of Landlord shall not be subject to any liens for improvements contracted by Tenant.

23. HARASSMENT. Tenant shall not do any acts to intentionally harass the Landlord or other tenants.

24. ATTORNEYS FEES. In the event of legal action, the prevailing party (shall) (shall not) recover reasonable attorney's fees in addition to any other recovery.

25. SEVERABILITY. In the event any section of this agreement shall be held to be invalid, all remaining provisions shall remain in full force and effect.

26. RECORDING. This agreement shall not be recorded in any public records.

27. WAIVER. Any failure by Landlord to exercise any rights under this agreement shall not constitute a waiver of Landlord's rights.

28. SUBORDINATION. Tenants interest in the premises shall be subordinate to any encumbrances now or hereafter placed on the premises, to any advances made under such encumbrances, and to any extensions or renewals thereof. Tenant agrees to sign any documents indicating such subordination which may be required by lenders.

29. ATTACHMENTS: The following attachments are incorporated and made a part of this agreement. (Tenant should initial) A. _____ B. _____ C. _____ D. _____

30. ENTIRE AGREEMENT. This rental agreement, including the above initialed attachments, constitutes the entire agreement between the parties and may not be modified except in writing signed by all parties.

31. OWNER OR MANAGER. The owner or manager for service of legal notices is: _____ _____.

WITNESS the hands and seals of the parties hereto as of this _____ day of _____, _____.

LANDLORD: TENANT:

_____   _____

_____   _____

CONDOMINIUM RENTAL AGREEMENT

LANDLORD:_____   TENANT:_____

_____   _____

PROPERTY:_____
IN CONSIDERATION of the mutual covenants and agreements herein contained, Landlord hereby rents to Tenant and Tenant hereby rents from Landlord the above-described property under the following terms:

    1. TERM. This Rental Agreement shall be for a month-to-month tenancy. Unless prohibited by law, this agreement may be terminated by either party or modified by Landlord upon service of 30 days written notice.

    2. RENT. The rent shall be $_____ per month and shall be due on or before the _____ day of each month. If rent is received more than three days late, a late charge of $_____ shall be paid.

    3. PAYMENT. Payment must be received by Landlord on or before the due date at the following address: _____ or such place as designated by Landlord in writing. Tenant understands that this may require early mailing. If a check bounces, Tenant agrees to pay a late charge of $_____, and Landlord may require future payments in cash, money order, or certified funds. Tenant is hereby notified that default of financial obligations under this agreement may be reported to credit reporting companies and may result in derogatory information on Tenant's credit report.

    4. DEFAULT. In the event Tenant defaults under any terms of this agreement, Landlord may recover possession as provided by Law and seek monetary damages.

    5. SECURITY. Landlord acknowledges receipt of the sum of $_____ as security deposit. This deposit may not be used as last month's rent. Landlord may withhold from the security deposit amounts necessary to cover unpaid rent, damages to the premises caused by the Tenant beyond ordinary wear and tear and cleaning of the premises, if necessary. Within three weeks after Landlord retakes possession of the premises, Landlord shall furnish Tenant with a written statement itemizing the amounts withheld with explanation and returning any unused portion of the deposit to Tenant.

    6. UTILITIES. Tenant agrees to pay all utility charges on the property except: _____
_____.

    7. MAINTENANCE. Tenant has examined the premises and has found them to be clean, safe, and in good repair and condition with the exception of the following:_____
_____

    Tenant agrees to return the premises to Landlord at the termination of the tenancy in the same clean, safe, good repair and condition, except for normal wear and tear.

    8. LOCKS. If Tenant adds or changes locks on the premises, Landlord shall be given copies of the keys. Landlord shall at all times have keys for access to the premises in case of emergencies.

    9. ASSIGNMENT AND SUBLETTING. Tenant may not sublet the premises nor any portion of the premises, nor may Tenant assign this agreement without written permission of Landlord.

    10. COMMON INTEREST PROPERTY . Tenant acknowledges that the premises are subject to a Declaration of Covenants, Conditions and Restrictions and Association Rules and Regulations. Copies of these documents are attached to and made part of this agreement. Tenant agrees to comply with the requirements of these documents and to reimburse Landlord for any fines or charges levied against Landlord for Tenant's failure to comply with these requirements.

    11. USE. Tenant shall not use the premises for any illegal purpose or any purpose which will increase the rate of insurance and shall not cause a nuisance for Landlord or neighbors. Tenant shall not create any environmental hazards on the premises.

    12. LAWN (CHECK AND INITIAL): Tenant agrees to maintain the lawn and other landscaping on the premises at Tenant's expense.   Yes _____   No _____   Initials _____

    13. LIABILITY. Tenant shall be responsible for insurance on his own property and agrees not to hold Landlord liable for any damages to Tenant's property on the premises.

    14. ACCESS. Landlord reserves the right to enter the premises in an emergency and also to inspect the premises as well as show the premises to prospective purchasers, tenants, and workers. Except in emergency, Landlord shall give Tenant at least 24 hours notice and shall enter only between 8am and 6pm, Monday through Saturday, except holidays.

15. PETS. No pets shall be allowed on the premises except: _____.

16. WATERBEDS: No waterbeds or liquid filled furniture shall be allowed on the premises without Landlord's written permission.

17. OCCUPANCY. The premises shall be occupied as a residence only, and shall be occupied only by the following persons. (List all occupants, both adults and minors) _____
_____.

18. TENANT'S APPLIANCES. Tenant agrees not to use any heaters, fixtures or appliances drawing excessive current without consent of the Landlord.

19. PARKING. Tenant agrees that no parking is allowed on the premises except: _____
_____. No boats, recreation vehicles or disassembled automobiles may be stored on the premises.

20. FURNISHINGS. Any articles provided to tenant and listed on attached schedule are to be returned in good condition at the termination of this agreement.

21. ALTERATIONS AND IMPROVEMENTS. Tenant shall make no alterations to the property without the written consent of the Landlord and any such alterations or improvements shall become the property of the Landlord.

22. SMOKE DETECTORS. Tenant shall be responsible for keeping smoke detectors operational and for changing battery when needed.

23. LIENS. The estate of Landlord shall not be subject to any liens for improvements contracted by Tenant.

24. HARASSMENT. Tenant shall not do any acts to intentionally harass the Landlord or other tenants.

25. ATTORNEYS FEES. In the event of legal action, the prevailing party (shall) (shall not) recover reasonable attorney's fees in addition to any other recovery.

26. SEVERABILITY. In the event any section of this agreement shall be held to be invalid, all remaining provisions shall remain in full force and effect.

27. RECORDING. This agreement shall not be recorded in any public records.

28. WAIVER. Any failure by Landlord to exercise any rights under this agreement shall not constitute a waiver of Landlord's rights.

29. SUBORDINATION. Tenants interest in the premises shall be subordinate to any encumbrances now or hereafter placed on the premises, to any advances made under such encumbrances, and to any extensions or renewals thereof. Tenant agrees to sign any documents indicating such subordination which may be required by lenders.

30. ATTACHMENTS: The following attachments are incorporated and made a part of this agreement. (Tenant should initial) A. _____ B. _____
C. _____ D. _____

31. ENTIRE AGREEMENT. This rental agreement, including the above initialed attachments, constitutes the entire agreement between the parties and may not be modified except in writing signed by all parties.

32. OWNER OR MANAGER. The owner or manager for service of legal notices is: _____
_____.

WITNESS the hands and seals of the parties hereto as of this _____ day of
_____, _____.

LANDLORD: TENANT:

_____   _____

_____   _____

AMENDMENT TO LEASE/RENTAL AGREEMENT

The undersigned parties to that certain agreement dated _____,
_____ on the premises known as _____,
hereby agree to amend said agreement as follows:

WITNESS the hands and seals of the parties hereto this _____ day of _____,
_____.

Landlord: Tenant:

_____   _____

_____   _____

Guarantee of Lease/Rental Agreement

The undersigned Guarantor(s), in consideration of the Lease or Rental Agreement between _____ as Landlord and _____ as Tenant, dated _____, _____, and other good and valuable consideration, receipt whereof is hereby acknowledged, does/do hereby guaranty to Landlord, his/her/its successors and assigns, the faithful performance of the Lease or Rental Agreement and all sums due thereunder.

In the event of breach by Tenant of any of the terms of said Lease or Rental Agreement, including damage to the premises and attorney fees paid in enforcement of said agreement, Guarantor(s) shall be liable, and Landlord, his/her/its successors and assigns may have recourse against Guarantor(s) without first taking action against Tenant.

It is understood between the parties that this Guaranty does not confer any right to possession of the premises, or to require any notices to be served upon Guarantor(s), but only serves as an inducement for Landlord to enter into a Lease or rental Agreement with Tenant.

This Guaranty shall remain in effect until Tenant has fully complied with the Lease or Rental Agreement or until released in writing by landlord, his/her/its successors or assigns.

Date: _____, _____.

Guarantor(s):

_____

_____

Disclosure of Information on Lead-Based Paint and/or Lead-Based Paint Hazards

Lead Warning Statement
Housing built before 1978 may contain lead-based paint. Lead from paint, paint chips, and dust can pose health hazards if not managed properly. Lead exposure is especially harmful to young children and pregnant women. Before renting pre-1978 housing, lessors must disclose the presence of known lead-based paint and/or lead-based paint hazards in the dwelling. Lessees must also receive a federally approved pamphlet on lead poisoning prevention.

Lessor's Disclosure
(a) Presence of lead-based paint and/or lead-based paint hazards (Check (i) or (ii) below):

(i)_____ Known lead-based paint and/or lead-based paint hazards are present in the housing (explain).

_____

(ii)_____ Lessor has no knowledge of lead-based paint and/or lead-based paint hazards in the housing.

(b) Records and reports available to the lessor (Check (i) or (ii) below):

(i)_____ Lessor has provided the lessee with all available records and reports pertaining to lead-based paint and/or lead-based paint hazards in the housing (list documents below).

_____

(ii)_____ Lessor has no reports or records pertaining to lead-based paint and/or lead-based paint hazards in the housing.

Lessee's Acknowledgment (initial)
(c)_____ Lessee has received copies of all information listed above.
(d)_____ Lessee has received the pamphlet Protect Your Family from Lead in Your Home.

Agent's Acknowledgment (initial)
(e)_____ Agent has informed the lessor of the lessor's obligations under 42 U.S.C. 4852d and is aware of his/her responsibility to ensure compliance.

Certification of Accuracy
The following parties have reviewed the information above and certify, to the best of their knowledge, that the information they have provided is true and accurate.

Lessor	Date	Lessor	Date
Lessee	Date	Lessee	Date
Agent	Date	Agent	Date

CALIFORNIA LANDLORD DISCLOSURES

Date:

To:

  The undersigned owner(s) of the property located at _____

_____ make the following disclosures regarding

this property:

1. The property ❑ is ❑ is not within one mile of a former military base where ammunition

or explosives were kept.

2. ❑ Your electric bill only includes electricity used in your unit.

  ❑ You electric bill includes electricity used outside your unit as follows: _____

_____.

3. Other _____

_____

_____

_____

_____

_____

_____

_____ _____
Owner   date   Owner   date

The undersigned tenant(s) acknowledge receipt and understanding of the above disclosures.

_____ _____
Tenant   date   Tenant   date

INSPECTION REQUEST

Date:

To:

It will be necessary to enter your dwelling unit for the purpose of _____

_____

_____. If possible we would like

access on _____ at ____o'clock ___.m.

In the event this is not convenient, please call to arrange another time.

Sincerely,

_____

Address: _____

Phone: _____

PROOF OF SERVICE

I, the undersigned, being at least 18 years of age, served this notice, of which this is a true copy, on _____, the person(s) named above. The notice was served by:

- ❏ Personal delivery of a copy to the above named person(s).
- ❏ Delivery of a copy for each of the above named to a person of suitable age and discretion at the above named person(s) residence/business after attempting to personally serve the above named person(s) at his/her/their residence and place of business (if known) and mailing by first class mail a second copy to his/her/their residence.
- ❏ Posting a copy for each of the above named person(s) in a conspicuous place on the above identified property, being unable to personally serve a person of suitable age or discretion at the residence or known place(s) of business of the above named person(s) and mailing on the same date by first class mail a second copy to each above named person(s) to the address of the above identified property.

I declare under penalty of perjury that the above proof of service is true and correct.

Name _____   Date _____

STATEMENT FOR REPAIRS

Date:

To:

It has been necessary to repair damage to the premises which you occupy which was caused by you or your guests. The costs for repairs were as follows:

This amount is your responsibility under the terms of the lease and California law and should be forwarded to us at the address below.

Sincerely,

_____

Address:

Phone:

PROOF OF SERVICE

I, the undersigned, being at least 18 years of age, served this notice, of which this is a true copy, on _____, the person(s) named above. The notice was served by:

- ❏ Personal delivery of a copy to the above named person(s).
- ❏ Delivery of a copy for each of the above named to a person of suitable age and discretion at the above named person(s) residence/business after attempting to personally serve the above named person(s) at his/her/their residence and place of business (if known) and mailing by first class mail a second copy to his/her/their residence.
- ❏ Posting a copy for each of the above named person(s) in a conspicuous place on the above identified property, being unable to personally serve a person of suitable age or discretion at the residence or known place(s) of business of the above named person(s) and mailing on the same date by first class mail a second copy to each above named person(s) to the address of the above identified property.

I declare under penalty of perjury that the above proof of service is true and correct.

Name _____   Date _____

NOTICE OF CHANGE OF TERMS
CIVIL CODE SECTION 827

DATE:

To:

Dear

You are hereby notified that effective _____ the terms

of your rental agreement will be changed as follows:

❑   Rent: From $_____ per _____ To: $_____ per _____.

❑   Other Changes:

Sincerely,

_____

Address:

Phone:

PROOF OF SERVICE

I, the undersigned, being at least 18 years of age, served this notice, of which this is a true copy, on
_____, the person(s) named above. The notice was served by:

❑   Personal delivery of a copy to the above named person(s).

❑   Delivery of a copy for each of the above named to a person of suitable age and discretion at the above named person(s) residence/business after attempting to personally serve the above named person(s) at his/her/their residence and place of business (if known) and mailing by first class mail a second copy to his/her/their residence.

❑   Posting a copy for each of the above named person(s) in a conspicuous place on the above identified property, being unable to personally serve a person of suitable age or discretion at the residence or known place(s) of business of the above named person(s) and mailing on the same date by first class mail a second copy to each above named person(s) to the address of the above identified property.

I declare under penalty of perjury that the above proof of service is true and correct.

Name _____   Date _____

Letter to Vacating Tenant

DATE:

To:

Dear _____

    This letter is to remind you that your lease will expire on _____.

Please be advised that we do not intend to renew or extend the lease.

    The keys should be delivered to us at the address below on or before the end of the

lease along with your forwarding address. We will inspect the premises for damages, deduct

any amounts necessary for repairs and cleaning, and refund any remaining balance as

required by law.

                                      Sincerely,

                                _____

                                Address:

                                Phone:

Proof of Service

I, the undersigned, being at least 18 years of age, served this notice, of which this is a true copy, on
_____, the person(s) named above. The notice was served by:

- ❑ Personal delivery of a copy to the above named person(s).
- ❑ Delivery of a copy for each of the above named to a person of suitable age and discretion at the above named person(s) residence/business after attempting to personally serve the above named person(s) at his/her/their residence and place of business (if known) and mailing by first class mail a second copy to his/her/their residence.
- ❑ Posting a copy for each of the above named person(s) in a conspicuous place on the above identified property, being unable to personally serve a person of suitable age or discretion at the residence or known place(s) of business of the above named person(s) and mailing on the same date by first class mail a second copy to each above named person(s) to the address of the above identified property.

I declare under penalty of perjury that the above proof of service is true and correct.

Name _____   Date _____

ANNUAL LETTER—CONTINUATION OF TENANCY

Date:

To:

Dear _____

    This letter is to remind you that your lease will expire on _____.
Please advise us within _____ days as to whether you intend to renew your lease. If so, we
will prepare a new lease for your signature(s).

    If you do not intend to renew your lease, the keys should be delivered to us at the
address below on or before the end of the lease along with your forwarding address. We will
inspect the premises for damages, deduct any amounts necessary for repairs and cleaning, and
refund any remaining balance as required by law.

    If we have not heard from you as specified above we will assume that you will be
vacating the premises and will arrange for a new tenant to move in at the end of your term.

Sincerely,

_____

Address:

Phone:

PROOF OF SERVICE

I, the undersigned, being at least 18 years of age, served this notice, of which this is a true copy, on
_____, the person(s) named above. The notice was served by:

    ❑   Personal delivery of a copy to the above named person(s).

    ❑   Delivery of a copy for each of the above named to a person of suitable age and discretion at the
above named person(s) residence/business after attempting to personally serve the above named
person(s) at his/her/their residence and place of business (if known) and mailing by first class mail
a second copy to his/her/their residence.

    ❑   Posting a copy for each of the above named person(s) in a conspicuous place on the above identi-
fied property, being unable to personally serve a person of suitable age or discretion at the residence
or known place(s) of business of the above named person(s) and mailing on the same date by first
class mail a second copy to each above named person(s) to the address of the above identified property.

I declare under penalty of perjury that the above proof of service is true and correct.

Name _____   Date _____

Notice of Termination of Agent

Date:

To:

    You are hereby advised that _____ is no longer our agent effective _____. On and after this date he or she is no longer authorized to collect rent, accept notices or to make any representations or agreements regarding the property.

    Rent should thereafter be paid to us directly at _____.

    If you have any questions you may contact us at the address or phone number below.

            Sincerely,

_____

Address:

Phone:

NOTICE OF APPOINTMENT OF AGENT

Date:

To:

You are hereby advised that effective _____, our agent
for collection of rent and other matters regarding the property will be _____
_____. Rent should be paid at:

_____

_____

_____

However, no terms of the written lease may be modified or waived without our written signature(s).

If you have any questions you may contact us at the address or phone number below.

Sincerely,

_____

Address:

Phone:

NOTICE OF DISHONORED CHECK
AND DEMAND FOR PAYMENT

Date:

To:

    You are advised that your check number _____, dated _____,

_____ in the amount of _____

dollars ($_____) was returned unpaid.

    Unless this check is paid within thirty (30) days you may be liable for the amount of

the check plus triple the amount of the check in damages, but in no case less that one hun-

dred dollars ($100) or more than one thousand, five hundred dollars ($1,500).

    Additionally, a report of your failure to pay this debt be made to a credit reporting

agency.

The applicable part of California Civil Code Section 1719 is as follows:

1719. (a) (1) Notwithstanding any penal sanctions that may apply, any person who passes a check on insufficient funds shall be liable to the payee for the amount of the check and a service charge payable to the payee for an amount not to exceed twenty-five dollars ($25) for the first check passed on insufficient funds and an amount not to exceed thirty-five dollars ($35) for each subsequent check to that payee passed on insufficient funds.

(2) Notwithstanding any penal sanctions that may apply, any person who passes a check on insufficient funds shall be liable to the payee for damages equal to treble the amount of the check if a written demand for payment is mailed by certified mail to the person who had passed a check on insufficient funds and the written demand informs this person of (A) the provisions of this section, (B) the amount of the check, and (C) the amount of the service charge payable to the payee. The person who had passed a check on insufficient funds shall have 30 days from the date the written demand was mailed to pay the amount of the check, the amount of the service charge payable to the payee, and the costs to mail the written demand for payment. If this person fails to pay in full the amount of the check, the service charge payable to the payee, and the costs to mail the written demand within this period, this person shall then be liable instead for the amount of the check, minus any partial payments made toward the amount of the check or the service charge within 30 days of the written demand, and damages equal to treble that amount, which shall not be less than one hundred dollars ($100) nor more than one thousand five hundred dollars ($1,500). When a person becomes liable for treble damages for a check that is the subject of a written demand, that person shall no longer be liable for any service charge for that check and any costs to mail the written demand.

_____

Payee
Address:

Phone:

ITEMIZED SECURITY DEPOSIT DISPOSITION
(CIVIL CODE SECTION 1950.5)

Date: _____

To: _____

_____

_____

Property Address: _____

Amount held as security: $_____
Interest: $_____
Total: $_____

DEDUCTIONS

1. Unpaid Rent: $_____ for (Dates) _____

_____

2. Repairs: $_____ for (Explanation) _____

_____

3. Cleaning: $_____ for (Explanation) _____

_____

4. Judgment: $_____ for (Explanation) _____

_____

Total Deductions: $_____
Amount owed by Tenant $_____
Amount owed to Tenant $_____

Further comments or explanations: _____

_____

_____

From: _____

_____

_____

Phone: _____

THREE DAY NOTICE TO PAY RENT OR QUIT

To: _____

Tenants' and Subtenants' Full Names and Names of all Other Residents

_____

Address

_____

City, State, Zip Code

From: _____

Date: _____

You are hereby notified that you are indebted to me in the sum of $_____

(insert amount owed by Tenant)

for the rent from _____ of the premises_____

(date)   (insert address of leased premises, including county)

now occupied by you and that I demand payment of the rent or possession of the premises within three days from the date of service of this notice, to-wit: on or before the _____ day of _____, _____ [insert the date which is three days from the service of this notice, excluding the date of service, Saturday, Sunday, and legal holidays].

_____

Signature

_____

Name of Landlord/Property manager
(Circle one)

_____

Address

_____

City, State, Zip Code

_____

Phone Number

PROOF OF SERVICE

I, the undersigned, being at least 18 years of age, served this notice, of which this is a true copy, on _____, the person(s) named above. The notice was served by:

- ❑ Personal delivery of a copy to the above named person(s).
- ❑ Delivery of a copy for each of the above named to a person of suitable age and discretion at the above named person(s) residence/business after attempting to personally serve the above named person(s) at his/her/their residence and place of business (if known) and mailing by first class mail a second copy to his/her/their residence.
- ❑ Posting a copy for each of the above named person(s) in a conspicuous place on the above identified property, being unable to personally serve a person of suitable age or discretion at the residence or known place(s) of business of the above named person(s) and mailing on the same date by first class mail a second copy to each above named person(s) to the address of the above identified property.

I declare under penalty of perjury that the above proof of service is true and correct.

Name _____   Date _____

THREE DAY NOTICE TO COMPLY OR QUIT

To: _____
Tenant's Name

_____
Address

_____
City, State, Zip Code

From: _____
Date: _____

You are hereby notified that you are not complying with your lease or rental agreement in that (insert noncompliance) _____ _____ _____. Demand is hereby made that you remedy the noncompliance within three days of service of this notice or your lease or rental agreement shall be deemed terminated and you shall vacate the premises upon such termination. Failure to vacate and surrender possession shall result in legal action to recover possession as well as damages and court costs.

_____

Landlord's Name_____

Address _____

_____

Phone Number _____

PROOF OF SERVICE

I, the undersigned, being at least 18 years of age, served this notice, of which this is a true copy, on _____, the person(s) named above. The notice was served by:
- ❏   Personal delivery of a copy to the above named person(s).
- ❏   Delivery of a copy for each of the above named to a person of suitable age and discretion at the above named person(s) residence/business after attempting to personally serve the above named person(s) at his/her/their residence and place of business (if known) and mailing by first class mail a second copy to his/her/their residence.
- ❏   Posting a copy for each of the above named person(s) in a conspicuous place on the above identified property, being unable to personally serve a person of suitable age or discretion at the residence or known place(s) of business of the above named person(s) and mailing on the same date by first class mail a second copy to each above named person(s) to the address of the above identified property.

I declare under penalty of perjury that the above proof of service is true and correct.

Name _____   Date _____

THREE DAY NOTICE TO QUIT

(Tenant's Name and Address)

Dear _____:
            (Tenant's Name)

      You are hereby notified that your lease is terminated immediately. You shall have three (3) days from delivery of this letter to vacate the premises. This action is taken because:

_____

Landlord's Name_____

Address _____

Phone Number _____

PROOF OF SERVICE

I, the undersigned, being at least 18 years of age, served this notice, of which this is a true copy, on _____, the person(s) named above. The notice was served by:

   ❑   Personal delivery of a copy to the above named person(s).

   ❑   Delivery of a copy for each of the above named to a person of suitable age and discretion at the above named person(s) residence/business after attempting to personally serve the above named person(s) at his/her/their residence and place of business (if known) and mailing by first class mail a second copy to his/her/their residence.

   ❑   Posting a copy for each of the above named person(s) in a conspicuous place on the above identified property, being unable to personally serve a person of suitable age or discretion at the residence or known place(s) of business of the above named person(s) and mailing on the same date by first class mail a second copy to each above named person(s) to the address of the above identified property.

I declare under penalty of perjury that the above proof of service is true and correct.

Name _____   Date _____

30 Day Notice of Termination of Tenancy

To: _____

(Full names of tenants, subtenants, and all others in possession)

Rental Property: _____ Unit _____

(Street address, City, County, Zip)

You are notified that your tenancy of the above property is terminated effective 30 days from service of this notice or _____, whichever is later. At that time

(Date)

you must surrender possession of the premises. If you do not, an action for unlawful detainer will be filed. This may result in eviction as well as a judgment against you for payment of court costs.

You are obligated to continue to pay rent on the property until the date of termination.

_____

Date

_____

Landlord/Agent

PROOF OF SERVICE

I, the undersigned, being at least 18 years of age, served this notice, of which this is a true copy, on _____, the person(s) named above. The notice was served by:

❑   Personal delivery of a copy to the above named person(s).

❑   Delivery of a copy for each of the above named to a person of suitable age and discretion at the above named person(s) residence/business after attempting to personally serve the above named person(s) at his/her/their residence and place of business (if known) and mailing by first class mail a second copy to his/her/their residence.

❑   Posting a copy for each of the above named person(s) in a conspicuous place on the above identified property, being unable to personally serve a person of suitable age or discretion at the residence or known place(s) of business of the above named person(s) and mailing on the same date by first class mail a second copy to each above named person(s) to the address of the above identified property.

I declare under penalty of perjury that the above proof of service is true and correct.

Name _____   Date _____

Notice of Belief of Abandonment
(Real Property—Civil Code Sec. 1951.3)

To: _____

(Full names of tenants, subtenants, and all others in possession)

Rental Property: _____ Unit _____

(Street address, City, County, Zip)

Pursuant to Civil Code Section 1951.3 you are notified that the rent on the above identified property rented by you has not been paid for 14 or more consecutive days and the Landlord believes that you have abandoned the property.

Pursuant to Civil Code Section 1951.2 the property will be deemed abandoned and your lease or rental agreement will terminate on _____, _____, which date is not less than 18 days after the mailing of this notice, unless prior to this date the undersigned receives written notice from you at the address below stating:

1. Your intent not to abandon the property and
2. An address where you may be served by certified mail for unlawful detainer of the property.

You are required to pay the rent due on this property as required by your lease or rental agreement and failure to do so may result in court action against you.

_____

Date

_____

Landlord/Agent

_____

Address

Proof of Service

I, the undersigned, being at least 18 years of age, served this notice, of which this is a true copy, on _____, the person(s) named above. The notice was served by:

❏ Personal delivery of a copy to the above named person(s).

❏ Delivery of a copy for each of the above named to a person of suitable age and discretion at the above named person(s) residence/business after attempting to personally serve the above named person(s) at his/her/their residence and place of business (if known) and mailing by first class mail a second copy to his/her/their residence.

❏ Posting a copy for each of the above named person(s) in a conspicuous place on the above identified property, being unable to personally serve a person of suitable age or discretion at the residence or known place(s) of business of the above named person(s) and mailing on the same date by first class mail a second copy to each above named person(s) to the address of the above identified property.

I declare under penalty of perjury that the above proof of service is true and correct.

Name _____   Date _____

ATTORNEY OR PARTY WITHOUT ATTORNEY *(Name and Address)*:

TELEPHONE NO.:

FOR COURT USE ONLY

ATTORNEY FOR *(Name)*:

INSERT NAME OF COURT, JUDICIAL DISTRICT, AND BRANCH COURT, IF ANY:

CASE NAME:

CASE NUMBER:

CIVIL CASE COVER SHEET
(Case Cover Sheets)

1. ☐ Case category *(Insert code from list below for the ONE case type that best describes the case)*:

01 Abuse of Process
02 Administrative Agency Review
03 Antitrust/Unfair Business Practices
04 Asbestos
05 Asset Forfeiture
06 Breach of Contract/Warranty
07 Business Tort
08 Civil Rights *(Discrimination, False Arrest)*
09 Collections *(Money Owed, Open Book Accounts)*
10 Construction Defect
11 Contractual Arbitration
12 Declaratory Relief
13 Defamation *(Slander, Libel)*
14 Eminent Domain/Inverse Condemnation
15 Employment *(Labor Commissioner Appeals, EDD Actions, Wrongful Termination)*
16 Fraud
17 Injunctive Relief

18 Insurance Coverage/Subrogation
19 Intellectual Property
20 Enforcement of Judgment *(Sister State, Foreign, Out-of-Country Abstracts)*
21 Partnership and Corporate Governance
22 PI/PD/WD—Auto *(Personal Injury/Property Damage/ Wrongful Death)*
23 PI/PD/WD—Nonauto
24 Product Liability
25 Professional Negligence *(Medical or Legal Malpractice, etc.)*
26 Real Property *(Quiet Title)*
27 RICO
28 Securities Litigation
29 Tax Judgment
30 Toxic Tort/Environmental
31 Unlawful Detainer—Commercial
32 Unlawful Detainer—Residential
33 Wrongful Eviction
34 Other: _____

2. Type of remedies sought *(check all that apply)*: a. ☐ Monetary b. ☐ Nonmonetary c. ☐ Punitive
3. Number of causes of action:
4. Is this a class action suit? ☐ Yes ☐ No

Date:

▶

....
(TYPE OR PRINT NAME)

_____
(SIGNATURE OF PARTY OR ATTORNEY FOR PARTY)

NOTE TO PLAINTIFF

- This cover sheet shall accompany each civil action or proceeding, except those filed in small claims court or filed under the Probate Code, Family Law Code, or Welfare and Institutions Code.
- File this cover sheet in addition to any cover sheet required by local court rule.
- Do not serve this cover sheet with the complaint.
- This cover sheet shall be used for statistical purposes only and shall have no effect on the assignment of the case.

Form Adopted by Rule 982.2
Judicial Council of California
982.2(b)(1) [New July 1, 1996]

CIVIL CASE COVER SHEET
(Case Cover Sheets)

215

ATTORNEY OR PARTY WITHOUT ATTORNEY *(Name and Address):*	TELEPHONE NO.:	FOR COURT USE ONLY

ATTORNEY FOR *(Name):*

NAME OF COURT:

STREET ADDRESS:

MAILING ADDRESS:

CITY AND ZIP CODE:

BRANCH NAME:

PLAINTIFF:

DEFENDANT:

☐ DOES 1 TO _____

COMPLAINT—Unlawful Detainer*	CASE NUMBER:

1. a. Plaintiff is
   (1) ☐ an individual over the age of 18 years (4) ☐ a partnership
   (2) ☐ a public agency   (5) ☐ a corporation
   (3) ☐ other *(specify)*:

   b. ☐ Plaintiff has complied with the fictitious business name laws and is doing business under the fictitious name of
   (specify):

2. Defendants named above are in possession of the premises located at *(street address, apt. No., city, and county):*

3. Plaintiff's interest in the premises is ☐ as owner ☐ other *(specify):*

4. The true names and capacities of defendants sued as Does are unknown to plaintiff.

5. a. On or about *(date):*   defendants *(names):*

   (1) agreed to rent the premises for a ☐ month-to-month tenancy ☐ other tenancy *(specify):*
   (2) agreed to pay rent of $ payable ☐ monthly ☐ other *(specify frequency):*
       The rent is due on the ☐ first of the month ☐ other day *(specify):*
   b. This ☐ written ☐ oral agreement was made with
   (1) ☐ plaintiff   (3) ☐ plaintiff's predecessor in interest
   (2) ☐ plaintiff's agent   (4) ☐ other *(specify):*
   c. ☐ The defendants not named in item 5a are
      (1) ☐ subtenants (2) ☐ assignees (3) ☐ other *(specify):*
   d. ☐ The agreement was later changed as follows *(specify):*

   e. ☐ A copy of the written agreement is attached and labeled Exhibit 1.

6. ☐ a. Defendants *(names):*
      were served the following notice on the same date and in the same manner:
      (1) ☐ 3-day notice to pay rent or quit   (4) ☐ 3-day notice to quit
      (2) ☐ 3-day notice to perform covenants or quit (5) ☐ 30-day notice to quit
      (3) ☐ other *(specify):*
   b. (1) On *(date):*   the period stated in the notice expired at the end of the day.
      (2) Defendants failed to comply with the requirements of the notice by that date.
   c. All facts stated in the notice are true.
   d. ☐ The notice included an election of forfeiture.
   e. ☐ A copy of the notice is attached and labeled Exhibit 2.
   f. ☐ One or more defendants was served (1) with a different notice, or (2) on a different date, or (3) in a different manner,
      as stated in attachment 6f. *(Check item 7c and attach a statement providing the information required by items 6a-e
      and 7 for each defendant.)*

*NOTE: Do not use this form for evictions after sale (Code Civ. Proc., § 1161a).

(Continued on reverse)

Form Approved by the
Judicial Council of California
982.1(90) [Rev. July 1, 1996]

COMPLAINT—Unlawful Detainer

Civil Code, § 1940 et seq.;
Code of Civil Procedure, § 425.12

217

PLAINTIFF (Name):	CASE NUMBER:
DEFENDANT (Name):	

7. a. ☐ The notice in item 6a was served on the defendants named in item 6a as follows:

(1) ☐ by personally handing a copy to defendant on (date):

(2) ☐ by leaving a copy with (name or description): , a person of suitable age and discretion, on (date): at defendant's ☐ residence ☐ business AND mailing a copy to defendant at defendant's place of residence on (date): because defendant cannot be found at defendant's residence or usual place of business.

(3) ☐ by posting a copy on the premises on (date): (☐ and giving a copy to a person found residing at the premises) AND mailing a copy to defendant at the premises on (date):

    (a) ☐ because defendant's residence and usual place of business cannot be ascertained OR

    (b) ☐ because no person of suitable age or discretion can be found there.

(4) ☐ (not for 3-day notice; see Civil Code section 1946 before using) by sending a copy by certified or registered mail addressed to defendant on (date):

(5) ☐ (not for residential tenancies; see Civil Code section 1953 before using) in the manner specified in a written commercial lease between the parties.

b. ☐ (Name): was served on behalf of all defendants who signed a joint written rental agreement.

c. ☐ Information about service of notice on the defendants named in item 6f is stated in attachment 7c.

8. ☐ Plaintiff demands possession from each defendant because of expiration of a fixed-term lease.

9. ☐ At the time the 3-day notice to pay rent or quit was served, the amount of **rent due** was $

10. ☐ The fair rental value of the premises is $ per day.

11. ☐ Defendants' continued possession is malicious, and plaintiff is entitled to statutory damages under Code of Civil Procedure section 1174(b). (State specific facts supporting a claim up to $600 in attachment 11.)

12. ☐ A written agreement between the parties provides for attorney fees.

13. ☐ Defendants' tenancy is subject to the local rent control or eviction control ordinance of (city or county, title of ordinance, and date of passage):

Plaintiff has met all applicable requirements of the ordinances.

14. ☐ Other allegations are stated in attachment 14.

15. Plaintiff remits to the jurisdictional limit, if any, of the court.

16. PLAINTIFF REQUESTS

a. possession of the premises.

b. costs incurred in this proceeding.

c. ☐ past due rent of $

d. ☐ reasonable attorney fees.

e. ☐ forfeiture of the agreement.

f. ☐ damages at the rate stated in item 10 from (date): for each day defendants remain in possession through entry of judgment.

g. ☐ statutory damages up to $600 for the conduct alleged in item 11.

h. ☐ other (specify):

17. ☐ Number of pages attached (specify):

UNLAWFUL DETAINER ASSISTANT (Business and Professions Code sections 6400-6415)

18. (must be answered in all cases) An unlawful detainer assistant ☐ did **not** ☐ did for compensation give advice or assistance with this form. (If plaintiff has received **any** help or advice for pay from an unlawful detainer assistant, state):

a. Assistant's name: b. Telephone No.:

c. Street address, city, and ZIP:

d. County of registration: e. Registration No.:   f. Expires on (date):

▶

....
(TYPE OR PRINT NAME)   (SIGNATURE OF PLAINTIFF OR ATTORNEY)

VERIFICATION

(Use a different verification form if the verification is by an attorney or for a corporation or partnership.)

I am the plaintiff in this proceeding and have read this complaint. I declare under penalty of perjury under the laws of the State of California that the foregoing is true and correct.

Date:

▶

....
(TYPE OR PRINT NAME)   (SIGNATURE OF PLAINTIFF)

SUMMONS
(CITACION JUDICIAL)

UNLAWFUL DETAINER—EVICTION
(PROCESO DE DESAHUCIO—EVICCION)

NOTICE TO DEFENDANT: *(Aviso a acusado)*

FOR COURT USE ONLY
(SOLO PARA USO DE LA CORTE)

YOU ARE BEING SUED BY PLAINTIFF:
(A Ud. le está demandando)

You have **5 DAYS** after this summons is served on you to file a typewritten response at this court. (To calculate the five days, count Saturday and Sunday, but do not count other court holidays.)	*Después de que le entreguen esta citación judicial usted tiene un plazo de 5 DIAS para presentar una respuesta escrita a máquina en esta corte. (Para calcular los cinco días, cuente el sábado y el domingo, pero no cuente ningún otro día feriado observado por la corte.)*
A letter or phone call will not protect you. Your typewritten response must be in proper legal form if you want the court to hear your case.	*Una carta o una llamada telefónica no le ofrecerá protección; su respuesta escrita a máquina tiene que cumplir con las formalidades legales apropiadas si usted quiere que la corte escuche su caso.*
If you do not file your response on time, you may lose the case, you may be evicted, and your wages, money, and property may be taken without further warning from the court.	*Si usted no presenta su respuesta a tiempo, puede perder el caso, le pueden obligar a desalojar su casa, y le pueden quitar su salario, su dinero y otras cosas de su propiedad sin aviso adicional por parte de la corte.*
There are other legal requirements. You may want to call an attorney right away. If you do not know an attorney, you may call an attorney referral service or a legal aid office *(listed in the phone book)*.	*Existen otros requisitos legales. Puede que usted quiera llamar a un abogado inmediatamente. Si no conoce a un abogado, puede llamar a un servicio de referencia de abogados o a una oficina de ayuda legal (vea el directorio telefónico).*

The name and address of the court is: *(El nombre y dirección de la corte es)*

CASE NUMBER: *(Número del caso)*

The name, address, and telephone number of plaintiff's attorney, or plaintiff without an attorney, is:
(El nombre, la dirección y el número de teléfono del abogado del demandante, o del demandante que no tiene abogado, es)

(Must be answered in all cases) An **unlawful detainer assistant (B&P 6400-6415)** ☐ did **not** ☐ did for compensation give advice or assistance with this form. *(If plaintiff has received **any** help or advice for pay from an unlawful detainer assistant, state)*:

a. Assistant's name:

c. Street address, city, and ZIP:

b. Telephone No.:

d. County of registration:

e. Registration No.:

f. Expires on *(date)*:

Date:
(Fecha)

Clerk, by _____ , Deputy
(Actuario) *(Delegado)*

[SEAL]

NOTICE TO THE PERSON SERVED: You are served
1. ☐ as an individual defendant.
2. ☐ as the person sued under the fictitious name of *(specify)*:

3. ☐ on behalf of *(specify)*:

under: ☐ CCP 416.10 (corporation)   ☐ CCP 416.60 (minor)
☐ CCP 416.20 (defunct corporation)   ☐ CCP 416.70 (conservatee)
☐ CCP 416.40 (association or partnership)   ☐ CCP 416.90 (individual)
☐ other:
4. ☐ by personal delivery on *(date)*:
(See reverse for Proof of Service)

Form Adopted by Rule 982
Judicial Council of California
982(a)(11) [Rev. January 1, 1997]

SUMMONS—UNLAWFUL DETAINER

Code of Civil Procedure, §§ 412.20, 1167

219

PLAINTIFF:	CASE NUMBER:
DEFENDANT:	

PROOF OF SERVICE

1. At the time of service I was at least 18 years of age and not a party to this action, and **I served copies** of the *(specify documents)*:

2. a. Party served *(specify name of party as shown on the documents served)*:

   b. Person served: ☐ party in item 2a   ☐ other *(specify name and title or relationship to the party named in item 2a)*:

   c. Address:

3. I served the party named in item 2
   a. ☐ **by personally delivering** the copies (1) on *(date)*:   (2) at *(time)*:
   b. ☐ **by leaving** the copies with or in the presence of *(name and title or relationship to person indicated in item 2b)*:

      (1) ☐ **(business)** a person at least 18 years of age apparently in charge at the office or usual place of business of the person served. I informed him or her of the general nature of the papers.
      (2) ☐ **(home)** a competent member of the household (at least 18 years of age) at the dwelling house or usual place of abode of the person served. I informed him or her of the general nature of the papers.
      (3) on *(date)*:   (4) at *(time)*:
      (5) ☐ A **declaration of diligence** is attached. *(Substituted service on natural person, minor, conservatee, or candidate.)*
   c. ☐ **by mailing** the copies to the person served, addressed as shown in item 2c, by first-class mail, postage prepaid,
      (1) on *(date)*:   (2) from *(city)*:
      (3) ☐ with two copies of the *Notice and Acknowledgment of Receipt* and a postage-paid return envelope addressed to me.
      (4) ☐ to an address outside California with return receipt requested.   ← *(Attach completed form.)* ⬏
   d. ☐ **by** causing copies to be mailed. A declaration of mailing is attached.
   e. ☐ **other** *(specify other manner of service and authorizing code section)*:

4. The "Notice to the Person Served" (on the summons) was completed as follows:
   a. ☐ as an individual defendant.
   b. ☐ as the person sued under the fictitious name of *(specify)*:
   c. ☐ on behalf of *(specify)*:
      under: ☐ CCP 416.10 (corporation)   ☐ CCP 416.60 (minor)   ☐ other:
                ☐ CCP 416.20 (defunct corporation)   ☐ CCP 416.70 (conservatee)
                ☐ CCP 416.40 (association or partnership)   ☐ CCP 416.90 (individual)

5. **Person serving** *(name, address, and telephone number)*:
              a. **Fee** for service: $
              b. ☐ Not a registered California process server
              c. ☐ Exempt from registration under B&P § 22350(b)
              d. ☐ Registered California process server
                   (1) ☐ Employee or independent contractor
                   (2) Registration No.:
                   (3) County:
                   (4) Expiration *(date)*:

6. ☐ **I declare** under penalty of perjury under the laws of the State of California that the foregoing is true and correct.

7. ☐ **I am a California sheriff, marshal, or constable and** I certify that the foregoing is true and correct.

Date:

▶ _____
                                   (SIGNATURE)

NOTICE: EVERYONE WHO LIVES IN THIS RENTAL UNIT MAY BE EVICTED BY COURT ORDER. READ THIS FORM IF YOU LIVE HERE AND IF YOUR NAME IS NOT ON THE ATTACHED SUMMONS AND COMPLAINT.
1. If you live here and you do not complete and submit this form within 10 days of the date of service shown on this form, you will be evicted without further hearing by the court along with the persons named in the Summons and Complaint.
2. If you file this form, your claim will be determined in the eviction action against the persons named in the Complaint.
3. If you do not file this form, you will be evicted without further hearing.

CLAIMANT OR CLAIMANT'S ATTORNEY *(Name and Address)*:	TELEPHONE NO.:	*FOR COURT USE ONLY*

ATTORNEY FOR *(Name)*:

NAME OF COURT:
STREET ADDRESS:
MAILING ADDRESS:
CITY AND ZIP CODE:
BRANCH NAME:

PLAINTIFF:

DEFENDANT:

PREJUDGMENT CLAIM OF RIGHT TO POSSESSION	CASE NUMBER:

Complete this form only if ALL of these statements are true: 1. **You are NOT named in the accompanying Summons and Complaint.** 2. **You occupied the premises on or before the date the unlawful detainer (eviction) Complaint was filed.** 3. **You still occupy the premises.**	*(To be completed by the process server)* DATE OF SERVICE: *(Date that this form is served or delivered, and posted, and mailed by the officer or process server)*

I DECLARE THE FOLLOWING UNDER PENALTY OF PERJURY:
1. My name is *(specify)*:

2. I reside at *(street address, unit No., city and ZIP code)*:

3. The address of "the premises" subject to this claim is *(address)*:

4. On *(insert date)*: _____ , the landlord or the landlord's authorized agent filed a complaint to recover possession of the premises. *(This date is the court filing date on the accompanying Summons and Complaint.*

5. I occupied the premises on the date the complaint was filed *(the date in item 4)*. I have continued to occupy the premises ever since.

6. I was at least 18 years of age on the date the complaint was filed *(the date in item 4)*.

7. I claim a right to possession of the premises because I occupied the premises on the date the complaint was filed *(the date in item 4)*.

8. I was not named in the Summons and Complaint.

9. I understand that if I make this claim of right to possession, I will be added as a defendant to the unlawful detainer (eviction) action.

10. *(Filing fee)* I understand that I must go to the court and pay a filing fee of $ _____ or file with the court the form "Application for Waiver of Court Fees and Costs." I understand that if I don't pay the filing fee or file with the court the form for waiver of court fees within 10 days from the date of service on this form (excluding court holidays), I will not be entitled to make a claim of right to possession.

(Continued on reverse)

CP10.5 [New January 1, 1991]	**PREJUDGMENT CLAIM OF RIGHT TO POSSESSION**	Code of Civil Procedure §§ 415.46, 715.010, 715.020, 1174.25

PLAINTIFF *(Name)*:	CASE NUMBER:
DEFENDANT *(Name)*:	

> **NOTICE: If you fail to file this claim, you will be evicted without further hearing.**

11. *(Response required within five days after you file this form)* I understand that I will have *five days* (excluding court holidays) to file a response to the Summons and Complaint after I file this Prejudgment Claim of Right to Possession form.

12. **Rental agreement.** I have *(check all that apply to you)*:
   a. ☐ an oral rental agreement with the landlord.
   b. ☐ a written rental agreement with the landlord.
   c. ☐ an oral rental agreement with a person other than the landlord.
   d. ☐ a written rental agreement with a person other than the landlord.
   e. ☐ other *(explain)*:

I declare under penalty of perjury under the laws of the State of California that the foregoing is true and correct.

> WARNING: Perjury is a felony punishable by imprisonment in the state prison.

Date:

. . . . ▶ _____
           (TYPE OR PRINT NAME)   (SIGNATURE OF CLAIMANT)

> **NOTICE:** If you file this claim of right to possession, the unlawful detainer (eviction) action against you will be determined at trial. At trial, you may be found liable for rent, costs, and, in some cases, treble damages.

— NOTICE TO OCCUPANTS —

YOU MUST ACT AT ONCE if all the following are true:
   1. **You are NOT named in the accompanying Summons and Complaint.**
   2. **You occupied the premises on or before the date the unlawful detainer (eviction) complaint was filed.** *(The date is the court filing date on the accompanying Summons and Complaint.)*
   3. **You still occupy the premises.**

(Where to file this form) You can complete and SUBMIT THIS CLAIM FORM WITHIN 10 DAYS from the date of service (on the reverse of this form) at the court where the unlawful detainer (eviction) complaint was filed.

(What will happen if you do not file this form) If you do not complete and submit this form and pay a filing fee or file the form for proceeding in forma pauperis if you cannot pay the fee), YOU WILL BE EVICTED.

After this form is properly filed, you will be added as a defendant in the unlawful detainer (eviction) action and your right to occupy the premises will be decided by the court. *If you do not file this claim, you will be evicted without a hearing.*

ATTORNEY OR PARTY WITHOUT ATTORNEY *(Name and Address)*:	TELEPHONE NO.:	*FOR COURT USE ONLY*

ATTORNEY FOR *(Name)*:

Insert name of court and name of judicial district and branch court, if any:

PLAINTIFF:

DEFENDANT:

REQUEST FOR (Application)	☐ ENTRY OF DEFAULT ☐ COURT JUDGMENT	☐ CLERK'S JUDGMENT	CASE NUMBER:

1. TO THE CLERK: On the complaint or cross-complaint filed

  a. On *(date)*:

  b. By *(name)*:

  c. ☐ Enter default of defendant *(names)*:

  d. ☐ I request a court judgment under CCP 585(b), (c), 989, etc. *(Testimony required. Apply to the clerk for a hearing date, unless the court will enter a judgment on an affidavit under CCP 585(d).)*

  e. ☐ Enter clerk's judgment

    (1) ☐ For restitution of the premises only and issue a writ of execution on the judgment. CCP 1174(c) does not apply. (CCP 1169) ☐ Include in the judgment all tenants, subtenants, named claimants, and other occupants of the premises. The Prejudgment Claim of Right to Possession was served in compliance with CCP 415.46.

    (2) ☐ Under CCP 585(a). *(Complete the declaration under CCP 585.5 on the reverse (item 4).)*

    (3) ☐ For default previously entered on *(date)*:

2. **Judgment to be entered**

	Amount	Credits Acknowledged	Balance
a. Demand of complaint · · · · · · · · · ·	$	$	$
b. Statement of damages (CCP 425.11) *(superior court only)*†			
(1) Special · · · · · · · · · · · · · ·	$	$	$
(2) General · · · · · · · · · · · · · · ·	$	$	$
c. Interest · · · · · · · · · · · · · · · · · ·	$	$	$
d. Costs *(see reverse)* · · · · · · · · · · ·	$	$	$
e. Attorney fees · · · · · · · · · · · · · · ·	$	$	$
f. **TOTALS** · · · · · · · · · · · · · · · · ·	$	$	$

  g. **Daily damages** were demanded in complaint at the rate of: $ per day beginning *(date)*:

3. ☐ *(check if filed in an unlawful detainer case)* **UNLAWFUL DETAINER ASSISTANT** information is on the reverse *(complete item 3).*

Date:

▶

. . . .

(TYPE OR PRINT NAME)   (SIGNATURE OF PLAINTIFF OR ATTORNEY FOR PLAINTIFF)

† *Personal injury or wrongful death actions only.*

FOR COURT USE ONLY	(1) ☐ Default entered as requested on *(date)*:
	(2) ☐ Default NOT entered as requested *(state reason)*:
	Clerk, by: _____

(Continued on reverse)

Form Adopted by the Judicial Council of California
982(a)(6) [Rev. July 1, 1996*]

REQUEST FOR ENTRY OF DEFAULT
(Application to Enter Default)

Code of Civil Procedure, §§ 585-587, 1169

*See note on reverse.

223

SHORT TITLE:	CASE NUMBER:

3. **UNLAWFUL DETAINER ASSISTANT** *(Business and Professions Code sections 6400-6415)* An **unlawful detainer assistant**
[ ] did **not** [ ] did for compensation give advice or assistance with this form. *(If declarant has received **any** help or advice for pay from an unlawful detainer assistant, state):*
a. Assistant's name:　　　　　　　　　　　　　　　　b. Telephone No.:
c. Street address, city, and ZIP:

d. County of registration:　　　　　e. Registration No.:　　　　f. Expires on *(date)*

4. [ ] **DECLARATION UNDER CCP 585.5** *(Required for clerk's judgment under CCP 585(a))* This action
a. [ ] is [ ] is not on a contract or installment sale for goods or services subject to CC 1801, etc. (Unruh Act).
b. [ ] is [ ] is not on a conditional sales contract subject to CC 2981, etc. (Rees-Levering Motor Vehicle Sales and Finance
c. [ ] is [ ] Act).
is not on an obligation for goods, services, loans, or extensions of credit subject to CCP 395(b).

5. **DECLARATION OF MAILING (CCP 587)** A copy of this Request for Entry of Default was
a. [ ] **not mailed** to the following defendants whose addresses are **unknown** to plaintiff or plaintiff's attorney *(names):*

b. [ ] **mailed** first-class, postage prepaid, in a sealed envelope addressed to each defendant's attorney of record or, if none, to each defendant's last known address as follows:
(1) Mailed on *(date):*　　　　　　(2) To *(specify names and addresses shown on the envelopes):*

I declare under penalty of perjury under the laws of the State of California that the foregoing items 3, 4, and 5 are true and correct.
Date:

....　　　▶ _____
(TYPE OR PRINT NAME)　　　　　　　(SIGNATURE OF DECLARANT)

6. **MEMORANDUM OF COSTS** *(Required if judgment requested)* **Costs and Disbursements** are as follows (CCP 1033.5):
a. Clerk's filing fees · · · · · · · · · · · · · · · · · · $
b. Process server's fees · · · · · · · · · · · · · · · $
c. Other *(specify):* · · · · · · · · · · · · · · · · · · $
d · $
e. **TOTAL** · $
f. [ ] Costs and disbursements are waived.

I am the attorney, agent, or party who claims these costs. To the best of my knowledge and belief this memorandum of costs is correct and these costs were necessarily incurred in this case.

I declare under penalty of perjury under the laws of the State of California that the foregoing is true and correct.
Date:

....　　　▶ _____
(TYPE OR PRINT NAME)　　　　　　　(SIGNATURE OF DECLARANT)

7. [ ] **DECLARATION OF NONMILITARY STATUS** *(Required for a judgment)* No defendant named in item 1c of the application is in the military service so as to be entitled to the benefits of the Soldiers' and Sailors' Civil Relief Act of 1940 (50 U.S.C.appen. § 501 et seq.).

I declare under penalty of perjury under the laws of the State of California that the foregoing is true and correct.
Date:

....　　　▶ _____
(TYPE OR PRINT NAME)　　　　　　　(SIGNATURE OF DECLARANT)

NOTE: Continued use of form 982(a)(6) (Rev. Sept. 30, 1991) is authorized until June 30, 1997, *except* in unlawful detainer proceedings.

982(a)(6) [Rev. July 1, 1996*]　　　**REQUEST FOR ENTRY OF DEFAULT**　　　Page two
(Application to Enter Default)

ATTORNEY OR PARTY WITHOUT ATTORNEY *(Name and Address)*:	FOR COURT USE ONLY
ATTORNEY FOR *(Name)*:	
Insert name of court and name of judicial district and branch court, if any:	
PLAINTIFF: DEFENDANT:	

CLERK'S JUDGMENT FOR POSSESSION UNLAWFUL DETAINER	CASE NUMBER

The defendant(s) in this cause having been served with a summons and complaint, having failed to appear and answer the complaint within the time allowed by law, and default having been entered against them, upon application having been filed pursuant to Code of Civil procedure §1169, the Clerk hereby enters the following judgment:

ADJUDGED that plaintiff(s) _____
have and recover from defendant(s) _____
the restitution and possession of those premises situated in the county of _____,
state of California, more particularly described as follows: _____
_____

This judgment was entered on

_____
in _____Book _____
at Page _____

_____
                                   Clerk
By:

_____
                        Deputy Clerk

ATTORNEY OR PARTY WITHOUT ATTORNEY *(Name and Address):* TELEPHONE NO.: **FOR RECORDER'S USE ONLY**

☐ Recording requested by and return to:

☐ ATTORNEY FOR ☐ JUDGMENT CREDITOR ☐ ASSIGNEE OF RECORD

NAME OF COURT:

STREET ADDRESS:

MAILING ADDRESS:

CITY AND ZIP CODE:

BRANCH NAME:

PLAINTIFF:

DEFENDANT:

WRIT OF	☐ **EXECUTION (Money Judgment)**
	☐ **POSSESSION OF** ☐ **Personal Property**
	☐ **Real Property**
	☐ **SALE**

CASE NUMBER:

FOR COURT USE ONLY

1. **To the Sheriff or any Marshal or Constable of the County of:**

   You are directed to enforce the judgment described below with daily interest and your costs as provided by law.

2. **To any registered process server:** You are authorized to serve this writ only in accord with CCP 699.080 or CCP 715.040.

3. *(Name):*

   is the ☐ judgment creditor ☐ assignee of record

   whose address is shown on this form above the court's name.

4. **Judgment debtor** *(name and last known address):*

☐ additional judgment debtors on reverse

5. **Judgment entered** on *(date):*

6. ☐ **Judgment renewed** on *(dates):*

7. **Notice of sale** under this writ

   a. ☐ has not been requested.

   b. ☐ has been requested *(see reverse).*

8. ☐ Joint debtor information on reverse.

[SEAL]

9. ☐ See reverse for information on real or personal property to be delivered under a writ of possession or sold under a writ of sale.

10. ☐ This writ is issued on a sister-state judgment.

11. Total judgment . . . . $

12. Costs after judgment (per filed order or memo CCP 685.090) . . . . $

13. Subtotal *(add 11 and 12)* . . . . $ _____

14. Credits . . . . $

15. Subtotal *(subtract 14 from 13)* . . . . . $ _____

16. Interest after judgment (per filed affidavit CCP 685.050) . . . . $

17. Fee for issuance of writ . . . . $

18. **Total** *(add 15, 16, and 17)* . . . . . $ _____

19. Levying officer:

    (a) Add daily interest from date of writ *(at the legal rate on 15)* of . . . . . $

    (b) Pay directly to court costs included in 11 and 17 (GC 6103.5, 68511.3; CCP 699.520(i)) . . . . $

20. ☐ The amounts called for in items 11-19 are different for each debtor. These amounts are stated for each debtor on Attachment 20.

Issued on *(date):*   Clerk, by _____, Deputy

— NOTICE TO PERSON SERVED: SEE REVERSE FOR IMPORTANT INFORMATION. —

(Continued on reverse)

WRIT OF EXECUTION

Form Approved by the
Judicial Council of California
EJ-130 [Rev. January 1, 1997*]

Code of Civil Procedure, §§ 699.520, 712.010, 715.010

See note on reverse.

227

SHORT TITLE:	CASE NUMBER:

— Items continued from the first page —

4. ☐ **Additional judgment debtor** *(name and last known address)*:

7. ☐ **Notice of sale** has been requested by *(name and address)*:

8. ☐ **Joint debtor** was declared bound by the judgment (CCP 989-994)
    a. on *(date)*:
    b. name and address of joint debtor:

    a. on *(date)*:
    b. name and address of joint debtor:

    c. ☐ additional costs against certain joint debtors *(itemize)*:

9. ☐ *(Writ of Possession or Writ of Sale)* **Judgment** was entered for the following:
    a. ☐ Possession of real property: The complaint was filed on *(date)*:   **(Check (1) or (2))**:
        (1) ☐ The Prejudgment Claim of Right to Possession was served in compliance with CCP 415.46.
                The judgment includes all tenants, subtenants, named claimants, and other occupants of the premises.
        (2) ☐ The Prejudgment Claim of Right to Possession was NOT served in compliance with CCP 415.46.
            (a) $ was the daily rental value on the date the complaint was filed.
            (b) The court will hear objections to enforcement of the judgment under CCP 1174.3 on the following
                dates *(specify)*:
    b. ☐ Possession of personal property
        ☐ If delivery cannot be had, then for the value *(itemize in 9e)* specified in the judgment or supplemental order.
    c. ☐ Sale of personal property
    d. ☐ Sale of real property
    e. Description of property:

— NOTICE TO PERSON SERVED —

WRIT OF EXECUTION OR SALE. Your rights and duties are indicated on the accompanying Notice of Levy.
WRIT OF POSSESSION OF PERSONAL PROPERTY. If the levying officer is not able to take custody of the property, the levying officer will make a demand upon you for the property. If custody is not obtained following demand, the judgment may be enforced as a money judgment for the value of the property specified in the judgment or in a supplemental order.
WRIT OF POSSESSION OF REAL PROPERTY. If the premises are not vacated within five days after the date of service on the occupant or, if service is by posting, within five days after service on you, the levying officer will remove the occupants from the real property and place the judgment creditor in possession of the property. Except for a mobile home, personal property remaining on the premises will be sold or otherwise disposed of in accordance with CCP 1174 unless you or the owner of the property pays the judgment creditor the reasonable cost of storage and takes possession of the personal property not later than 15 days after the time the judgment creditor takes possession of the premises.
► *A Claim of Right to Possession form accompanies this writ (unless the Summons was served in compliance with CCP 415.46).*

EJ-130 [Rev. January 1, 1997*]   * NOTE: Continued use of form EJ-130 (Rev. July 1, 1996) is authorized through December 31, 1997.   Page two
WRIT OF EXECUTION

ATTORNEY OR PARTY WITHOUT ATTORNEY *(Name and Address)*:	FOR COURT USE ONLY
ATTORNEY FOR *(Name)*:	
Insert name of court and name of judicial district and branch court, if any:	
PLAINTIFF: DEFENDANT:	
DEFAULT JUDGMENT **UNLAWFUL DETAINER**	CASE NUMBER

The defendant(s) in this cause having been served with a summons and complaint, having failed to appear and answer the complaint within the time allowed by law, and default having been entered against them, upon application having been filed by plaintiff(s), and the Court having ☐ heard the testimony and considered the evidence
   ☐ received the declaration submitted by plaintiff(s)   it is,

ORDERED AND ADJUDGED that plaintiff(s) _____
_____ have and recover from defendant(s) _____
_____ the restitution and possession of those premises situated in the county of
_____, state of California, more particularly described as follows: _____
_____

for costs in the amount of $_____ and rent/damages in the amount of $_____
for a total of $_____.

Date:_____

_____
                                 Judge

This judgment was entered on

_____
in _____Book _____
at Page _____
_____
                                 Clerk
By:
_____
                          Deputy Clerk

ATTORNEY OR PARTY WITHOUT ATTORNEY *(Name and Address)*:	FOR COURT USE ONLY
ATTORNEY FOR *(Name)*:	
Insert name of court and name of judicial district and branch court, if any:	
PLAINTIFF: DEFENDANT:	

DECLARATION IN SUPPORT OF DEFAULT JUDGMENT IN LIEU OF TESTIMONY	CASE NUMBER

The undersigned, after first being sworn, deposes and says:

1. I am the plaintiff in the above styles case and the owner of the premises at _____ _____, in the city of _____, County of _____, state of California.

2. Defendant(s) rented the premises from me on _____ by _____ agreement to pay $_____ per _____, payable in advance on the _____ of each _____.

3. The current rent on the premises is ☐ the same ☐ $_____, having been raised:
    ☐ by agreement and subsequent payment
    ☐ by 30 days written notice

4. The daily rental value on the date of filing the complaint was $_____.

5. Defendant went into possession of the premises pursuant to the aforementioned agreement and remains in possession.

6. On _____ defendant(s) were in default in payment of rent in the amount of $_____ and I caused defendants to be served with written notice to pay the amount due or surrender possession of the premises within three days after service of the notice.

7. After Defendant(s) failed to pay said rent within said three days, I caused to be filed and served upon defendant(s) complaint(s) and summon(es) for unlawful detainer in the cause, in compliance with any applicable local rent control or eviction protection ordinance.

8. Defendant(s) have failed to answer or respond to said complaint as allowed by law.

9. Defendant(s)   ☐ vacated the premises on _____
    ☐ have not yet vacated the premises.

10. Rent remains unpaid for the period of from _____ to _____ _____ in the total amount of $_____ plus $_____ per day until defendant(s) vacate the premises.

I declare under penalty of perjury under the laws of the state of California that the above statements are true and correct. and that if sworn as a witness I could swear to the above facts.

WHEREFORE I pray that judgment be entered against defendant(s) for possession of said premises, filing fees, service or process fees and other costs in this action of $_____, and past due rent of $_____.

Dated this ____ day of _____, _____, at _____, county of _____, state of California.

_____
Plaintiff

ATTORNEY OR PARTY WITHOUT ATTORNEY *(Name and Address)*:	FOR COURT USE ONLY
ATTORNEY FOR *(Name)*:	
Insert name of court and name of judicial district and branch court, if any:	
PLAINTIFF: DEFENDANT:	

JUDGMENT AFTER TRIAL **UNLAWFUL DETAINER**	CASE NUMBER

This cause came on for hearing on this date at the request of plaintiff(s) in courtroom _____
before the Honorable _____,
with plaintiff(s) _____
appearing in pro per and defendant(s) _____
_____ having

       ☐ not appeared

       ☐ appeared in pro per

       ☐ appeared through counsel _____

and the court having heard the testimony and considered the evidence, it is

ORDERED AND ADJUDGED that plaintiff(s)
_____ have and recover from defendant(s)
_____ the restitution and possession of
those premises situated in the county of _____, state of California, more particularly described as follows: _____
_____,
costs in the amount of $_____ and damages in the amount of $_____.

Date:_____

_____
Judge

This judgment was entered on

_____

in _____Book _____
at Page _____

_____
                           Clerk

By:

_____
               Deputy Clerk

ATTORNEY OR PARTY WITHOUT ATTORNEY *(Name and Address)*:	FOR COURT USE ONLY

ATTORNEY FOR *(Name)*:

Insert name of court and name of judicial district and branch court, if any:

PLAINTIFF:

DEFENDANT:

STIPULATION FOR ENTRY OF JUDGMENT	CASE NUMBER

The parties to this action hereby stipulate as follows:

1. The defendant(s) acknowledge the sum of $_____ to be due and owing to the plaintiff(s).

2. In partial payment of the above debt, the defendant(s) agree(s) to immediately pay to the plaintiff(s) the amount of $_____, and the balance of the above debt will be paid as follows:
$_____ due on _____ $_____ due on _____
$_____ due on _____ $_____ due on _____
In addition to the above-stated amounts, the defendant, as a further condition hereof, agrees to pay to the plaintiffs the sum of $_____ on the ___ day of each month, in cash, representing periodic installments payable under the rental agreement between the parties for rent of the subject residential premises.

3. If all of the foregoing sums are paid as set out above, in full, and when due, this action shall be dismissed with prejudice, and each party does hereby release the other by a general release as if set out here in full.

4. If any of the above sums are not paid as set out above, the plaintiff(s) shall be entitled to a Judgment Pursuant to Stipulation for possession and or amounts due under this Stipulation. Defendant(s) hereby consent to the entry of said Judgment upon filing by Plaintiff(s) of an affidavit stating that the Stipulation has not been complied with and the amounts due. Defendant(s) hereby waive the right to notice or hearing before entry of said judgment.

Dated: _____, _____.

_____   _____
Plaintiff   Defendant

_____   _____
Plaintiff   Defendant

ATTORNEY OR PARTY WITHOUT ATTORNEY *(Name and Address)*:	FOR COURT USE ONLY
ATTORNEY FOR *(Name)*:	
Insert name of court and name of judicial district and branch court, if any:	
PLAINTIFF: DEFENDANT:	

JUDGMENT PURSUANT TO STIPULATION	CASE NUMBER

Pursuant to the stipulation entered into between the plaintiff(s) and defendant(s) in this cause, it is

ORDERED AND ADJUDGED that plaintiff(s) _____
have and recover from defendant(s) _____
the restitution and possession of those premises situated in the county of _____,
state of California, more particularly described as follows: _____
_____,

costs in the amount of $_____ and damages in the amount of $_____.

Date:_____

_____
Judge

This judgment was entered on

_____
in _____ Book _____
at Page _____
_____
Clerk
By:
_____
Deputy Clerk

ATTORNEY OR PARTY WITHOUT ATTORNEY *(Name and Address):*	TELEPHONE NO.:	*FOR COURT USE ONLY*

ATTORNEY FOR *(Name)*:

NAME OF COURT:
STREET ADDRESS:
MAILING ADDRESS:
CITY AND ZIP CODE:
BRANCH NAME:

PLAINTIFF:

DEFENDANT:

CASE NUMBER:

APPLICATION AND ORDER FOR APPEARANCE AND EXAMINATION

[ ] **ENFORCEMENT OF JUDGMENT** [ ] **ATTACHMENT (Third Person)**

[ ] **Judgment Debtor** [ ] **Third Person**

ORDER TO APPEAR FOR EXAMINATION

1. TO *(name)*:

2. YOU ARE ORDERED TO APPEAR personally before this court, or before a referee appointed by the court, to

   a. [ ] furnish information to aid in enforcement of a money judgment against you.

   b. [ ] answer concerning property of the judgment debtor in your possession or control or concerning a debt you owe the judgment debtor.

   c. [ ] answer concerning property of the defendant in your possession or control or concerning a debt you owe the defendant that is subject to attachment.

Date: Time: Dept. or Div.: Rm.:
Address of court [ ] shown above [ ] is:

3. This order may be served by a sheriff, marshal, constable, registered process server, **or** the following specially appointed person *(name)*:

Date: _____

▶ _____
(SIGNATURE OF JUDGE OR REFEREE)

This order must be served not less than 10 days before the date set for the examination.

IMPORTANT NOTICES ON REVERSE

APPLICATION FOR ORDER TO APPEAR FOR EXAMINATION

1. [ ] Judgment creditor [ ] Assignee of record [ ] Plaintiff who has a right to attach order
   applies for an order requiring *(name)*: to appear and furnish information
   to aid in enforcement of the money judgment or to answer concerning property or debt.

2. The person to be examined is
   [ ] the judgment debtor
   [ ] a third person (1) who has possession or control of property belonging to the judgment debtor or the defendant or (2) who owes the judgment debtor or the defendant more than $250. An affidavit supporting this application under CCP § 491.110 or § 708.120 is attached.

3. The person to be examined resides or has a place of business in this county or within 150 miles of the place of examination.

4. [ ] This court is **not** the court in which the money judgment is entered or *(attachment only)* the court that issued the writ of attachment. An affidavit supporting an application under CCP § 491.150 or § 708.160 is attached.

5. [ ] The judgment debtor has been examined within the past 120 days. An affidavit showing good cause for another examination is attached.

I declare under penalty of perjury under the laws of the State of California that the foregoing is true and correct.

Date: _____

. . . .   ▶ _____
(TYPE OR PRINT NAME)   *(SIGNATURE OF DECLARANT)*

Form Approved by the
Judicial Council of California
AT-138, EJ-125 [New July 1, 1984]

**APPLICATION AND ORDER
FOR APPEARANCE AND EXAMINATION**
(Attachment—Enforcement of Judgment)

CCP 491.110, 708.110, 708.120

239

APPEARANCE OF JUDGMENT DEBTOR (ENFORCEMENT OF JUDGMENT)

NOTICE TO JUDGMENT DEBTOR If you fail to appear at the time and place specified in this order, you may be subject to arrest and punishment for contempt of court, and the court may make an order requiring you to pay the reasonable attorney fees incurred by the judgment creditor in this proceeding.

APPEARANCE OF A THIRD PERSON
(ENFORCEMENT OF JUDGMENT)

(1) NOTICE TO PERSON SERVED If you fail to appear at the time and place specified in this order, you may be subject to arrest and punishment for contempt of court, and the court may make an order requiring you to pay the reasonable attorney fees incurred by the judgment creditor in this proceeding.

(2) NOTICE TO JUDGMENT DEBTOR The person in whose favor the judgment was entered in this action claims that the person to be examined pursuant to this order has possession or control of property which is yours or owes you a debt. This property or debt is as follows *(Describe the property or debt using typewritten capital letters)*:

If you claim that all or any portion of this property or debt is exempt from enforcement of the money judgment, you must file your exemption claim in writing with the court and have a copy personally served on the judgment creditor not later than three days before the date set for the examination. You must appear at the time and place set for the examination to establish your claim of exemption or your exemption may be waived.

APPEARANCE OF A THIRD PERSON (ATTACHMENT)

NOTICE TO PERSON SERVED If you fail to appear at the time and place specified in this order, you may be subject to arrest and punishment for contempt of court, and the court may make an order requiring you to pay the reasonable attorney fees incurred by the plaintiff in this proceeding.

APPEARANCE OF A CORPORATION, PARTNERSHIP,
ASSOCIATION, TRUST, OR OTHER ORGANIZATION

It is your duty to designate one or more of the following to appear and be examined: officers, directors, managing agents, or other persons who are familiar with your property and debts.

AT-138, EJ-125
[New July 1, 1984]

APPLICATION AND ORDER FOR APPEARANCE AND EXAMINATION
(Attachment—Enforcement of Judgment)

Page two

Judgment Debtor Questionnaire

Full name: _____

Driver's license number: _____

List any other names used by you: _____

Are you married? Yes_____ No_____

If yes, complete the following:

Spouse's full name: _____

Spouse's driver's license number: _____

List any other names used by your spouse: _____

Employment

Your occupation: _____ Employed _____ Self Employed _____

Name of your business or employer: _____

Address: _____ City: _____

County: _____ State: _____ Zip code: _____

Gross monthly income: _____ Take home pay: _____

How often are you paid? Weekly____ Every two weeks ____ Twice monthly ____ Monthly ____

How long at this business or job? _____

If less than two years, Previous business or employer:

Name of your business or employer: _____

Address: _____ City: _____

County: _____ State: _____ Zip code: _____

Job Title: _____

Gross monthly income: _____

Spouse's Occupation: _____ Employed _____ Self Employed _____

Name of spouse's business or employer: _____

Address: _____ City: _____

County: _____ State: _____ Zip code: _____

Gross monthly income: _____ Take home pay: _____

How often paid? Weekly____ Every two weeks ____ Twice monthly ____ Monthly ____

How long at this business or job? _____

If less than two years, Previous business or employer:

Name of spouse's business or employer: _____

Address: _____ City: _____

County: _____ State: _____ Zip code: _____

Job Title: _____

Gross monthly income: _____

FINANCIAL ASSETS

How much money do you have with you now? _____

How much money do you or your spouse have in banks, savings and loans, credit unions and other financial institutions, either in your name or jointly? List:

Names and Addresses Financial institution	Account Number	Type of Account (Checking/Savings)	Balance
1._____	_____	_____	_____
2._____	_____	_____	_____
3._____	_____	_____	_____
4._____	_____	_____	_____

Do you have any credit cards? Yes _____ No _____

If yes, list all credit cards:

Credit Card Name	Account Number	Maximum Credit	Amount Owed
1._____	_____	_____	_____
2._____	_____	_____	_____
3._____	_____	_____	_____

Do you have any checkbooks with you? Yes _____ No _____
Do you have any credit cards with you? Yes _____ No _____

Do you or your spouse have a safe deposit box? Yes _____ No _____
Name of institution and address where the box is located _____
List of all persons allowed into the box: _____
List what is kept in the box: _____
_____
_____

Do you or your spouse own any stocks, bonds, or other securities? Yes _____ No _____
Where are these securities kept?_____
If with a broker, name and address _____
_____

Approximate total value _____

Do you or your spouse have a life insurance policy? Yes _____ No _____
Can you borrow against the policy? Yes _____ No _____
If yes, how much can you borrow? _____

Do you or your spouse own any notes, mortgages, trust deeds or any other financial instruments on which you are owed money and/or receiving payments? Yes _____ No _____

If yes, list these instruments, the total amount owing to you and the amount of payments you are receiving:
_____
_____

OTHER PERSONAL PROPERTY

Do you or your spouse own any automobiles, trucks, recreational vehicles, boats or any other vehicles either separately or jointly? Yes _____ No _____

If yes, list all of these items:

Make and Year	License Number	Value	Owner	Amount Owed
1._____	_____	_____	_____	_____
2._____	_____	_____	_____	_____
3._____	_____	_____	_____	_____

Where are these items located?

1. _____

2. _____

3. _____

REAL PROPERTY

Do you or your spouse own any real estate? Yes _____ No _____

If yes, list all such property:

Address or Location	Market Value	Amount Owing and to Whom
1._____	_____	_____
2._____	_____	_____

Which of these properties is your home? 1. _____ 2. _____ None _____

Do you receive any income from any of these properties? Yes _____ No _____

If yes, list all sources of income and the amounts: _____

_____

_____

Do you rent your residence? Yes _____ No _____

If yes, complete the following:

Do you rent month to month or lease? _____

If you lease, how long is your lease? _____

Amount of monthly rent? _____ Is your payment current? Yes _____ No _____

If no, amount in arrears: _____

Name and address of landlord: _____

_____

Do you receive any income from roommates or tenant? Yes _____ No _____

If yes, amount received and from whom: _____

Other Assets and Income

List all property not yet listed that you own, except household furniture, which has a value of $100 or more (include jewelry, machinery, business inventory, and any other items): _____

_____

_____

List all income not yet listed which you are receiving or expect to receive (include judgments, settlements, bequests, inheritances or any other income), the amount and source of the income and when you expect it.

_____

_____

_____

_____   _____
              Signature   Date

ATTORNEY OR PARTY WITHOUT ATTORNEY *(Name and Address)*:

TELEPHONE NO.:

LEVYING OFFICER *(Name and Address)*:

ATTORNEY FOR *(Name)*:

NAME OF COURT, JUDICIAL DISTRICT OR BRANCH COURT, IF ANY:

PLAINTIFF:

DEFENDANT:

APPLICATION FOR EARNINGS WITHHOLDING ORDER **(Wage Garnishment)**	LEVYING OFFICER FILE NO.:	COURT CASE NO.:

TO THE SHERIFF OR ANY MARSHAL OR CONSTABLE OF THE COUNTY OF
OR ANY REGISTERED PROCESS SERVER

1. The judgment creditor *(name)*:

requests issuance of an Earnings Withholding Order directing the employer to withhold the earnings of the judgment debtor (employee).

Name and address of employer

Name and address of employee

Social Security Number *(if known)*:

2. The amounts withheld are to be paid to
   a. ☐ The attorney (or party without an attorney) named at the top of this page.
   b. ☐ Other *(name, address, and telephone)*:

3. a. Judgment was entered on *(date)*:
   b. Collect the amount directed by the Writ of Execution unless a lesser amount is specified here:
      $

4. ☐ The Writ of Execution was issued to collect delinquent amounts payable for the **support** of a child, former spouse, or spouse of the employee.

5. ☐ Special instructions *(specify)*:

6. *(Check a or b)*
   a. ☐ I have not previously obtained an order directing this employer to withhold the earnings of this employee.
      —OR—
   b. ☐ I have previously obtained such an order, but that order *(check one)*:
      ☐ was terminated by a court order, but I am entitled to apply for another Earnings Withholding Order under the provisions of Code of Civil Procedure section 706.105(h).
      ☐ was ineffective.

▶

....
(TYPE OR PRINT NAME)

_____
(SIGNATURE OF ATTORNEY OR PARTY WITHOUT ATTORNEY)

I declare under penalty of perjury under the laws of the State of California that the foregoing is true and correct.

Date:

▶

....
(TYPE OR PRINT NAME)

_____
(SIGNATURE OF DECLARANT)

Form Adopted by the
Judicial Council of California
982.5(1) [Rev. January 1, 1993]

APPLICATION FOR EARNINGS WITHHOLDING ORDER
(Wage Garnishment)

CCP 706.121

245

ATTORNEY OR PARTY WITHOUT ATTORNEY *(Name and Address)*:	TELEPHONE NO.:	FOR RECORDER'S OR SECRETARY OF STATE'S USE ONLY

ATTORNEY FOR *(Name)*:

NAME OF COURT:
STREET ADDRESS:
MAILING ADDRESS:
CITY AND ZIP CODE:
BRANCH NAME:

PLAINTIFF:

DEFENDANT:

CASE NUMBER:

ACKNOWLEDGMENT OF SATISFACTION OF JUDGMENT
☐ FULL   ☐ PARTIAL   ☐ MATURED INSTALLMENT

FOR COURT USE ONLY

1. Satisfaction of the judgment is acknowledged as follows *(see footnote* before completing)*:
  a. ☐ Full satisfaction
    (1) ☐ Judgment is satisfied in full.
    (2) ☐ sThe judgment creditor has accepted payment or performance other than that specified in the judgment in full satisfaction of the judgment.
  b. ☐ Partial satisfaction
    The amount received in partial satisfaction of the judgment is
    $
  c. ☐ Matured installment
    All matured installments under the installment judgment have been satisfied as of *(date)*:
2. Full name and address of judgment creditor:

3. Full name and address of assignee of record, if any:

4. Full name and address of judgment debtor being fully or partially released:

5. a. Judgment entered on *(date)*:
    ☐ (1) in judgment book volume no.:   (2) page no.:
  b. ☐ Renewal entered on *(date)*:
    ☐ (1) in judgment book volume no.:   (2) page no.:

6. ☐ An ☐ abstract of judgment ☐ certified copy of the judgment has been recorded as follows *(complete all information for each county where recorded)*:
COUNTY	DATE OF RECORDING	BOOK NUMBER	PAGE NUMBER

7. ☐ A notice of judgment lien has been filed in the office of the Secretary of State as file number *(specify)*:

NOTICE TO JUDGMENT DEBTOR: If this is an acknowledgment of full satisfaction of judgment, it will have to be recorded in each county shown in item 6 above, if any, in order to release the judgment lien, and will have to be filed in the office of the Secretary of State to terminate any judgment lien on personal property. ▶

Date:

_____
(SIGNATURE OF JUDGMENT CREDITOR OR ASSIGNEE OF CREDITOR OR ATTORNEY)

*The names of the judgment creditor and judgment debtor must be stated as shown in any Abstract of Judgment which was recorded and is being released by this satisfaction. **A separate notary acknowledgment must be attached for each signature.**

Form Approved by the
Judicial Council of California
EJ-100 [Rev. July 1, 1983] (Cor. 7/84)

ACKNOWLEDGMENT OF SATISFACTION OF JUDGMENT

CCP 724.060, 724.120, 724.250

247

Notice of Right to Reclaim Abandoned Property
(Under $300)
(Personal Property — Civil Code Sec. 1984)

To: _____
(Full names of tenants, subtenants, and all others in possession)

Rental Property: _____ Unit _____
(Street address, City, County, Zip)

When the above-identified premises was vacated by you, the personal property described below remained.

Unless you pay reasonable storage costs and take possession of the property not later than 18 days after the mailing of this notice, the property may be disposed of pursuant to Civil Code section 1988.

Because the property is believed to be worth less than $300, it may be kept, sold, or destroyed without further notice to you if you fail to reclaim it within the above indicated time limit.

Address where you may
claim the property: _____
(Street Address)   (City)   (County)   (State)   (Zip)

The personal property is described as follows: _____
_____
_____
_____
_____

Mailing Date _____

Landlord/Agent _____

Address _____

_____

Notice of Right to Reclaim Abandoned Property
($300 or More)
(Personal Property — Civil Code Sec. 1984)

To: _____
(Full names of tenants, subtenants, and all others in possession)

Rental Property: _____ Unit _____
(Street address, City, County, Zip)

When the above-identified premises was vacated by you, the personal property described below remained.

Unless you pay reasonable storage costs and take possession of the property not later than 18 days after the mailing of this notice, the property may be disposed of pursuant to Civil Code section 1988.

The property is believed to be worth more than $300. It will be sold at public sale after notice by publication if you fail to reclaim it within the time indicated above. You have the right to bid on the property at the sale. After the costs of storage, advertising, and sale are deducted from the sale proceeds, the remaining balance will be paid to the county. You may claim this money within one year of its receipt by the county.

Address where you may
claim the property: _____
         (Street Address)   (City)   (County)   (State)   (Zip)

The personal property is described as follows: _____
_____
_____
_____
_____

Mailing Date _____

Landlord/Agent _____

Address _____

_____

ATTORNEY OR PARTY WITHOUT ATTORNEY *(Name and Address)*:

TELEPHONE NO.:

FOR RECORDER'S USE ONLY

☐ Recording requested by and return to:

☐ ATTORNEY FOR ☐ JUDGMENT CREDITOR ☐ ASSIGNEE OF RECORD

NAME OF COURT:

STREET ADDRESS:

MAILING ADDRESS:

CITY AND ZIP CODE:

BRANCH NAME:

PLAINTIFF:

DEFENDANT:

ABSTRACT OF JUDGMENT

CASE NUMBER:

FOR COURT USE ONLY

1. The ☐ judgment creditor ☐ assignee of record
applies for an abstract of judgment and represents the following:
   a. Judgment debtor's

   Name and last known address

   b. Driver's license No. and state: ☐ Unknown
   c. Social Security No.:   ☐ Unknown
   d. Summons or notice of entry of sister-state judgment was personally served or
   mailed to *(name and address)*:

   e. ☐ Additional judgment debtors are shown on reverse.

Date:

. . . .
(TYPE OR PRINT NAME)

▶ _____
(SIGNATURE OF APPLICANT OR ATTORNEY)

2. a. ☐ I certify that the following is a true and correct
abstract of the judgment entered in this action.
   b. ☐ A certified copy of the judgment is attached.
3. Judgment creditor *(name)*:

   whose **address** appears on this form above the court's name.
4. Judgment debtor *(full name as it appears in judgment)*:

6. Total amount of judgment as entered or last renewed:
$
7. ☐ An ☐ execution ☐ attachment lien
is endorsed on the judgment as follows:
   a. Amount: $
   b. In favor of *(name and address)*:

[SEAL]

5. a. Judgment entered on
      (date):
   b. Renewal entered on
      (date):
   c. Renewal entered on
      (date):

   This abstract issued on
   (date):

8. A stay of enforcement has
   a. ☐ not been ordered by the court.
   b. ☐ been ordered by the court effective until
      (date):
9. ☐ This judgment is an installment judgment.

Clerk, by _____, Deputy

Form Adopted by Rule 982
Judicial Council of California
982(a)(1) [Rev. January 1, 1991]

ABSTRACT OF JUDGMENT
(CIVIL)

Code of Civil Procedure, §§ 488.480,
674. 700.190

251

PLAINTIFF:	CASE NUMBER:
DEFENDANT:	

INFORMATION ON ADDITIONAL JUDGMENT DEBTORS

10.   Name and last known address

Driver's license No. & state: ☐ Unknown
Social Security No.: ☐ Unknown
Summons was personally served at or mailed to (address):

14.   Name and last known address

Driver's license No. & state: ☐ Unknown
Social Security No.: ☐ Unknown
Summons was personally served at or mailed to (address):

11.   Name and last known address

Driver's license No. & state: ☐ Unknown
Social Security No.: ☐ Unknown
Summons was personally served at or mailed to (address):

15.   Name and last known address

Driver's license No. & state: ☐ Unknown
Social Security No.: ☐ Unknown
Summons was personally served at or mailed to (address):

12.   Name and last known address

Driver's license No. & state: ☐ Unknown
Social Security No.: ☐ Unknown
Summons was personally served at or mailed to (address):

16.   Name and last known address

Driver's license No. & state: ☐ Unknown
Social Security No.: ☐ Unknown
Summons was personally served at or mailed to (address):

13.   Name and last known address

Driver's license No. & state: ☐ Unknown
Social Security No.: ☐ Unknown
Summons was personally served at or mailed to (address):

17.   Name and last known address

Driver's license No. & state: ☐ Unknown
Social Security No.: ☐ Unknown
Summons was personally served at or mailed to (address):

18. ☐ Continued on attachment 18.

ABSTRACT OF JUDGMENT
(CIVIL)

PRELIMINARY LIEN NOTICE

TO   _____
                  (occupant)

         _____
                  (address)

         _____
                  (state)

You owe and have not paid rent and/or other charges for the use of storage _____ (space number) at _____ (name and address of storage facility). These charges total $ _____ (amount) and have been due for more than 14 days. They are itemized as follows:

Due Date	Description	Amount

                                                                 TOTAL: $ _____

If this sum is not paid in full before _____ (date at least 14 days from mailing) your right to use the storage space will terminate, you will be denied access, and an owner's lien on any stored property will be imposed.

You may pay this sum and may contact the owner at:

_____
               (name)

_____
               (address)

_____
               (state)

_____
            (telephone)

_____
        (date)

                                                _____
                                                 (owner's signature)

THREE DAY/SIXTY DAY NOTICE

THREE DAY NOTICE TO PAY RENT OR QUIT

TO _____

And all other tenants, subtenants, and others in possession of the property located at:

Address _____ Space number _____

City of _____ County of _____

State of California

Rent on the above described property is due and owing from _____ *(date)* in the amount of $ _____.

You are required to pay the amount owing in full within three (3) days after the service of this notice to _____ *(Owner/Agent/Park Manager)* or quit and deliver possession of the premises to the above party.

Failure to deliver up the premises will result in legal action against you to recover all monies owed as well as the premises and all other damages allowed by law. Failure to pay the money owed will also result in the termination of your lease/rental agreement.

You are also notified that negative information may be submitted to a credit reporting agency which may result in a negative credit report if you fail to meet your financial obligations.

_____   _____
Owner/Agent   Date

NOTICE OF TERMINATION OF TENANCY

TO _____

And all other tenants, subtenants, and others in possession of the property located at:

Address _____ Space number _____

City of _____ County of _____

State of California

This notice to you that your tenancy of space number _____ at _____

_____ *(address)*, in the City of _____,

County of _____, California is terminated and that your mobile home must be removed from the above address not later than _____ *(Date more than 60 days after receipt of notice)*.

Reason(s) for termination *(Detail all reasons for termination)*: _____

_____

_____

Signature _____   Date _____
                      Owner/Agent

PROOF OF SERVICE

I, the undersigned, being at least 18 years of age, served this notice, of which this is a true copy, on _____, the person(s) named above. The notice was served by:

❑   Personal delivery of a copy to the above named person(s).

❑   Delivery of a copy for each of the above named to a person of suitable age and discretion at the above named person(s) residence/business after attempting to personally serve the above named person(s) at his/her/their residence and place of business (if known) and mailing by first class mail a second copy to his/her/their residence.

❑   Posting a copy for each of the above named person(s) in a conspicuous place on the above identified property, being unable to personally serve a person of suitable age or discretion at the residence or known place(s) of business of the above named person(s) and mailing on the same date by first class mail a second copy to each above named person(s) to the address of the above identified property.

I declare under penalty of perjury that the above proof of service is true and correct.

Name _____   Date _____

Index

Your #1 Source for Real World Legal Information...

SPHINX® PUBLISHING
A Division of Sourcebooks, Inc.®

• Written by lawyers
• Simple English explanation of the law
• Forms and instructions included

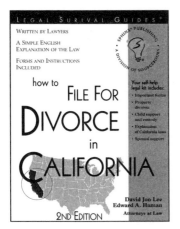

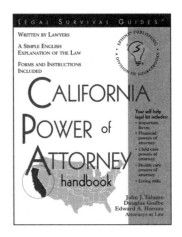

HOW TO FILE FOR DIVORCE IN CALIFORNIA, 2ND ED.

This book provides a step-by-step guide for obtaining a divorce in California without a lawyer. Learn about alimony; child support, custody and visitation; property division; simplified procedures; emergency procedures and more.

208 pages; $19.95;
ISBN 1-57248-136-9

HOW TO WIN IN SMALL CLAIMS COURT IN CALIFORNIA

File and defend your own small claims case by learning critical information about California small claims court. Lists mediators and small claims advisors. Includes forms with instructions.

257 pages; $14.95;
ISBN 1-57071-358-8

CALIFORNIA POWER OF ATTORNEY HANDBOOK

Now it is easier than ever to authorize someone to act on your behalf for your convenience or necessity. With forms and instructions, this book allows you to draft your own power of attorney for financial matters, health care, real estate and child care.

128 pages; $12.95;
ISBN 1-57071-360-X

See the following order form for books written specifically for California, Florida, Georgia, Illinois, Massachusetts, Michigan, Minnesota, New York, North Carolina, Pennsylvania, and Texas! *Coming soon—Ohio and New Jersey!*

What our customers say about our books:

"It couldn't be more clear for the lay person." —R.D.

"I want you to know I really appreciate your book. It has saved me a lot of time and money." —L.T.

"Your real estate contracts book has saved me nearly $12,000.00 in closing costs over the past year." —A.B.

"...many of the legal questions that I have had over the years were answered clearly and concisely through your plain English interpretation of the law." —C.E.H.

"If there weren't people out there like you I'd be lost. You have the best books of this type out there." —S.B.

"...your forms and directions are easy to follow." —C.V.M.

Sphinx Publishing's Legal Survival Guides
are directly available from the Sourcebooks, Inc., or from your local bookstores.
For credit card orders call 1–800–43–BRIGHT, write P.O. Box 4410, Naperville, IL 60567-4410,
or fax 630-961-2168

SPHINX® PUBLISHING'S NATIONAL TITLES

Valid in All 50 States

LEGAL SURVIVAL IN BUSINESS

How to Form a Limited Liability Company	$19.95
How to Form Your Own Corporation (2E)	$19.95
How to Form Your Own Partnership	$19.95
How to Register Your Own Copyright (3E)	$19.95
How to Register Your Own Trademark (3E)	$19.95
Most Valuable Business Legal Forms You'll Ever Need (2E)	$19.95
Most Valuable Corporate Forms You'll Ever Need (2E)	$24.95
Software Law (with diskette)	$29.95

LEGAL SURVIVAL IN COURT

Crime Victim's Guide to Justice	$19.95
Debtors' Rights (3E)	$12.95
Defend Yourself against Criminal Charges	$19.95
Grandparents' Rights (2E)	$19.95
Help Your Lawyer Win Your Case (2E)	$12.95
Jurors' Rights (2E)	$9.95
Legal Malpractice and Other Claims against Your Lawyer	$18.95
Legal Research Made Easy (2E)	$14.95
Simple Ways to Protect Yourself from Lawsuits	$24.95
Winning Your Personal Injury Claim	$19.95

LEGAL SURVIVAL IN REAL ESTATE

How to Buy a Condominium or Townhome	$16.95
How to Negotiate Real Estate Contracts (3E)	$16.95
How to Negotiate Real Estate Leases (3E)	$16.95
Successful Real Estate Brokerage Management	$19.95

LEGAL SURVIVAL IN PERSONAL AFFAIRS

Guia de Inmigracion a Estados Unidos (2E)	$19.95
How to File Your Own Bankruptcy (4E)	$19.95
How to File Your Own Divorce (3E)	$19.95
How to Fire Your First Employee	$19.95
How to Hire Your First Employee	$19.95
How to Make Your Own Will (2E)	$12.95
How to Write Your Own Living Will (2E)	$9.95
How to Write Your Own Premarital Agreement (2E)	$19.95
How to Win Your Unemployment Compensation Claim	$19.95
Living Trusts and Simple Ways to Avoid Probate (2E)	$19.95
Neighbor v. Neighbor (2E)	$12.95
The Nanny and Domestic Help Legal Kit	$19.95
The Power of Attorney Handbook (3E)	$19.95
Simple Ways to Protect Yourself from Lawsuits	$24.95
Social Security Benefits Handbook (2E)	$14.95
Unmarried Parents' Rights	$19.95
U.S.A. Immigration Guide (3E)	$19.95
Your Right to Child Custody, Visitation and Support	$19.95

Legal Survival Guides are directly available from Sourcebooks, Inc., or from your local bookstores.

For credit card orders call 1–800–43–BRIGHT, write P.O. Box 4410, Naperville, IL 60567-4410
or fax 630-961-2168

SPHINX® PUBLISHING ORDER FORM

BILL TO:		SHIP TO:		
Phone #	Terms	F.O.B.	Chicago, IL	Ship Date

Charge my: ☐ VISA ☐ MasterCard ☐ American Express

☐ **Money Order or Personal Check**

Credit Card Number

Expiration Date

Qty	ISBN	Title	Retail	Ext.
		SPHINX PUBLISHING NATIONAL TITLES		
_____	1-57071-166-6	Crime Victim's Guide to Justice	$19.95	_____
_____	1-57071-342-1	Debtors' Rights (3E)	$12.95	_____
_____	1-57071-162-3	Defend Yourself against Criminal Charges	$19.95	_____
_____	1-57248-082-3	Grandparents' Rights (2E)	$19.95	_____
_____	1-57248-087-4	Guia de Inmigracion a Estados Unidos (2E)	$19.95	_____
_____	1-57248-103-X	Help Your Lawyer Win Your Case (2E)	$12.95	_____
_____	1-57071-164-X	How to Buy a Condominium or Townhome	$16.95	_____
_____	1-57071-223-9	How to File Your Own Bankruptcy (4E)	$19.95	_____
_____	1-57071-224-7	How to File Your Own Divorce (3E)	$19.95	_____
_____	1-57248-083-1	How to Form a Limited Liability Company	$19.95	_____
_____	1-57248-100-5	How to Form a DE Corporation from Any State	$19.95	_____
_____	1-57248-101-3	How to Form a NV Corporation from Any State	$19.95	_____
_____	1-57248-099-8	How to Form a Nonprofit Corporation	$24.95	_____
_____	1-57071-227-1	How to Form Your Own Corporation (2E)	$19.95	_____
_____	1-57071-343-X	How to Form Your Own Partnership	$19.95	_____
_____	1-57248-125-0	How to Fire Your First Employee	$19.95	_____
_____	1-57248-121-8	How to Hire Your First Employee	$19.95	_____
_____	1-57248-119-6	How to Make Your Own Will (2E)	$12.95	_____
_____	1-57071-331-6	How to Negotiate Real Estate Contracts (3E)	$16.95	_____
_____	1-57071-332-4	How to Negotiate Real Estate Leases (3E)	$16.95	_____
_____	1-57248-124-2	How to Register Your Own Copyright (3E)	$19.95	_____
_____	1-57248-104-8	How to Register Your Own Trademark (3E)	$19.95	_____
_____	1-57071-349-9	How to Win Your Unemployment Compensation Claim	$19.95	_____
_____	1-57248-118-8	How to Write Your Own Living Will (2E)	$9.95	_____
_____	1-57071-344-8	How to Write Your Own Premarital Agreement (2E)	$19.95	_____
_____	1-57071-333-2	Jurors' Rights (2E)	$9.95	_____
_____	1-57248-032-7	Legal Malpractice and Other Claims against...	$18.95	_____
_____	1-57071-400-2	Legal Research Made Easy (2E)	$14.95	_____
_____	1-57071-336-7	Living Trusts and Simple Ways to Avoid Probate (2E)	$19.95	_____

Qty	ISBN	Title	Retail	Ext.
_____	1-57071-345-6	Most Valuable Bus. Legal Forms You'll Ever Need (2E)	$19.95	_____
_____	1-57071-346-4	Most Valuable Corporate Forms You'll Ever Need (2E)	$24.95	_____
_____	1-57248-089-0	Neighbor v. Neighbor (2E)	$12.95	_____
_____	1-57071-348-0	The Power of Attorney Handbook (3E)	$19.95	_____
_____	1-57248-020-3	Simple Ways to Protect Yourself from Lawsuits	$24.95	_____
_____	1-57071-337-5	Social Security Benefits Handbook (2E)	$14.95	_____
_____	1-57071-163-1	Software Law (w/diskette)	$29.95	_____
_____	0-913825-86-7	Successful Real Estate Brokerage Mgmt.	$19.95	_____
_____	1-57248-098-X	The Nanny and Domestic Help Legal Kit	$19.95	_____
_____	1-57071-399-5	Unmarried Parents' Rights	$19.95	_____
_____	1-57071-354-5	U.S.A. Immigration Guide (3E)	$19.95	_____
_____	0-913825-82-4	Victims' Rights	$12.95	_____
_____	1-57071-165-8	Winning Your Personal Injury Claim	$19.95	_____
_____	1-57248-097-1	Your Right to Child Custody, Visitation and Support	$19.95	_____
		CALIFORNIA TITLES		
_____	1-57071-360-X	CA Power of Attorney Handbook	$12.95	_____
_____	1-57248-126-9	How to File for Divorce in CA (2E)	$19.95	_____
_____	1-57071-356-1	How to Make a CA Will	$12.95	_____
_____	1-57071-408-8	How to Probate an Estate in CA	$19.95	_____
_____	1-57248-116-1	How to Start a Business in CA	$16.95	_____
_____	1-57071-358-8	How to Win in Small Claims Court in CA	$14.95	_____
_____	1-57071-359-6	Landlords' Rights and Duties in CA	$19.95	_____
		FLORIDA TITLES		
_____	1-57071-363-4	Florida Power of Attorney Handbook (2E)	$12.95	_____
_____	1-57248-093-9	How to File for Divorce in FL (6E)	$21.95	_____
_____	1-57248-086-6	How to Form a Limited Liability Co. in FL	$19.95	_____
_____	1-57071-401-0	How to Form a Partnership in FL	$19.95	_____
_____	1-57071-380-4	How to Form a Corporation in FL (4E)	$19.95	_____
		Form Continued on Following Page	**SUBTOTAL**	_____

To order, call Sourcebooks at 1-800-43-BRIGHT or FAX (630)961-2168 (Bookstores, libraries, wholesalers—please call for discount)

SPHINX® PUBLISHING ORDER FORM

Qty	ISBN	Title	Retail	Ext.
		FLORIDA TITLES (CONT'D)		
____	1-57071-361-8	How to Make a FL Will (5E)	$12.95	____
____	1-57248-088-2	How to Modify Your FL Divorce Judgment (4E)	$22.95	____
____	1-57071-364-2	How to Probate an Estate in FL (3E)	$24.95	____
____	1-57248-081-5	How to Start a Business in FL (5E)	$16.95	____
____	1-57071-362-6	How to Win in Small Claims Court in FL (6E)	$14.95	____
____	1-57071-335-9	Landlords' Rights and Duties in FL (7E)	$19.95	____
____	1-57071-334-0	Land Trusts in FL (5E)	$24.95	____
____	0-913825-73-5	Women's Legal Rights in FL	$19.95	____
		GEORGIA TITLES		
____	1-57071-376-6	How to File for Divorce in GA (3E)	$19.95	____
____	1-57248-075-0	How to Make a GA Will (3E)	$12.95	____
____	1-57248-076-9	How to Start a Business in Georgia (3E)	$16.95	____
		ILLINOIS TITLES		
____	1-57071-405-3	How to File for Divorce in IL (2E)	$19.95	____
____	1-57071-415-0	How to Make an IL Will (2E)	$12.95	____
____	1-57071-416-9	How to Start a Business in IL (2E)	$16.95	____
____	1-57248-078-5	Landlords' Rights & Duties in IL	$19.95	____
		MASSACHUSETTS TITLES		
____	1-57071-329-4	How to File for Divorce in MA (2E)	$19.95	____
____	1-57248-115-3	How to Form a Corporation in MA	$19.95	____
____	1-57248-108-0	How to Make a MA Will (2E)	$12.95	____
____	1-57248-109-9	How to Probate an Estate in MA (2E)	$19.95	____
____	1-57248-106-4	How to Start a Business in MA (2E)	$16.95	____
____	1-57248-107-2	Landlords' Rights and Duties in MA (2E)	$19.95	____
		MICHIGAN TITLES		
____	1-57071-409-6	How to File for Divorce in MI (2E)	$19.95	____
____	1-57248-077-7	How to Make a MI Will (2E)	$12.95	____
____	1-57071-407-X	How to Start a Business in MI (2E)	$16.95	____
		MINNESOTA TITLES		
____	1-57248-039-4	How to File for Divorce in MN	$19.95	____
____	1-57248-040-8	How to Form a Simple Corporation in MN	$19.95	____
____	1-57248-037-8	How to Make a MN Will	$9.95	____
____	1-57248-038-6	How to Start a Business in MN	$16.95	____

Qty	ISBN	Title	Retail	Ext.
		NEW YORK TITLES		
____	1-57071-184-4	How to File for Divorce in NY	$19.95	____
____	1-57248-105-6	How to Form a Corporation in NY	$19.95	____
____	1-57248-095-5	How to Make a NY Will (2E)	$12.95	____
____	1-57071-185-2	How to Start a Business in NY	$16.95	____
____	1-57071-187-9	How to Win in Small Claims Court in NY	$14.95	____
____	1-57071-186-0	Landlords' Rights and Duties in NY	$19.95	____
____	1-57071-188-7	New York Power of Attorney Handbook	$19.95	____
____	1-57248-122-6	Tenants' Rights in NY	$14.95	____
		NORTH CAROLINA TITLES		
____	1-57071-326-X	How to File for Divorce in NC (2E)	$19.95	____
____	1-57071-327-8	How to Make a NC Will (2E)	$12.95	____
____	1-57248-096-3	How to Start a Business in NC (2E)	$16.95	____
____	1-57248-091-2	Landlords' Rights & Duties in NC	$19.95	____
		OHIO TITLES		
____	1-57248-102-1	How to File for Divorce in OH	$19.95	____
		PENNSYLVANIA TITLES		
____	1-57248-127-7	How to File for Divorce in PA (2E)	$19.95	____
____	1-57248-094-7	How to Make a PA Will (2E)	$12.95	____
____	1-57248-112-9	How to Start a Business in PA (2E)	$16.95	____
____	1-57071-179-8	Landlords' Rights and Duties in PA	$19.95	____
		TEXAS TITLES		
____	1-57071-330-8	How to File for Divorce in TX (2E)	$19.95	____
____	1-57248-009-2	How to Form a Simple Corporation in TX	$19.95	____
____	1-57071-417-7	How to Make a TX Will (2E)	$12.95	____
____	1-57071-418-5	How to Probate an Estate in TX (2E)	$19.95	____
____	1-57071-365-0	How to Start a Business in TX (2E)	$16.95	____
____	1-57248-111-0	How to Win in Small Claims Court in TX (2E)	$14.95	____
____	1-57248-110-2	Landlords' Rights and Duties in TX (2E)	$19.95	____

SUBTOTAL THIS PAGE ____

SUBTOTAL PREVIOUS PAGE ____

Illinois residents add 6.75% sales tax ____

Florida residents add 6% state sales tax plus applicable discretionary surtax ____

Shipping— $4.00 for 1st book, $1.00 each additional ____

TOTAL ____